Just One Thing

Just One Thing

To: Ann

[signature]

ANNA SCHAEFFER

— Isaiah 43:1-2

Copyright © 2019 Anna Schaeffer.
www.annaschaefferwrites.com

All rights reserved. No part of this book may be used or reproduced by any means without the written permission of the copyright owner except for the use of brief quotations in book reviews.

This is a work of fiction. All of the characters, names, incidents, organizations, and dialogue in this novel are either the products of the author's imagination or are used fictitiously. Any resemblance to actual persons, living or dead, is coincidental.

Scriptures taken from the Holy Bible, New International Version®, NIV®. Copyright © 1973, 1978, 1984, 2011 by Biblica, Inc.™ Used by permission of Zondervan. All rights reserved worldwide. www.zondervan.com. The "NIV" and "New International Version" are trademarks registered in the United States Patent and Trademark Office by Biblica, Inc.™

Author photo by Hannah Adkins
Cover and interior design by Roseanna White Designs
Cover images from Shutterstock.com

ISBN (paperback): 978-1-7333657-0-3
ISBN (EPUB): 978-1-7333657-1-0
ISBN (Kindle): 978-1-7333657-2-7

Library of Congress Control Number: 2019911575

Published in Wake Forest, NC

To Ronald and Helen Hasty, my grandparents:
Because of your story, I write mine.

Chapter One

If God had given Moses an eleventh commandment, it would've been: *Thou shalt not give Sadie Franklin a driver's license.*

I bopped my head against the steering wheel a couple of times, backed up the old blue Buick, and made a second attempt at pulling into the driveway. Dumb mailbox. And dumb distractions running through my brain.

I finally put the car in park and pulled my grocery bags out of the backseat, mentally running through my list of life goals for the next few months:

1. Build a relationship with Dad.
2. Survive Fall Semester.
3. Get the heck out of Seattle.

And on days when I felt particularly ambitious:

4. Make some friends who don't want to toss me into the Puget Sound.

I aimed high, for sure. I repeated my goals like a mantra as I sprawled across the back seat to retrieve a rogue can of green beans that had rolled under the seat.

I dared a glance at the right-side car mirror, which dangled by a wire. I'd have to get some duct tape for that later.

Taking a deep breath, I grabbed the bags and headed for the front door, ready to focus on Goal #1.

"Hi, Dad." I stepped into the kitchen and plopped the bags onto the counter. "I got grapes…and squeeze cheese!" The Franklins were super classy like that.

Dad glanced up from where he sat at the small kitchen table, working through bills. He nodded, his eyes already back on the laptop screen.

I pulled his Visa and the grocery receipt from my pocket and set them in front of him, making sure the part where the cashier highlighted the savings took the spotlight, rather than the party-size bag of dark chocolate M&M's.

"Do you have everything you need for school tomorrow?" Dad asked.

I nodded and stacked the cans in the cabinet by the refrigerator. "Yeah, I'm good." A can slipped out of my grip, and I barely caught it before it hit the counter. I was so not ready for senior year to start the next day, mainly because it meant I'd have to start working on my other goals. The first one may have seemed impossible, but the others made me want to hide under the car seat with the green beans.

Clutching a bag of grapes in my shaking hand, I opened the fridge, pulled open the fruit crisper drawer, and froze.

I set the bag of grapes on the counter and tucked my sandy blonde bangs behind my ear. "Um, Dad?"

And here's where Goal #1 gets real…

He looked up from his number-crunching. "Yeah?"

How could I say this without seeming disrespectful or like I had an ego? "So…I was gonna put these grapes into the fruit drawer." I motioned at the fridge. "But it's actually filled with…beer."

It wasn't that I didn't know my dad drank, because I did. And it wasn't like he didn't know that I, at seventeen, already had a history with the hard stuff, because I'd just returned from a summer on the other side of the country, where I'd finally gotten a grip on my life. It's just that he'd never kept alcohol in the house before.

We were both silent for a moment, looking at each other, trying to figure out who exactly we shared a house with.

There's this thing about eye contact. Sometimes it's comforting, sometimes it's reassuring in an I-get-you kind of way, and sometimes it's creepy. And then other times, like during this potential showdown in my kitchen, it said all of the things I wanted to say but couldn't. Things like: *I've stayed sober for a couple of months now. I cleaned up like you wanted me to.* And the kicker: *I'm scared I'm not strong enough to stay away from it when it's right here waiting for me.*

Dad pulled dark brown eyes away from my gray ones and looked at the stash in the fridge. He rubbed the back of his neck. "What are you trying to say, Sadie?"

I drew in a deep breath. Here was the defining moment. I could tell him an easy answer—a snarky, pre-summer Sadie answer, in which I mouth off and call him a hypocrite...or I could work toward the goal of actually having a relationship with my own father, which involved honesty and vulnerability. My heart thudded against my ribs, and my choice was obvious, but painful. *New Sadie it is.*

"My life completely changed," I confessed. Dad knew I met God while in Pecan Creek, Georgia, but it wasn't a topic up for discussion. The idea of a loving Creator had always been a sore subject in a house where tragedy had visited and never packed her bags of grief and gone away. So I left it at, "I quit drinking this summer. But I don't trust myself yet."

I also didn't trust myself to say anything else, so I turned back to the fridge. My heart rate was still berserk as I quietly put away the rest of the groceries—the grapes moved in with the lettuce—and retreated to my bedroom, away from the beer and the stranger I called Dad, feeling like a foreigner in the place I'd always lived.

———— oOo ————

"Hi, do you know how to get to this room?"

I jumped at the voice next to my ear, nearly dropping my textbook. The owner of the voice shoved a schedule under my nose, and I came to a halt. I took the paper, lowering it so I could actually read it, and turned to face purple-streaked auburn hair, slightly sunburned skin, and freckles that looked like someone dipped a brush in tan paint and channeled their inner Georges Seurat. Apparently I was staring, because the girl squinted at me and pointed to the syllabus. "Can you help?"

Blinking, I glanced at the paper. "British Literature. Oh, yeah, I'm in there too. Follow me." I handed back the schedule and speed-walked down the hallway, sliding into my desk about two seconds before the bell.

The girl plopped down in the desk in front of me and focused her hazel eyes on mine. "Thanks!" she mouthed as Mrs. Zurich began talking. She whipped around to face the teacher and knocked her textbook to the floor. This girl was a hurricane.

While Mrs. Zurich introduced the course, I took a couple of minutes to catch my breath. This was it. Senior year. I'd made it, hallelujah. I fixed my gaze on a tree outside the classroom window. The weather was extra sunny and warm for Washington, but I couldn't help the shiver that went through me when I thought about the semester ahead.

Senior year was supposed to mean livin' it up with friends, but when the cops show up at your party, you learn pretty quickly who your real friends are. And in my case, that left my friend bank in the negative at the end of junior year. But I still might be able to accomplish my friend-making goal, as long as everyone at school hadn't heard about my reputation and the literal smack down that happened in my living room this past May.

After class, Hurricane walked next to me, needing directions to her next class. "So where's this one?" She handed me the crumpled page. "I'm new here, and this place is nuts."

"I hear ya," I muttered as I looked at her schedule. "Yeah, I'm actually headed in that direction. I'll show you." I handed back the schedule and offered a small smile.

"Thanks. I'm Fynnigan, by the way."

"Sadie." I smiled for real this time and shifted my backpack to my other shoulder. Desperate for conversation while we walked, I asked, "So, where are you from?"

Fan-Again—or whatever Hurricane's real name was—stuck close to me in the menagerie of students crushing through the hall and leaned in to answer. Instinctively, I drew back a little. I had a relatively large personal bubble. Came with years of avoiding letting people see me vulnerable.

"I'm from the area, just a different school," she said. "Private school. I'm here for a change of scenery, you know?"

Oh, I *so* knew.

We reached my classroom. "Okay, this is me. You're two doors down, on the left." I pointed in the direction of her class.

"Thank you! Seriously, I looked at this schedule and was like, what even." She grinned. It was genuine, but she had an impish, free-spirited gleam in her lake-water brown eyes. Which made me wonder what kind of "fresh start" she was after. "See ya, Sadie!"

I sighed as I slid into the next class just before the bell again. "Thanks, God," I whispered. I didn't know if I'd just made an ally or met someone crazy enough to drag me into another mess, but for now, I had a friendship prospect. Whatever her name was.

———— ○○○ ————

That night, I called Becca Shepherd, one of my few true friends I'd made while in Pecan Creek, Georgia, for the summer.

"Sadie! Hey!" Her sweet Southern drawl slipped through the phone. "Just a sec, let me switch it off speaker. I'm ironing my shorts."

"Who irons their *shorts*?"

"Me." She sighed. "I procrastinated on folding my laundry, so they were at the bottom of the pile for a while and got creased. And I don't put them in the dryer because they get too tight."

I laughed, not because she was all that funny, but because she was so authentic. Becca was naturally beautiful and it shone through her personality, including her quirks. Even though I'd only met her at the beginning of summer, she was there for me. Even when I was deceitful and judgmental Old Sadie, she was there. I just hoped nearly three thousand miles and a three-hour time difference didn't put any distance between me and one of the realest friends I'd ever had.

I made a salad for dinner while I talked to her, telling her about the awkward conversation with Dad and how the girl named Fynnigan decided we'd be lunch buddies from now on.

I stuck the salad ingredients back in the fridge and carried my bowl into the living room. "So how's everyone in Pecan Creek?" I asked. Becca nannied for my aunt and uncle, who I'd stayed with, so she'd have a full report. I tucked my legs under me on the couch and took a bite of romaine.

"Your cousins are always wild," she sighed, "but it's like the new baby has made them crave attention or something.

Trissy is sassier than ever, and Jackson and Cooper are all into everything. Then baby Evelyn was worried they'd steal the show, so she got colic. Your poor aunt."

My laughter from earlier caught in my throat. I wanted to be there so badly it was like a physical ache. I'd been there for Evelyn's birth and stayed in Pecan Creek a few weeks longer than planned so I could help my aunt Melina and uncle Kurt while everyone adjusted to life with the new baby. My cousins were eight, six, two, and newborn, and I really enjoyed hanging around them. But all too soon, I had to pack my bags and head back to the Pacific Northwest. The birthday/going away party they threw for me was one of the most bittersweet things I'd experienced in my life.

Speaking of bittersweet... "Hey, Becca? I'd better let you go. I promised Truitt I'd call him, too."

After ending the call, I finished dinner and made a sandwich to leave on the counter for Dad whenever he got off work later. I called Truitt as I was climbing into bed and got his voicemail.

Rather than leave a message, I hung up and put my phone on the nightstand, slid beneath the cool sheets, and pulled the green and purple bedspread I'd had since I was a little girl up to my chin.

I felt so torn. The place where I'd lived for seventeen years felt so unfamiliar, while the place I'd known for only a few months was where my heart felt at home. My throat tightened, and the distance between there and here threatened to suffocate me. I tried to pray about it all but ended up tossing and turning until I finally fell asleep.

A couple of hours later, I woke up feeling like my beat-up mailbox. I lay still for a moment, trying to figure out what woke me up. Outside my window, the moon shone. It always reminded me of my mom, who once told me that the moon reflected the sun. Whenever I was scared of the darkness surrounding me, all I had to do was look at the moon and know the warm sun wasn't far away. The moon spilled into the room through my open curtains and cast a gray light across my bed. I heard footsteps in the hallway. *Dad.* He must've just come home from work. I'd started to think he might work all night, but we hadn't exactly met for coffee and swapped schedules since I'd come home.

I checked the time on my phone and saw a text from Truitt waiting: *Sorry I missed you. Went out to pizza and the batting cages with the guys. Gotta stay pro. Miss you…been too long since I've had a good yelling match. Becca just can't get into it.*

Though I wanted to cry for missing him, I also couldn't help but laugh. Truitt Peyton could irritate me just by breathing the same air. But he also knew me like no one else. Even though it was late, I texted a reply.

It hadn't even been two weeks since we'd said goodbye, but I was already starting to lose the feel of our pop-rock kiss the night Evelyn was born and those sturdy arms that held me close and whispered, "Don't throw grapes at just any granola guy out there," before my flight. I didn't know where all of that left us. The tears finally won out and I pressed my cheek into my pillow, my fingers tracing the letters of his text even after my eyes were too swollen to read it.

Chapter Two

○○○

Sticking with tradition, I slid into a seat in precalculus nanoseconds before the bell the next day. I really wanted to be on time, but I'd stepped in gum in the parking lot and got distracted scraping my shoe on the pavement.

I was definitely not a front-row sitter, but that was the only seat left. I exhaled like I'd just scaled a building as the teacher began taking roll.

"Sadie Franklin?"

"Here." I raised my hand, and Mr. Sanders glanced at me just long enough to put a face to the name. I went back to searching my backpack for a pen.

"Gavin Tyler?"

My hand involuntarily dropped the pen back into my bag, and I felt the color drain from my face. *Don't turn around, Sadie. Don't turn around...*

Mr. Sanders marked something on his roster.

I clamped my hands together to try to get them to stop shaking. So Gavin was in my class? I refused to turn around to verify. I would need more than an extra cup of coffee to survive this year. A teleportation device would suffice.

Mr. Sanders finished going through the roster and began reading the syllabus. Terms like "cofunction" and "matrix" and "derivative" spun in my brain like laundry in a washing machine.

Why was I even taking precalculus, anyway? Who was I to think I belonged in such a class? Until this summer, I hadn't even cared about grades. But then my aunt and uncle had made me believe it wasn't too late to work hard and graduate with a respectable GPA. After all, math had been the class I didn't need to repeat over the summer. Only now, not only was I near tears after just hearing an overview of the year, I was also taking the class with the one male I needed to most avoid at this school.

As soon as the bell rang, I beelined for my political science class so I wouldn't have to face Gavin. I went for a seat in the middle of the room.

"Sadie! Hi!" Fynnigan reached over and grabbed my arm. "We're in this class together too!"

"Oh, hi, Fynnigan." I retrieved my arm from her grip so I could have plenty of time to locate my pen.

"You can call me Fyn, if you want," she said. "Most people do, and I'm glad because it's weird being a girl named after her grandfather."

"Noted." Though it would be nice to know where my first name came from. I knew Grey, my middle name, had to do with God showing my mom how something good could come out of even the most confusing situations in life—out of the gray. But Sadie? Who knows.

"Gonna be honest," Fyn lowered her voice. "I'm not super excited about this class. I'm more of a creative spirit."

I glanced at her purple strands of hair. "How about that."

I turned back to face the front of the room...just in time to see Ruby Anderson walk in. What was this? National Give-Sadie-a-Panic-Attack Day? I quickly turned back to Fyn.

"So, you're creative? That's cool. I'm not really into crafts or anything. I'm more into movies and stuff. Like—" I listened to myself ramble, unable to stop the flow of words. Without her compatriots, who graduated last year, Ruby might've been harmless. But it was a risk I couldn't take. Not today, after the scare in precalculus.

Thankfully, Fyn didn't know anything about my history or how foreign the art of babble was to me. She just nodded her head vigorously, inserting "uh-huh," and "yeah, I so get that!" at appropriate times.

After school, I nearly sprinted to my car. Day two had gone better than I thought, I just needed to get my head under control. I needed to run.

I climbed into the car and threw my backpack in the passenger's seat. Putting my key in the ignition, I cranked the car. It made a clicking noise then shut off. *Huh.* I tried again, only to have the same results. My knowledge of automobiles extended to seatbelts and turn signals, and a couple of awkward moments with a stick shift truck in Georgia, but I climbed out and opened the hood anyway. Nothing looked abnormal, although that may have been the first time I'd ever looked under a hood. But nothing was in flames, and no smoke came from what I assumed to be the engine. Bad luck with cars was kind of my thing. This was what I got for trying to avoid riding the bus.

I checked the trunk for jumper cables but came up empty. "God, is this a test?" I muttered. "Are You testing me to see if I'll still cuss in stressful situations? Because I might lose this one. Can I get some help?"

I thought of Gavin's number still in my phone. He would probably come to my rescue, but it wasn't worth the risk of interacting with him and giving him the wrong impression.

Just then, a girl came up to her car parked next to me. "Hey," I called over the top of my car, "Do you have any cables? My car won't start."

She fished around in her trunk and produced a tangled

mess of orange cables. "Good luck," she said, handing them to me. "'Cause I don't have a clue how to use them. Hey, wait, we have a couple classes together, don't we?"

I squinted up at her in the afternoon sun. Her dark hair was cut close to her face, but she had the type of head that could pull it off. If I did that, I'd look like a cue ball. Her eyes were deep and sharp, like she missed nothing. She looked like someone you'd want on your team and not against you.

"Maybe?" I said because, let's be real, I'd been a little preoccupied with the ex-friends situations today.

She shrugged. "Anyway, I'm Liz Solomon. You know how to use these?"

I shook my head. "I've never even held them before."

Liz thought for a minute, rolling her neck around. "Well, this'll be fun." She pulled up a how-to video on her phone and we leaned our heads in to watch what we were supposed to do.

After Liz clamped the ends of the cables to my car's battery and hers, I sat in my car and tried to crank it. Nothing happened. We tried a few more times, Liz in her car and I in mine, only to end up right where we started.

Liz slid out of her car. "I don't know what to tell you, Sadie. Sorry about that."

"I'll figure it out. Thank you for your help, though, seriously."

Liz nodded. "I've gotta run, but do you have someone who could give you a lift?"

I shook my head. "Not really, no…Actually, yeah, I might be good."

I held my hand up in a wave as she drove off, then reached into my pocket for my phone.

---○○○---

"Thanks for the ride, Fyn. I owe you one." I pulled my

backpack onto my lap and slid out of Fyn's car later that afternoon.

She draped her arms over the steering wheel and tilted her head. "No offense, but after hearing about your car's freak-out session, I'd rather not take you up on a ride offer. But it's not a problem at all. I knew it'd be a good idea to have each other's numbers, although I thought it'd be for homework questions. Like, what is a political pundit? I've already forgotten."

I propped my arm on the top of her little lime green car. "Can I at least get you a snack or something as a thanks?"

Fyn grinned, and my heartbeat tripped as I realized somehow, someway, God had already given me a friend. I knew nothing about her other than her crazy name and wild approach to life, but for now it was enough. Although I was not above bribing her with after-school snacks.

We reached the porch, and I paused for a minute before opening the front door. This wasn't gonna be pretty, but if I wanted friends I needed them to like me for me, jacked-up situation and all.

"So, um, we're kinda in the middle of a remodel…" I explained as we stepped into the living room. It was close enough to honesty.

I watched Fyn's eyes take in her surroundings. I tried to see it from her point of view, but my breath hitched and time felt like it stood still as I had a flashback to right before I left for the summer. To our right sat the slouchy beige sofa, and I couldn't unsee the stuff that'd happened on that couch the night of the party. Stuff involving intoxication and teenage hormones and things that now made my skin crawl. To our left, mercifully just shy of the television, a fist-sized hole gaped at eye level like a portal to the moment my ex was too quick for Gavin's fist. And I wished with all my heart the stains on the carpet were from a puppy or something and not from the sloshing of red plastic cups.

I'd managed to avoid these thoughts since I came home, but now it all rushed back. I knew I'd have to face my choices, but I'd hoped Dad would've at least patched up the physical evidence while I was gone so I could focus on dealing with the mental baggage.

Man, things just got real.

I felt Fyn's eyes on me and turned. She raised a full eyebrow. "You okay?"

I coughed to clear my head. "Oh, um, yeah. Just remembering how much DIY we still have left. Gotta get some supplies this weekend..." I trailed off as I headed toward the kitchen.

"Oh! Can I help? Please? I even have spackle!"

I turned back around. "What? Seriously?" Like I even knew what spackle was.

"Yes!" Fyn actually jumped up and down. "My grandma lived in the attic, and she got tired of doing the stairs, and so she traded rooms with me."

I quickly ushered Fyn into the kitchen, far away from the hole in the wall. "What were you saying about spackle?" I motioned for her to have a seat at the table while I went to the fridge and retrieved two sparkling waters.

"Oh, right. Well, we did some remodeling in the attic before I moved up there, and we have all this leftover stuff. I could come over Saturday and help, if you want?"

I handed her a can. "You don't already have plans?" She was crazy, but she had that magnetic personality that drew people to you. For all I knew, she was popular at her old school. The good kind of popular.

"Nah." She tapped the top of the can with her nail. "We've

been in school three days. I haven't met many people yet. Do you have plans already?"

I popped the top on my own can. "No, not really..."

The conversation ended there as Fyn jumped into a commentary on the day's political science class. But I had a feeling we both knew we weren't telling each other everything, especially since we'd both grown up in Seattle and should have plenty of friends by now.

───── ○○○ ─────

"So, yeah, it just wouldn't start. We even tried using those cable things." I glanced up at the windowsill where my phone sat propped up, Truitt Peyton's face filling the screen.

He leaned back in his chair and stretched his arms behind his head. "Cable things, huh? I'm impressed. Did you line up the positive and negative ends right?"

Even though he was nearly three thousand miles away, I could hear the teasing in his voice.

"What?" I said in my best clueless girl voice as I inspected a coffee mug. "I thought the plus sign meant good and the minus sign meant bad." I shrugged dramatically. "Guess that's why the car exploded. Oh, well."

Truitt rolled his eyes.

"Of course, Yard Man," I said, using the nickname I gave him when I first learned about his job maintaining lawns. "We watched a video."

"Atta girl." He took off his ever-present ball cap and ran a hand through his thick brown hair before putting the cap back on. What was the purpose of guys doing that? "Next time, don't hesitate to call me. I'm not a mechanic or anything, but I know my way around a vehicle."

I set the last mug on the drying rack and wiped my hands

on my t-shirt. "How could I forget? The way you love that older woman in your life is relationship goals for us all."

He winked, and my mind went back to the summer when he taught me how to drive his old, dilapidated stick-shift truck. Her name was Beulah—which, according to Truitt, meant *beautiful* in Hebrew. She looked like a sunburned traffic cone.

Truitt was obsessed with Beulah and talked about it like it was his girlfriend or something. Kinda made me uncomfortable. How could I compete with *that?*

The driving lesson came shortly after I met Truitt and couldn't stand being in his presence. He was just so…*good*. His hero complex made him want to fix my life before he even knew the extent of it. But, as I later learned, it also covered up the broken parts of his own life he couldn't control.

That stick-shift lesson was the start of something we never saw coming. We high-fived at the end of that adventure then found ourselves in another argument about fifteen seconds later, but it was the beginning of all of this. Whatever *this* was.

"I thought you were fixin' to shove me out and run over me just for the heck of it," Truitt said, using a Southern term that still made absolutely zero sense to me.

"Don't think the thought didn't cross my mind. I—"

The front door opened, and I looked up from wiping the countertop.

"Everything okay?"

"Oh, yeah. Sorry. I think my dad's home. I'll talk to you later."

Truitt looked like he wanted to ask about how Dad and I were doing, but he knew better than to bring it up. Instead, he waved as I ended the call.

Dad walked into the kitchen. "Hey, Dad." I hung the dishrag on the edge of the sink. "I didn't know when you'd be back, but I put some of that stir-fry mix stuff in the fridge for you."

"Thanks, Sadie." He opened the fridge and rummaged around. "Talking to yourself in here?"

"No, that was Truitt from Georgia. We were catching up."

Dad closed the fridge, stir-fry container in hand. "Good. I was going to say, might want to see about making some new friends if you've resorted to carrying on conversations with yourself." He twisted his mouth.

I laughed. "Good point. I'm not quite that far gone yet, thankfully."

Dad reached around me to grab a fork from the rack. "There's hope yet."

Who was this man, joking around with me? Did Mike Franklin have an identical twin? Was this an uncle I didn't know about? I quickly scanned the room for hidden cameras.

I felt a flicker of boldness and grabbed it before it extinguished. "So what'd they say about the car?" Look at me, bonding with my father.

Dad stuck the container in the microwave. "The battery is shot."

I slid up on the clean but damp counter. I shifted my weight to avoid the dampness. "Is that my fault?"

The microwave dinged, and he pulled out the bowl. Stirring the veggies and chicken, he said, "No, it was old anyway. We just had to pay to have it replaced."

"Yikes. Was it expensive?"

He shrugged. "Not really, compared to most car issues. But it wasn't an expense I expected this month. I think it might be a good idea if you—"

My phone vibrated in my damp back pocket, and I jumped, nearly hitting the floor. I didn't want to end this moment of civility with my dad, so I hoped whoever was calling would take a hint. No such luck. We looked at each other, my back pocket buzzing, Dad eating his dinner.

Finally, he sighed, "Better answer that," and went into the living room. I took a turn to sigh. We were making progress.

I slid my phone out of my pocket and redialed Fyn. No one ever actually *called* me unless we had significant catching up to do. Just another of Fyn's eccentricities.

She answered on the first ring. "I thought you might be dead. What were you doing?"

"Dramatic much?"

"Sorry, I just wanted to check and make sure we're still on for getting living room supplies tomorrow morning. I was going to text you, but wanted to make sure you got the message. However…"

While listening to Fyn go on about the art of a real conversation, I carried my phone and a glass of milk into my room to work on homework.

Chapter Three

○○○

The knocking wouldn't stop on Saturday morning. I finally rolled out of bed and shuffled to the door in my pajama shorts and giant t-shirt. I slapped my tangled hair out of my face and glanced at the clock. *6:30.*

I opened the door to find Fyn standing on my porch wearing an old pair of jean shorts that looked like she'd cut them off herself and a baggy plaid shirt. Her hair had blue streaks today and was pulled up in a messy bun on top of her head. She looked about a hundred times more awake than I was as she took in my bedraggled appearance, hands on her hips.

"What the heck, Fyn?" I mumbled, my voice groggy.

Fyn grinned. "It's demo day!"

This made my eyes pop open. "*Demo?*"

"I'm joking." She adjusted her bun. "You're clearly not conscious yet. Get dressed or we'll miss the good stuff."

"The—" I stifled a yawn with the back of my hand, "—good stuff?"

"Yes." She grabbed a grocery bag from the porch and pushed her way into my living room. "We're going yard-saleing."

I folded my arms across my chest, suddenly aware of the fact I was in my pajamas in front of someone I'd known less than a full week. "I just wanna shampoo the carpet, Fyn. What does yard-saleing have to do with anything?"

Ignoring me, she pulled a plastic container out of her bag and held it up to the fist-sized hole in the wall. "I think we're going to need more spackle."

I shuffled back to my room to change while she mumbled something about calling a cement truck.

By the time I'd thrown on some clothes, Fyn had made herself at home in my kitchen and made a pot of coffee. I couldn't figure out how she'd found all of the supplies so quickly.

She handed me a travel mug and shooed me out the door and into her car, telling me to hold her phone and pay attention to the directions it gave me in an Australian accent.

"I call him my boyfriend," she gushed as she flipped on her blinker and pulled into a sleepy-looking neighborhood.

After a few winding turns, Fyn pulled the car up to a curb in front of a yard decked out in all kinds of junk. A poster board read: *Estate Sale 7:00 a.m.–1:00 p.m.*

"The internet told me this one will be awesome," Fyn said as we climbed out of the car. Above us, the gray of the pre-dawn sky was just beginning to fade into light pinks and yellows as the sun began its climb. I shivered in my hoodie and wondered how Fyn wasn't frostbitten yet.

We walked up the driveway, passed some of those fake trees people keep in their living rooms, and I froze.

The girl standing at a table of dishes turned toward me. "Can I help you find—*oh*. Hi."

I swallowed hard and stuck my hands in hoodie pocket. "Sam. I didn't know this was your house."

She shook her head but didn't take her deep brown eyes off me, like she didn't trust me. "My great aunt's house. She passed away a few weeks ago."

"Oh, man. I'm sorry, Sam."

Her eyes softened just a tiny bit before going back to the intimidating glare.

We stood there in silence for a solid minute, not knowing what to say to each other. Sam had been one of my friends—or rather, a person who I got along with—before that party.

My breath quickened, and I had to turn my head. "Sam, I—"

"Just tell me what you're looking for."

Oh, okay. So we weren't going to mend this thing. She wasn't yelling at me, yet my palms still went clammy.

Fyn stepped up next to me. "We're hoping you've got a rug or something. Sadie's got these gnarly carpet stains in front of her sofa, and it's disgusting."

"Wow, thanks," I mumbled.

Sam shifted her glare to poor Fyn and pointed over her shoulder. "Back there."

While we wove between tables of random vases and picture frames, Fyn muttered, "I'd like to see how much she sells with *that* attitude toward her customers. Like she doesn't actually want to get rid of this junk. She could frost a room."

"Where were you just now?" I side-stepped a pale pink ottoman and shuddered. I hated anything pink.

Either Fyn didn't notice my irritated tone, or she chose to ignore it. "I saw this collection of ceramic cats I wanted to check out."

I didn't think that needed a response.

"That's it!" Fyn declared, making me jump.

Oh. My...

"We'll take it!" Fyn hopped over to a gray-haired lady sitting at a table with a cash box. The woman seemed really dazed and confused. "How much for that rug?"

The woman looked at the rolled rug for a moment,

considering Fyn's question. "It's older, so I'll give it to you for twenty dollars."

"Sold!" Fyn elbowed me. "Give her the money, Sadie."

The backside of the carpet faced outward, so I hadn't even had a good look at it yet. But scared to object and beyond ready to get away from Sam's presence, I paid for the rug and helped Fyn stick the roll in the car. Even with the back seat folded down and the rug shoved between the two front seats, it still stuck out of the trunk about two feet.

After stopping at the hardware store for a wall repair kit and paint strips, we went back to my house. I had to focus on keeping my breathing steady while we drove. It wasn't a bad encounter, necessarily, but since Sam was that frosty, I now dreaded seeing my ex-friends even more.

"So tell me about you, Sadie," Fyn used a box cutter to cut out a piece of drywall to patch the wall, where she'd used some tool to saw a square around the fist hole. She was a constant surprise. "I mean, I'm in your house and for all I know, you could really be a forty-year-old man."

I covered my mouth with my hand to muffle an unattractive snort. "I can assure you, I'm not a man."

Fyn cut the final edge of the dry wall square. "Then who are you?" she asked. "Why have you lived here your whole life, but you never hang out with anyone else?"

I drew in a deep, heavy breath. "I've made some bad choices. And then I really lost my grip earlier this year." I fixed my gaze on the carpet. "I hung out with the wrong people, did the wrong things…so my dad sent me to spend the summer in Georgia with my aunt and uncle and their family. It was that bad."

Fyn nodded slowly as she glanced at some instructions on her phone, silently telling me to continue.

"And, well…" I hesitated. I was so new at this New Sadie

thing. So new at talking about God and believing I had a purpose. What if Fyn thought of Christians the same way I did before I became one? I had no clue what I'd do if I had to start over *again* at making friends. But I knew I had to be real; I'd spent too many years wearing a mask.

"I became a Christian about a month ago. I came back to Seattle with a new perspective. I know it seems weird, but—"

"You're a *Christian?*" Fyn stopped working and raised both of her eyebrows at me.

"Yeah. Sorry, I just—"

"Girl, me too! Where do you go to church? You should come with me tomorrow! We meet downtown. I'll pick you up. Ooh, you *have* to meet…"

Even though I had to interrupt Fyn's rambling to ask her to please stop waving the box cutter at me, I released the deep breath I'd been holding. *Thank You,* I whispered to God. I mean, wow. Who would've thought off-the-wall Fyn was a Christian, too? Just wow.

Raining Grace Community Church had me doing double-takes all morning. Tucked inside a warehouse in the heart of the city, the place was the exact opposite of the more traditional Pecan Creek Baptist Church, which was the only real experience I'd had with church.

As I stood in the darkened room, my foot tapping on the concrete floor and my eyes trained on the lyrics of an unfamiliar song on the screens above the stage, I felt my shoulders relax for the first time all week.

My uncle Kurt told me a church didn't have to be a certain style or look a certain way, and there didn't have to be pews or a steeple or nice carpeting for God to be there. The people around me wore everyday street clothes and some looked like they actually came in off the streets. And I loved that.

Fyn tossed her head back, raised her hands, and sang with all she had, not even caring if she was off-key. Surrounding us, other teens sang and danced and smiled for invisible reasons. I wasn't used to that. Dancing? Sure. But out of pure joy? Not so much.

"Good morning and welcome to Raining Grace!" The pastor said, taking the stage in a pair of jeans and a button-down. "Thank you all for joining us this morning. If you've come before, you're family. If you're new here, you're family too."

Family. The word I'd desperately wanted to claim as my own for so long. The word that once made me shut off my thoughts before emotions strangled me. But now, I'd found that word over the summer in an old yellow house in a small southern town.

The pastor continued, "If you have your Bible or a phone or a friend to share with, let's get into God's Word this morning."

I pulled my Bible out of my bag. It had been a birthday gift from Kurt, Melina, and the rest of the Elliots. The spine was still stiff. Tucking a leg beneath me in the folding chairs, I used my finger to trace the table of contents. I was so lost when it came to navigating this book.

"Today," the pastor said as he walked to the other end of the stage, "we're going to continue our series on loving even when it's difficult."

My finger froze on the page, and I looked up, eyes wide. It was like he was talking to the nagging feeling I'd had ever since I came back to Seattle. The one that whispered, *love your dad.* Goal #1.

The time passed more quickly than I expected, and soon

Pastor Theo was closing his Bible and saying, "Remember, Jesus loved you enough to actually die for you, even when you'd rather love anything else. So serving the people around you in small ways may seem like dying sometimes—" he shook his head "—but do it anyway. Ask and God will give you the grace for the challenge."

Grace. I could use about a truckload of that stuff when it came to Dad. Honestly, I rarely ever saw the man. And when we were both home, I stayed in my room or at the kitchen table doing homework, while he watched TV. I wanted—needed—to escape back to Pecan Creek as soon as possible, but in the meantime, that goal stared me in the face. How was I supposed to actually build a relationship with him when there wasn't a relationship to begin with?

After the service ended, I stood, accidentally dropping my Bible.

"Here, I've got it." A hand reached down, picked up my Bible, and handed it back to me. My gaze trailed from the hand up an arm to a shoulder to a guy's face. I quickly brushed my tear-stained cheek with the back of my hand, since it's possible I'd kind of cried a little during church.

"That's a cool Bible," said the guy with the short, dark hair and warm smile. "My sister has the same one and loves it."

I held it close to my heart. "Yeah, it's awesome."

The boy smiled. "I'm Owen, and you're…"

"Sadie. It's my first time here. I came with Fynnigan Larcy. Do you know her?" I pointed my thumb over my shoulder where Fyn stood, talking to a girl from school.

Recognition registered in Owen's eyes. "Oh yeah, I know Fyn." He paused, waiting for her to turn around. We stood there awkwardly, me watching him and him watching her. After a couple of beats, he said, "Can you tell her I said hello? I've got to leave, but I haven't had a chance to talk to her in a while."

"Yeah, sure. Nice meeting you, Owen."

As super-polite Owen walked away, stopping to talk to several people on his way out, I turned to find Fyn still talking with the friend, but shifting her eyes between Owen and me.

Chapter Four

○○○

"Are you sure it's okay if I come over?" I asked for the fifth time since leaving Raining Grace.

"Yes, I'm sure. My parents told me they want you to come to lunch. They're excited I'm already making new friends." Fyn stopped at a traffic light and flipped on her turn signal.

At church, we sat with a group of Fyn's friends, then we stayed a while after the service to talk to them. I hadn't met the rest of the Larcy family yet, but Fyn insisted they wanted me to have lunch with them.

"Do you live downtown?" I pulled down the mirror to check my makeup.

"No, not exactly." We drove to just the sound of the radio for a little bit, before turning into…

"Whoa, cool. You live here in Queen Anne?" I asked, taking in the gorgeous homes with the super cute front porches and beautifully manicured yards. When I was little, we would walk through Queen Anne and I would daydream about living in one of these castles. "So you're like…" My tact kicked in before I could say the word *rich*. "Um…*affluent?*" SAT vocab for the win.

"Correct," Fyn said, her tone apologetic. She had, after all, seen *my* house. "We moved here when I was little. It's in a great location, and there are a lot of memories attached to this place."

"There's no way we're zoned to be in the same school."

Fyn didn't seem to hear me. "Here we are!" she announced.

Fyn pulled into the driveway of a large, deep blue home with a low brick wall surrounding the yard. Stonework lined the base of the house, as well as the columns on the porch. White trim surrounded the three stories' worth of windows. It was breathtaking, even under the overcast skies.

Fyn unfastened her seatbelt. "Before we go in, I should warn you that my family—"

Fyn was cut short when a boy jumped out from behind the shrubbery and took off across the yard, whistling with his eyes trained on the grass.

I glanced at Fyn and caught her mid eye-roll.

Fyn led me up the steps and opened the door to beautiful, polished hardwood floors in a spacious living area. The boy squeezed in behind us right as I closed the door.

He set something on the floor and looked up at us, his limp brown hair hanging over his glasses.

"Sadie, meet my twelve-year-old brother, Fig. Fig, meet my friend Sadie." She motioned between the two of us.

"Hi, uh, Fig?"

Fig grinned. "Nice to meet you." His cheeks tinged pink, and he brushed his hair out of his face. "And this is Walnut."

Something bumped into my foot. I jumped and barely held back a shriek. Glancing down, I saw a clear blue hamster ball, with what looked like a little brown pom-pom inside.

"Walnut!" Fig shook his head and bent down to pick up the ball. "Where are your manners?" He unscrewed the lid and fished out the hamster. "Sadie, this is Walnut. He escaped from his ball outside a minute ago, and I thought he was a goner. But he came back to me."

"Delusional rodent," Fyn mumbled under her breath as she pushed me into the kitchen. "And his psycho hamster."

I wanted to ask what was up with the unusual names in the family, but I figured I should probably wait until I met everyone.

In the kitchen, a lady stood stirring a pot at the stove. Her brown-haired bun looked effortless, but I knew from experience that a style like that took serious skill. She crossed the kitchen, one hand holding a ladle, the other extended to me. "Sadie!" She smiled. "I'm Fyn's mom, Aubrey." I shook her slender hand, which sent her bracelets jingling. "And there's my husband, Brian." She tilted her head in the direction of a distinguished man with graying dark hair, seated at the breakfast table. He glanced up from a stack of papers and smiled warmly.

"Nice to meet you, Sadie. Fyn speaks highly of you. It's great to see she's making good friends at school."

Fyn crossed her eyes so only I could see them. I stifled a laugh. "And here's Gran," Fyn walked over to the table where her grandmother sat across from her dad. She wrapped her arms around the older woman and kissed her on the cheek.

"Hello, Sadie." Fyn's grandmother smiled all the way to her eyes. She was petite and had to be at least in her late eighties, and on first impression, she seemed surprisingly normal for the Larcy family.

"Gran's my BFF."

Gran nodded. "We go way back, don't we, honey?" The older woman winked, and my heart probably could've melted right there in the kitchen. Aubrey would have to ladle me up.

Fyn tugged on my arm. "Let's go upstairs before lunch."

"Five minutes, Fyn!" Aubrey called after us.

As I followed Fyn up the staircase, I couldn't help but ask, "What do your parents do?"

"Dad is a surgeon, and Mom is a partner at a law firm."

Wow, Fyn's family was impressive. Ever since my mom

died when I was eight, Dad and I had been the only ones in our small, tired, single-story house. We didn't even have a goldfish. Fyn hit the jackpot in the good life department. I had another "wow" moment when I stepped onto the third floor of the Larcy home. The room had one big window overlooking the Seattle landscape out back and another window facing the front of the house. Lots of natural light on a sunny day. The walls were painted a light gray, which was hard to see given all of the artwork covering the walls. Pages torn out of sketchbooks were tacked to the slanted ceiling in a little nook, where an easel also stood by a window. It was busy, but artsy. Totally Fyn.

"We call it The Cave," Fyn said, "because I can disappear for hours in here."

"So you draw and paint?" I couldn't help it; I had to step further into the room and turn a full circle to take it all in.

"Sometimes. But sculpting is my main thing right now. I have a studio out back because clay can be a mess."

"Uh-huh." I zeroed in on a sketch of a woman who had to be Gran. "You have so much talent," I whispered, caught up in awe.

She shrugged, brushing off my compliment. "More like cheap therapy."

When Aubrey called us for lunch, we made our way to the large farm table in the kitchen. I sat between Fyn and Gran, who entertained us with stories from the nursing home where she led Bingo and karaoke once a week. Fyn rolled her eyes, although I could tell she thought her grandma was incredibly cool. I did, too. An eighty-seven-year-old woman volunteering at a nursing home? Gran was awesome.

"I know what you're thinking, Sadie Franklin," Gran said suddenly, in the middle of her story about the time Bart Millard called Bingo and threw his card off the table in excitement.

"Ma'am?" I asked. Politeness couldn't hurt.

"You think I should be in that nursing home, too, don't you." It wasn't a question.

I pulled my elbows off the table and sat up straight in my chair. "Um, no ma'am. I don't think…"

"You think I'm a raisin, too far over the other side of the hill." Gran's eyes squinted, nearly disappearing.

"No, that's not…" My voice wavered.

"Sadie! You are so rude!" Fyn gasped and glanced at her father. "Dad, do you see how she's disrespecting your mother? The one who birthed you?"

Okay, this was getting out of hand. I set my spoonful of beans back on my plate. "You guys, wait. I'm sorry. I—"

Gran burst into laughter and reached over my head to high-five her granddaughter. Fyn winked at me.

"Gotcha, Sadie Franklin!" Gran said, gently slapping me on the back. "Welcome to the Larcy family."

I really didn't know how to move on with normal life after that, so once the Larcys finished stuffing me with tacos and guac, I followed Fyn back up to her room so we could quiz each other for the SAT. As I sat at her desk, I noticed a picture of her and a group of friends at a restaurant. One of the guys looked familiar. "Oh, hey, I met that guy today." I pointed with my pen and looked down at the floor, where Fyn lay on her stomach, surrounded by flash cards. "That's Owen, right?"

Fyn squinted at the picture, as if she had to think about who the person was. "Yeah, that's Owen." She ducked her head back down to her flash cards, like she was too fascinated by them to think about anything else.

Her reaction seemed weird. I didn't know her well enough to pry, but I still couldn't shake the feeling all was not well in Fyn Land.

As I sat across from Dad at the small kitchen table that night, the contrast between the Franklins and the Larcys couldn't be more stark. Dad and I ate scrambled eggs and bacon—my attempt at a loving gesture—and he seemed detached, like he'd lost interest in everything. We weren't exactly close, obviously, but we were all each other had. And he was invested in me enough to send me away to get my life back on track. But now he ate his eggs in silence, put his plate in the dishwasher (which hadn't worked in a couple of years), and slipped out the door. It was better than arguing, but it didn't exactly help with The Goal.

After finishing up homework, I decided to work on the living room. The rug Fyn bought still sat in the corner, so after I vacuumed, I grabbed a pair of scissors and cut the tape. Then I called Fyn.

She answered on the second ring. "What's up?"

"This jank rug we bought. It looks like…I don't even know…" I trailed off as I tried to find an accurate description. The red, gold, and brown Persian rug pattern was dizzying, almost like it was moving. I blinked to be sure it wasn't. "Fyn, I gotta send you a picture of this thing."

"Does it have stains?"

"No."

"Is it faded?"

"No."

"Then count your blessings and cover up that nasty carpet. Besides, starting over isn't always pretty."

Oh, how true that was. I did as I was told and stood back to see the full effect. One word to summarize? *Ew.*

I could only hope the paint we bought for the walls had miracle dust in it and could transform the rest of this space.

Fyn had some kind of appointment after school Monday, and I quickly realized how attached I'd become to her friendship in just a week. After struggling through precalculus homework, I threw on a pair of gym shorts and a t-shirt. I laced up my old pair of running shoes, and slipped out of the house. I stretched my legs straight, each foot pressing against the side of the house, then started out in a light jog. I hadn't run since I'd been back in Seattle, but I had no idea how much I'd missed it until I treaded down the sidewalk. It was like coming up for air after being underwater. I didn't know how badly I'd needed to breathe.

I wove around some garbage cans, careful to not let my feet slip on the curb. The houses in my neighborhood were certainly different than the ones in Fyn's neighborhood. All small with fences and overgrown bushes. Not too sketchy or anything, but definitely a different atmosphere. When my parents first moved to the area, they rented a tiny apartment. Then the man who hired my dad gave him a good price on the house. I guess he took pity on such a young couple with a baby. Otherwise, there was no way we'd be able to afford living in the shadow of the city.

I waved to a man checking his mail then kicked it into a full-on run. Houses flew past, and worries flew out. I decided to pray, my thoughts rapid and constant like the rhythm of my feet pounding the pavement. I was so new at talking to God, and it still felt so strange. But when I prayed, I felt peace. And that was something I desperately needed.

Halfway through my loop around the neighborhood, my side started to ache. A reminder that I was broken. I slowed down to a trot, trying to massage the pain in my abdomen. I knew that wouldn't help because the pain was internal. I knew cysts cluttered up ultrasound images of my insides. The pain stemmed from the fact I hadn't been eating right, and it was all I could do not to whimper my way home. By the time I reached the house, sweat dripped down my face, only partially due to the exercise. The pain throbbed in my lower gut and made me light-headed. I needed to make an appointment with a doctor, but there was a problem: I was under eighteen—a minor—which meant I probably needed a parent to go with me.

I could totally picture *that* conversation: *So, uh, Dad, I thought it'd be fun if you came with me to the doctor's office so they could take a look at my ovaries. Maybe they'll let me keep the ultrasound pictures this time, and we can hang them on the fridge.*

It'd send him straight to the fruit drawer.

———— oOo ————

That evening, I called my Aunt Melina to try to figure out the whole doctor thing.

"Hello?" she answered. I could hear a baby whimpering in the background.

"Hi, Mel?" I pulled my phone away from my ear to look at the time. I forgot about the three-hour time difference. "Should I call back tomorrow?"

"Oh, no. Sorry, it's fine. Evie is just fussy. Try again, Mel." She had this thing about talking to herself. She cleared her throat. "Hey, Sadie Grey. What's up?"

I smiled at the use of my middle name. Ever since I went to stay with the Elliots this past summer, she'd called me Sadie Grey as a term of endearment. At first it made me bristle, because my mom had been the only one who had ever called me that, but it gradually grew on me. Every time Melina said it now, I knew she was saying she loved me.

"Is Evelyn's colon better?"

"You mean her *colic?*" Melina's grin came through her tired voice. "It's still hanging on, which is why we're up so late. Trissy, Becca, and I take turns walking her around the house. But Evie's a fighter. She gets it from her cousin."

I blushed at the compliment. "So what causes colic, anyway?"

The baby's whimpers gradually quieted, and Melina sighed. "I'm not really sure."

"She takes after me in the unexplainable medical diagnoses department, too. Which is actually why I called." I shifted my phone to my other ear and turned on the sink to rinse some grapes. "I need to find a doctor out here, and I'm not so sure Dad wants to hang out at the gynecologist."

"Oh, Sadie!" Melina gasped, and the baby whimpered again. "I meant to send that information to you, but it's been nuts here." She hummed a few beats of a lullaby to the baby. "You just need your dad to sign a consent form, and you're good to go. I'll send him everything once I put Evie down."

I exhaled. That was good news. "Thanks, Mel."

"No problem. Hey, Trissy needs to talk to you for a second. She's supposed to be in bed, but she wants—"

"Sadie! Guess what!"

I pulled the phone away from my ear as my eight-year-old cousin came on the line. In the background, I could hear Melina whisper-hiss: "Tristan Elise Elliot! Do you *want* to pull an all-nighter with your little sister?"

Laughing, I brought the phone back to my ear and grabbed a bottle of water out of the fridge. The chaos was way less stressful when it was on the other side of the continent. "How are things, Tris?"

"I think I have a crush," Trissy whispered.

I pictured her cheeks matching her bright red, curly hair as she said this.

"You like a guy?" Holding the phone between my ear and shoulder, I twisted the cap off the bottle and took a long sip.

"No, silly! A boy has a crush on *me*. He thinks I'm hot stuff."

I coughed, and the water I'd just sipped spewed out my nose. *Ow.* I leaned over the sink and pinched the bridge of my nose.

"Sadie? Did you just freak out?"

"No, I'm good," I sputtered, still hanging over the sink. "Tell me more about this guy."

"Yes, Mama, I already brushed my teeth. Sorry, Sadie. Well, he is always in my space at church. Every time I go to pick something up, he gets it before I can. He says my hair is pretty and tries to pet it, and I tell him to stop because that's super weird."

I leaned against the counter and put the cap back on the water. I wasn't that thirsty, anyway. "Do you like him back?"

"Have you not heard me, Sadie? For an almost grown-up, sometimes you're way slow. He *pets* my hair. And he's only seven. I'm fixin' to be nine. I need an older man, and I think you can see why. What do I *do?*"

Her whine rang all the way from Georgia to Washington. "Well, my experience from when I was your age was that these things usually pass. He'll like another girl soon. Just ride it out."

"Should I pray about it?"

"Oh. Sure. Prayer works." Boy, didn't I know it.

"I will. I'm also praying about how to get a really cute older man to like me, too, so I'll keep praying."

Truitt. The "older man" in her life. As far as I knew, she had no clue I knew she had this adorable little girl crush on him. It was fun to watch, but I couldn't let her know that. I also couldn't let her know that Truitt and I were…what, exactly, were we? I missed him—needed him—but so far we'd done nothing more than exchange a few texts. My heart ached in my chest at all of the not knowing. But for now, maybe I could learn more through Trissy.

"So…" I said casually. "How's the progress with that situation?"

"Well, good when he's at my house." Her Southern accent heightened in her distress, adding extra syllables to almost every word. "But when other girls are around him, I'm chopped liver."

What other girls were around him? Girls Trissy's age…or my age? I started to ask, but Trissy interrupted:

"But then—Oh, hold on." Something covered the phone and her voice was muffled for a minute. "Mama says I've got to go. Later, Sadie. Mama says we love you."

Trissy ended the call and Pecan Creek once again felt a world away.

Chapter Five

○○○

The Encounter happened at school the next day. And it happened in the school bathroom, of all places. My life was such a teen drama.

I opened the stall door, accidentally bumping someone's backpack as she exited the stall next to mine. "Oh, sorry, I—" My throat closed up, and I couldn't finish my apology.

"Hi…" Ruby stared at me for a full five seconds, her eyes narrowing.

I prayed for courage. "How was your summer?" Cliché back-to-school question, but better than puking, which was my other option.

She laughed dryly. "Terrible, thanks to you. My parents took my car after you got the party busted." She flipped her brown hair over her shoulder and started washing her hands. It's not like we'd never been at parties when the cops showed up. This was just the first time things had gotten violent.

"Ruby, I didn't call the cops. I just—"

"Can it, Sadie."

I nodded dumbly, and my long bangs fell into my eyes, covering the frustration that simmered. I shoved them out of my face, quickly ran my hands under the water, and left the bathroom. So if Ruby didn't want to even talk to me, that meant the others were probably done with me, too. Really, though, they had just liked me for my sans-parental parties. I was just thankful Alyssa had already graduated.

I had to admit, The Encounter could've been *much* worse. My biggest fear wasn't even Alyssa, who was kind of the queen of my friend group, even though she'd let me think I held some sway. Griffin was the one I was most afraid of. Last I'd heard, he'd spent the summer at some kind of camp for people with issues. I wasn't exactly holding out hope that he'd offer to pay for my wall repairs.

I shivered and slipped into Brit Lit behind Fyn.

"Want to go camp out downtown and watch tourists this afternoon? Fig and I have a point system. If they're taking a picture outside the oldest Starbucks, that's five points. You get five more points if you see them immediately post the picture. It's also five points if you see them hanging around the market looking for flying fish. If they ask you where the Gum Wall is, that's ten points. And fifteen if you see them wearing a Sasquatch hunter t-shirt. I'm the champ with fifty points in ten minutes. It's a blast."

I blinked at her for a minute, trying to figure out how someone could be so alive. Everything about Fynnigan Larcy screamed life, from her crazy hair that now sported an orange streak, to her vibrant eyes that missed nothing, to her wacky love of random adventures.

"Love to, Fyn, but I'm supposed to talk to a friend this afternoon before homework."

"I'll be thinking about you when I'm out photo-bombing tourist pictures."

Mrs. Zurich called class to order, and we faced the front, not daring to be caught distracted. "Class, like we talked about on the first day of the year, your midterm grade will be a project. Your job is to teach a topic to the rest of the class using whatever means you decide. You can lecture, or you can be more creative." She handed a stack of papers to a student in the front row for him to pass around. "These are the details. We'll talk more as the weeks go on, but I wanted you to have a head start, should you decide to finish your prep work before Thanksgiving break. Your project is due when we come back."

Stifled sighs and groans slowly filled the room as students received their copies of the assignment. I looked down at the instructions and slid a little lower in my seat. I didn't have an artistic bone in my body, and the thought of writing and performing a play or something made me feel like I would break out in hives.

"You'll do this in teams," Mrs. Zurich continued. "Against my better judgment, I'm letting students pick their partners this year so I don't have to put up with complaining."

The most creative person I'd ever met bounced in her seat in front of me. This was right up Fyn's alley.

Mrs. Zurich grabbed a marker for the whiteboard and raised her eyebrows. "Just know that if any sort of issue arises in your team, there will be absolutely no swapping partners. This time next year, you'll be in college, and you'll wish for the structure of high school."

I could almost feel all of the eyes rolling around me. Some kid behind me muttered, "Yeah, right."

Ignoring that guy, Mrs. Zurich said, "On your way out today, come write your name and your partner's name on the board for me to make note of. If you need help finding a partner, see me after class. Now, let's take out our copies of the text."

While backpacks unzipped and pages rustled, Fyn glanced back at me. "Partners?" she mouthed.

I nodded. "Let's do it."

Dad actually came home in time for dinner. I was so surprised when he opened the door, I spilled my coffee on my English notes.

"Dad. I didn't expect you back until late."

He shifted two McDonald's bags into his other hand so he could shut the door. "I was tired and decided to take off early. I brought dinner."

He looked at me—actually looked at me—and smiled. What was this life? He plopped the fast food bags onto the coffee table next to my homework. "Thought we could eat?"

I didn't tell him I had a quiz I desperately needed to study for. That could wait. I'd pull an all-nighter if it meant I could eat dinner with my dad. It was as if God was answering my prayers for helping us get along.

"I'll get us something to drink. Where do you want to sit?"

He gave me a look that said, "Are you *really* asking me that?" and pointed to his recliner.

I slipped into the kitchen and came back a few minutes later with a Diet Coke for Dad and a glass of water for me.

I handed him the can of pop, and he tossed a food bag to me.

"I didn't know what you'd want, so I got a couple things."

It was stupid, I know, but I felt like a giddy little girl opening a present. My dad brought me dinner. He got off work early and thought to bring his kid food. I wasn't into journaling, but I'd have to write this night down.

I reached into the bag and pulled out a cheeseburger, a large order of fries, and a ten-piece box of nuggets, followed by an assortment of sauces and ketchup packs.

"Wow, Dad. I won't have to grocery shop for a week." I smiled sideways at him, and he smiled back. "Thank you."

I wasn't supposed to eat any of the things in front of me, and I wouldn't have an update on anything health-related until my doctor's appointment. I didn't want to mess up. But my dad had tried. If I had to be up half the night with stomach pains from a Big Mac, so be it because Mike Franklin tried.

I decided if I was going to break all of my dietary rules in one fell swoop, I might as well enjoy the burger first. Unwrapping it, and avoiding eye contact with Dad, I asked, "Is it okay if I pray really quick?"

Dad swallowed a bite of burger, his brow furrowed. "Okay, Sadie."

I knew he wasn't happy with me mentioning God, but I couldn't help it. I closed my eyes and quickly mumbled a thank you for the food and for time with my dad, then said amen. Opening my eyes, I saw he was still looking at me.

"We can eat now..." I suggested.

Dad turned on the TV, and we chewed in silence while we watched the news. Dad surprised me when he said, "You did good on the wall, Sadie. Who taught you how to patch holes?"

"YouTube." I was surprised he'd even noticed. "And my friend Fyn helped me. She's into painting and stuff." Although, saying Fyn was into painting was like saying Seattle was rainy sometimes.

"Well, I'm impressed."

Okay, now I was *really* shocked. I almost choked on the nugget I'd stuffed in my mouth. Had Dad really just complimented me? Was he running a high fever?

"Thanks. I just...the house needed a little attention, so I decided I might as well start on the wall. I also got this rug."

"You know I'm gone a lot, Sadie," Dad said. "That's why I haven't fixed the place up."

"I know."

"I'm busy. And when I get home, I'm exhausted."

"I'm not saying you—"

"I know you probably think I don't do much around here, but I work long hours to take care of you."

Clearly, "take care of" was a subjective term. "Yes, Dad. Sometimes I think you work too much."

Dad set his pop can on the end table. "What does that mean?"

I felt my shoulder muscles tighten. "I just mean your schedule is hard on you and wears you out. Maybe if you worked less, we could spend more time together and have more time to do things like fix up the house."

He sat up straighter in the recliner. "If I worked less, I couldn't afford your lifestyle, Sadie. All those parties you somehow had the means to pay for. You think I didn't know you were taking my money?"

I swallowed. Yikes, I had been *so* messed up. "You're the one with beer in the fridge!"

As soon as the words left my mouth, I wanted to grab them back.

Dad stood. "You of all people can't talk about lifestyle choices. I know the kind of kid you are. I know what you did in Georgia. Kurt and Melina told me."

"Yeah?" I was standing now, too. It was true—I had snuck around, drank, partied, lied, gotten into a fight, and been too involved with the wrong type of guys. But there was more to the story. Dad had to believe that. "Did they tell you I changed?"

"You tell me that. A hundred times a day. But this 'change' of yours is new. You'll get tired of the idea of a good God as soon as the next thing goes wrong. Give it time."

"What are you saying?" I started stuffing dinner trash into the paper bag. I couldn't eat another bite, and it had nothing to do with a medical condition. "Are you saying I'm not really working hard to get it together? Isn't that what you wanted me to do?" I hated the edge in my voice.

Dad grabbed his own trash and wadded it into a ball. "That tone. Don't do that. I came home early to spend time with my daughter and you end up being hypocritical again. Pointing out my habits while forgetting who you really are. I'm not having this conversation with you." He turned and walked into the kitchen.

My blood boiled. Why could I not get along with that man for more than five minutes? Why couldn't we have a real conversation? And why couldn't I prove I was different now? I swallowed a foul word I would've said without hesitation a couple of months ago. Even though I was angry, I wouldn't disrespect my dad like that. Not again.

Instead, I walked over to the table by the front door and grabbed my keys. In my frustration, they clattered to the floor.

"Where are you going?" Dad leaned around the corner. He didn't look angry, just tired and frustrated.

"I have to go to the store."

He sighed, exasperated. "I decided to go out anyway. What do you need? I'll get it."

He reached for his own set of keys, and I fought the urge to ask why he was going out if he was off work. Did he want to get away from his kid that badly?

Besides, he couldn't go to the store for me. I had needs he didn't understand. There was no way he'd get it. But there was also no way he'd let me go if he was about to take the car.

"Okay," I finally resigned. I softened my voice and examined my fingernails. "I need...tea bags."

I hated sweet tea. Absolutely despised the syrupy stuff. It was like I could feel cavities forming with every sip. But at that moment, I just craved something familiar and comforting. Something that reminded me of Pecan Creek and my family.

Dad looked at me like I'd just told him I needed chest

implants. But to his credit, he didn't say anything; he just turned and walked out of the house, shutting the door behind him.

"So be honest with me." Truitt's voice came through my phone's video chat app extra loud, and I adjusted the volume. "How's it goin'?"

I watched him run his hand through his thick brown hair. I felt his eyes on mine, even though we were separated by a screen and nearly three thousand miles. "Okay, I guess. It's like my dad and I can't get along to save our lives, but I keep praying and working on it. School is school, and my friend Fyn has been awesome." I set my phone on my desk, propping it against my precalculus textbook, so I could collect the stray hairs that had worked their way loose during my run and tuck them into my ponytail. "Now it's your turn. How is your mom?"

Truitt dropped his gaze to his lap, then looked back up. "Last I heard, she was fine. She'll be in the rehab program for a while, but if it helps her get a handle on her—" he swallowed "—her addictions, it's worth it. Kurt and Mel feed me sometimes, and I hang out with the Shepherds a good bit, too. I'm also picking up some extra yards to try to keep my head above water. Child support only goes so far."

I stuck on him hanging out with the Shepherds. He hadn't hung out at their place that much all summer. So why now? But I didn't want to start something. "Wow, Truitt," I said. "That sounds so tough."

"Yeah. But I've got great support. People to check up on me."

"I'm proud of you for reaching out." And I meant that. I thought back to the night I'd learned Truitt was living with an abusive, strung-out mother and how he worked long hours to pay the bills since his mom couldn't hold down a job. He'd been embarrassed and ashamed to admit he couldn't handle it all, so getting help was huge for him.

"Thanks, Franklin. Make sure you do the same, you hear?"

"We'll see. Gotta finish homework now, though. Tomorrow night I'm going to try out youth group with Fyn."

He gave me a thumbs-up and smiled. I could barely make out that endearing dimple on his chin. "Sounds good. I'm fixin' to call Becca and walk her through her math study guide. Have a good time tomorrow."

My throat suddenly felt thick, and I blinked a couple of times. I wanted to be in Pecan Creek so badly. I wanted to be near Truitt and talk about us—about the future and if he'd be in mine. He'd never called me Franklin until this conversation. Was that a friendly nickname, or something else? We weren't officially a couple because of the whole distance thing. And because we both knew neither of us was probably emotionally healthy enough to handle a relationship right now. But it was clear we needed to be in each other's life.

And that feeling went a little deeper than friendship. He'd only kissed me once, but you don't kiss your friend on the mouth—and she doesn't go weak-kneed when it happens—unless there's something more involved. I'd give anything to just have him sling an arm around my shoulders and talk to me about the ideal height of grass blades or one of the other random things that fascinated him.

"You okay, Sadie?" His voice broke through my thoughts.

"Oh, yeah. Zoned out. I'm sorry." I couldn't tell him how much I missed him. He needed to know I was going to be all right. I could do this separation thing, learn to get along with my dad, and make new friends. He had enough going on without worrying about me. "Tell Becca I said hi and I'll call her tomorrow."

Truitt propped his chin in his palm. "Will do. Hey, Sadie?"

"Yeah?"

"Hang in there, okay? I'm praying for you. And I miss you somethin' crazy."

I smiled slowly, my mouth wobbling, my eyes saying things my lips didn't dare to speak. "Miss you, too."

———— ○○○ ————

"Welcome to Café Graffiti!" Fyn spread her arms wide as we stepped into Raining Grace. It was the same room we'd been in Sunday, but the place had been transformed. The rows of chairs still faced the stage, but café tables had been placed in the back, and the smell of coffee wafted from a station set up in the corner. Large drop cloths covered in graffiti and various art hung around the room, the paint glowing in the dim lighting.

"Like the art?" Fyn asked, leading me over to the coffee station.

I nodded, fascinated by it all.

"It was done by yours truly."

"No way."

Fyn flipped her green-streaked hair over her shoulder. "Don't praise me so much, Sadie. I'll get an ego."

After fixing cups of coffee, we walked over to a group of girls I recognized from either church or school.

"Sadie, right?" Liz asked. "How's the car holding up?" She smiled, the tiny stud in her nose reflecting the dim light. She was nearly a foot taller than me and in any other circumstance, I'd be intimidated by her. But something about her was warm and welcoming, despite the tough exterior.

I talked to Liz about school for a few minutes until a girl named Jen entered our conversation and introduced herself. Jen was slim and small, with long blond hair and eyes that reminded me of an owl—round and alert, yet cautious. I vaguely recognized her from my precalculus class at school. Before long, several others had joined our group, swapping stories about the teachers at school, and I was actually disappointed when Liz and Jen left to get ready to play in the band and everyone else made their way to the chairs.

I stood by Fyn during the music, feeling it pound in my chest. Owen was on the keyboard, Liz played bass, and quiet Jen had a voice that almost knocked me over.

I didn't know the lyrics, so I watched them on the screen and listened to Fyn's raspy, slightly flat voice.

Saving, healing, restoring, redeeming. Keep changing me, God, for the sake of Your name.

I wasn't sure what all of it meant, but those seemed like some solid lyrics. Restoration? I'd like to order a truckload of that, especially for my relationship with Dad. Although, was it really restoration if we'd never actually had much of anything worth restoring? And it's not like I wanted restoration with Ruby or Alyssa or Gavin or any of them. Those relationships were toxic, poisoning my identity and sense of worth and probably my liver, too.

During the next song, a slower one about rescue, I noticed something shining on Liz's face as she played and sang along. Tears. God had reached her heart, like He'd reached mine. And although I didn't know her story, I knew grace had caught her, too.

After the music, Jordan, the youth pastor, stepped onto the stage. "On Sundays recently, we've been talking about loving those it's hard to love. Loving those who don't deserve it. Let's take that even deeper tonight..."

I caught a laugh in my throat. "Okay, God," I whispered. "I'm listening."

Chapter Six

○○○

I froze in the middle of the school hallway. All of the noise and shuffling around me faded as Ruby and one of her cohorts walked toward me. I watched Ruby whisper something to the other girl as a guy from the baseball team walked past. Did she see me? There was no way she'd missed me. Why did I pick a bright green shirt to wear that day? You couldn't miss seeing me in the middle of a dark forest.

I practically ran to the nearest girls' restroom and locked myself in a stall. My heart beat wildly in my chest and beads of sweat broke out on my forehead. I perched on the edge of the toilet seat so I could put my head in my hands. I tried to focus on taking deep breaths, but my mind raced a million miles an hour. Dark spots danced in my vision, and I started to shake. What was happening? I tried to get myself under control, rocking back and forth. I'd never dealt with strong anxiety before. Was that what this was? I didn't know if I was going to throw up or pass out. All I knew was that I couldn't breathe, and I wanted to run. My forehead was clammy, and I couldn't swallow. Scenes from all of my past interactions with those girls flashed through my mind, mixed with the sound of sirens and yelling and Ruby and Alyssa threatening to get me back and slander my reputation for calling the cops.

Finally, I thought of Jesus. "Please help me," I whispered. "I'm freaking out. Please…" I mumbled and rocked until my heart rate finally started to calm down. Now it was more of a canter rather than a gallop.

My heart gradually stopped slamming against my ribs. I shakily stood up. I didn't know how long it'd been since the warning bell rang, but I knew I was in trouble. I splashed water on my face at the sink and hoped I didn't smell too much like sweat.

When I walked into British Literature, Mrs. Zurich stopped lecturing and the entire class turned to look at me.

"So glad you could join us today. Now we can start the party," Mrs. Zurich said dryly. She held out her hand. "Where's your note?"

My mouth felt like I'd been sucking on cotton balls. "I-I don't have one..." I stammered.

She looked hard at my face for what felt like a whole minute. Probably taking in my swollen eyes and pale, sweaty face. "Are you all right?" she asked quietly.

"I'll be fine," I whispered back.

"Then take your seat and do not let this happen again. Now, class, back to Dickens..."

I exhaled the breath I'd been holding ever since I walked into the room and slipped into my seat. *Thank you, God.* Mrs. Zurich could've busted me so hard. And from what I'd heard about how strict she was, it was a miracle she hadn't.

Fyn didn't say anything to me, but I could see her swinging her foot in anticipation of learning what I'd been up to.

Sure enough, after class she grabbed my arm in the hallway. "What's going on? You looked like a zombie when you came in!"

I shrugged her off. I'd never been all that touchy-feely with my friends. "It was nothing. I just don't feel well." I turned down the hall toward precalculus class.

"Unh-uh. I can read your face." Fyn stuck her own face way too close to mine. "What happened?"

I didn't want to be late for class again, and I also didn't want to have this conversation in the middle of the crowded hallway. As it was, I was already jumpy and afraid I'd run into the group again. "Let's go to my house after school and I'll tell you, okay?"

Even though Fyn did not look like she liked that idea, she nodded. "Okay."

———— ○○○ ————

"Is your dad at work again?" Fyn asked as she settled onto the couch.

"Probably. He'll get in late."

"Are you sure you have a dad?" Fyn asked. Her eyes went wide, and she quickly swiped a hand back and forth in front of her face to erase the words. "That was so inconsiderate. I'm sorry, Sadie."

I shook my head. "He works a lot, but it's whatever." *Although sometimes I wonder if I actually have a dad, too.*

Fyn raised her cup to her mouth and took a big gulp. Her eyes bulged again as she struggled to swallow. "Man, you weren't kidding when you said you made sweet tea. That's intense. I feel like the South just exploded in my mouth. All I need now is a giant monogrammed hair bow."

I laughed, remembering the first time I'd tasted the syrupy Southern drink.

"So about today…"

I sat sideways on the couch facing Fyn, my feet tucked into the couch cushion and my back against the arm of the couch. I pointed behind me. "That hole in the wall?"

"Yeah…"

"Right before I went to Georgia for the summer, I had

a party. It got way out of hand, and the cops showed up and everything. Basically, that ruined my friendships. I was known as the one who threw the best parties because…because my dad was never home…but I found out they bailed as soon as it got inconvenient. They just liked me for what I could offer. I saw some of them again today and, well, I freaked out."

Fyn watched me over the rim of her cup. "So that's why I don't see you hanging out with any of your friends, even though you've always lived here?"

I nodded and sipped my own tea, wincing as it went down. I wanted to remember the good times, but at what cost?

"You really were a wild child before you became a Christian, weren't you?" Fyn asked.

"Yeah. I partied, I drank, I basically did whatever I could to try to be okay with my life. But it left me feeling empty." I shook my head. "That's the past. I'm not going down that road anymore."

Fyn set her cup on the coffee table. "Thank God for grace, huh?"

"Yeah," I said as I turned to look at the patched-up wall. Even with a coat of paint over the hole, you could still see the outline. Like a scar that reminded me of what I'd been through, but didn't define me anymore. "Thank God for grace."

I grabbed a bag off the shelf and tried to decide if it was worth it, sale or not. *Green bean chips?* They looked disgusting, but they also looked healthy. But come on, *green bean* chips? I slipped my phone out of my pocket to send Becca a picture.

"Sadie, right?"

Owen stepped up next to me. "Yeah. Hi, Owen." I quickly placed the bag back on the shelf.

Awkward silence. Must. Break. Awkward. Silence.

"Um, so, how's it goin'?" I asked, recognizing the Southern twang that slipped out. Weird how you can live somewhere your whole life, then spend a few months in the South and come back tainted. Either that, or the sweet tea kicked in.

"Not bad. What are you up to?" He motioned toward the green bean chips.

"Trying to eat healthy. It's so weird." I grabbed the bag of chips. "Know anything about these?"

Owen smiled, one of his front teeth slightly crooked in an endearing way. "Not at all. I'm not a fan of imposters, and *these*"—he reached over and thumped the bag—"should feel ashamed for calling themselves chips."

My eyes met his since he was exactly my height. "So what would you recommend I buy in terms of healthy snacks? Beef jerky?"

Owen shook his head. "Oh, no. I'm a vegetarian."

I brought a hand to my chest. "Are you sure?"

He laughed, the sound slightly raspy. "Pretty sure."

"Then what would you suggest? Tofu? Because that's an imposter too."

"Negative. I'd check out the hummus. It'll change your life."

He reached out, and I thought he might touch my hand. But he pulled the package of thick-cut bacon out of my basket. "And this will shorten it."

I snatched the meat back. "I'm a fan of quality of life, Owen. And it's already dead whether I eat it or not. I don't want it to go to waste because *that* would be tragic."

For a second, I thought I'd offended him because, yikes, that came out strong, but he just laughed. "To each her own. I'll see you around, Sadie. Tell Fyn I asked about her if you see her?"

I shifted my basket to my other arm and pulled my phone

out of my pocket to read Becca's reply. "Sure, Owen." Weird, intriguing boy.

———○○○———

"So, Martin Luther King, Jr. Cool guy."

I jerked my head up from the biography I was reading to find Liz sitting in the chair across from me. Totally hadn't heard her sneak up on me in the library. It was easy to zone out to the music in my earbuds.

"Yeah," I said. "I've got an assignment on him. Fun fact: Where I lived in the South this summer, literally every town has at least one street named for him."

Liz cocked her head to the side, her nose ring catching the light, and I caught myself wondering what happened when she had a cold. Did she sneeze snot out of her piercing?

"You're stuck in Georgia, huh?" she asked.

"What do you mean?" A guy at the table next to us shot me a look, and I lowered my voice to a whisper.

Liz didn't. "At Café Graffiti, it's all you could talk about. It's the first thing you chose to talk about right now. I get the feeling you don't actually want to be here."

I slid an index card into the book to mark my place. "You're right. I'd rather be in Georgia. But I've gotta graduate, so here I am."

Liz glanced at the clock on the wall above the computer station behind me and stood. "'Wherever you are, be all there,'" she said as she grabbed her backpack off the floor.

"Are you a poet or something?" I blinked up at her. She was so tall.

"Actually, yes. I dabble in poetry. But that's a quote from Jim Elliot, who was a missionary in Ecuador."

"Elliot? That's actually my relatives' last name. The one's who live in—"

"Georgia. I know. Later, Sadie."

"But—"

The guy next to us cleared his throat.

As I watched Liz wander off into the stacks, I thought about what she'd said: *Wherever you are, be all there*. I wasn't sure what that meant, so I jotted it down on my index card and slipped it into the pocket of my jeans to think about later.

She was still loitering outside of the library half an hour later when I left to go grab dinner before meeting Fyn for coffee.

"Did you think about what I said?" she asked, using her foot to push herself away from the brick wall she reclined against.

"What are you, my guardian angel?"

She smiled. "Nah. Just looking out for a sister."

I fished my keys out of my backpack. "What's it mean, though?"

She whipped out her phone and replied to a text before answering me. "It means live fully wherever you are. Your body, heart, and mind need to be in the same place. That's half of the quote."

I put a hand on my hip. "You must be a pastor's kid or something," I said, although she was the polar opposite of Becca, the squeaky-clean PK I knew in Pecan Creek. *More like a PK gone wild.*

Liz tossed back her head and full-on laughed. "You're hilarious. Let's just say my dad wasn't passing out Bibles on the streets when the cops gave him a lift."

I didn't know what to do with that information, but I was starting to see Liz was not so different than me in how she also had big things to overcome.

I stepped into Goldfinch's Coffee Co. and inhaled deeply. This was my all-time favorite local coffee roaster. I'd spent hours studying for tests at one of the distressed wood corner tables. Countless Saturday mornings holding my head over a strong cup of coffee and a breakfast sandwich to fight off a hangover. It was like a haven for me, in a way. I'd definitely missed Goldfinch's.

After Fyn showed up and we ordered coffees, we went back to my old corner table near the front window and watched the world darken.

"What are your thoughts on Raining Grace and Café Graffiti so far?" Fyn asked, breaking my coffee trance.

"I liked it. It's a lot different from the last youth group I went to. Actually, Raining Grace is totally different from where I went to church this summer, except both places are pretty cool."

Fyn smiled over her cup of coffee and tucked a strand of dark blue hair behind her ear, showing off a row of earrings. Fyn's hair was a different color every week. It was always something vibrant, just like her personality.

"Yeah, I bet it's probably different. And Raining Grace is a church plant."

"What does that mean?" I blew on the top of my coffee.

"Another church started it a couple years ago. They put it downtown on purpose, so it's pretty urban. We get all kinds of people, and I think that's the most awesome thing ever. Some of us literally sleep on the streets. Some of us have been in jail, made drug deals, sold ourselves, and some of us—like my parents—are pretty well-known in the community. But I think that's what church should look like because I think that's what Heaven will look like, you know?"

I nodded slowly. "Yeah. That's cool." I took a cautious sip of coffee.

"The thing to remember, though," Fyn went on, "is that everyone has a story. Everyone comes from a different place. Everyone has a past. Sometimes that past is really dark or difficult. But that's what rocks about Jesus. He meets you where you are, but He loves you too much to leave you there. You wouldn't believe some of these people's stories, Sadie."

"Wow," I responded. I had never heard Fyn go this deep. She was always so over-the-top spirited and emotion-driven. To hear her talk about God's rescue made something stir inside of me. It felt similar to the first time I realized I had a true friend in Becca Shepherd.

"So. . ." I wrapped my fingers around my mug and watched the ripples in my coffee smooth out. "You know some of my story now. What's your story, Fyn?"

Fyn didn't look at me at first but rather fixed her eyes on something out the window. She blinked slowly, then looked straight at me. "I got into some trouble at my old school," she said slowly, like she was releasing a breath. "I got expelled. I grew up going to church, but it wasn't real for me. God used that terrible fall-out to get my attention. To get my heart. So starting over, like what you're doing? I totally get that." She nodded like she was finished talking and reached for her homework, eerily calm.

———— oOo ————

The next Sunday morning, I found myself back at Raining Grace. I knew I could've tried another new church, but Raining Grace was the one good thing in my life, and I decided not to mess with that. During his message, Pastor Theo talked about how to serve people who are difficult to deal with as a way of showing them God's love.

"Whenever you find yourself wanting to just give up, serve them. Channel that energy into doing something for them, rather than marinating in the anger and letting it control you," he said.

I'd already tried doing nice things for my dad, but now I had more of a focus for my goal: Build a relationship through serving him. If I could show him how much I had changed, then why wouldn't he change, too?

I was still mulling over it all as I rode to Fyn's house with her for lunch after church. "So where were you all day yesterday? I thought you might've been up for some more yard-saleing," Fyn said, breaking the silence.

"My room needed some serious cleaning, and then I worked on trying not to fail that Brit Lit project. How is your part coming?"

Fyn glanced over, giving me a blank expression. "Project?"

"You know. The one that's due mid-semester? The one we've been working on? You're designing the presentation?"

I wasn't used to being the one on top of homework assignments—it was giving me an identity crisis, actually—but I was so determined to do well this semester so I could graduate in the spring. Fyn didn't know about how I would've been repeating eleventh grade if I hadn't taken classes in Georgia over the summer.

She blinked. "Oh. Right."

"Oh! I forgot to tell you. I ran into Owen the other day and he said to tell you hello, but he probably told you himself today."

Fyn's grin froze. "Owen?" she said his name without moving her mouth. Impressive.

"Yeah. Apparently you've been avoiding him?"

"He said that?" Fyn turned into her driveway a little too quickly, and I grabbed the safety handle over the door.

"Well, no, but that's the impression I got."

She climbed out of the car and practically jogged to the

door. Something weird was up between the two of them and, although I was good at being nosy—I mean, *observant*—I was scared of doing anything that would hurt my relationship with Fyn. She was pretty much all I had.

In her room, a pile of paint-splattered newspapers lay in the middle of the floor.

"Sorry about the mess," she said, kicking aside last Tuesday's weather page. "I've been busy."

I took in the scene. Paint brushes lay scattered on her desk, like they'd spilled out of the cup and she hadn't bothered to put them back in. Tubes of paint sat in piles on the floor near a blank canvas, and sketches littered the bed. Everything smelled like acrylic.

"No wonder you haven't thought about our project," I breathed. "You've been creating."

She offered a half-smile. "Yeah. They were fixing a leak in the studio roof, so I've been up here working." She inspected the ceiling. "There's something you should know, Sadie."

I sat on the only open spot on her bed and nodded slowly. "What's up?"

"Owen's connected to my past. He goes to my old school and knows…well, my past. He could ruin me in a second."

"Would he?"

"I don't think so. But I just avoid him. It's easier."

I guess that made sense. But still…

"What happened that was so bad, Fyn?"

She walked over to her closet. Then back to me. Then back to her closet. She was pacing and it looked like she wanted to throw herself out the window.

"I—I—" She started to speak then stopped. I waited for her to finish, but all she said was, "I need to breathe." She brought a hand to her throat.

I jumped up. "Do you need an inhaler or something? Do you have asthma?"

She shook her head so jerkily her hair slapped her face. She took a deep breath and released it. Then she walked over to a pile of clothes in the corner and pulled a big t-shirt on over her clothes. After changing into a pair of paint-stained jeans and putting her hair into a knot on the top of her head, she finally spoke. "No. I need to sculpt."

Chapter Seven

Fyn's studio was surprisingly tidy for such a small space—and for belonging to a living hurricane. The walls were a light gray like her bedroom, and the distressed desk in the corner looked antique. A tall, paint-splattered bookshelf sat in one corner holding mason jars of brushes and tubes of paint. Blank canvases were wedged between the cabinet and an easel.

"This used to be a garage," Fyn said as I took in the space. "But we closed it off and installed heat and A/C so it's like an actual room. Now the art won't be damaged by the humidity or temperature outside."

I just nodded. I knew even less about art than I did about precalculus.

Fyn grabbed some clay and plopped it on a work table. Straddling a stool, she began to move her hands up and down the clay, smoothing and squishing the gooey mixture. She hummed while she worked, and it was like I wasn't even in the room. In fact, I'd just started turning around to leave and give her some space when she spoke.

"How do you breathe, Sadie?"

I blinked. "Usually through my nose, unless I have allergies."

She rolled her eyes. "No, I mean how do you *breathe*. How do you cope when life is crazy?"

Oh. "I run."

"Literally or metaphorically?"

"Huh?"

She gently pressed her fist into the center of the lump. "Do you actually lace up your shoes and run down the street, or do you run away in your mind to avoid stuff?"

Well, that was personal. "A little of both, I guess. But I do actually run. It helps me clear my head."

When running wasn't an option, I focused on my breathing. In and out, in and out. Breathing, like running, had kept me from freaking out so many times in the past, kept me from feeling emotions that scared me.

"Sadie," Fyn said. I couldn't take my eyes off the sculpture coming to life in front of me. It was tubby and bottom-heavy—the beginnings of a vase? "This is how I breathe. This is what I do when the world is spinning out of control. I guess in a way it makes me feel like I actually can control something. Especially last year when—"

The bowl caved in Fyn's grip, and she pounded her fist into it, mumbling something that sounded like a very creative substitute for a four-letter word.

"I'm sorry," she apologized. "When I think too deeply, I get too heavy-handed and ruin what I'm working on. I'm such a piece of work."

"I can relate," I admitted. I perched on the edge of the desk a safe distance away from the clay splatters.

"It's all in the sanctification," she said softly as she began reshaping the clay.

I raised my hand. "New Christian over here. I don't know churchy words yet."

Fyn laughed and flicked a piece of clay at me, which I dodged, nearly falling off the desk in the process.

"No worries. I just learned it, like, a few months ago. It's like…" She paused to think, squishing the clay like a stress reliever ball. "It's like the process of God making us into what He created us to be. Like, He slowly helps us get rid of the stuff that's no good. He keeps doing that until we get to Heaven. I don't know if that makes any sense how I'm describing it. But the main thing is that it's a process. You don't get saved and get sanctified all at once."

That made sense to me. It explained why I still struggled to love my dad and why I still couldn't manage to talk with any sort of a filter. Maybe it all took time.

Fyn dropped the clay on the table and faced me, her knees bumping up and down. She was always moving.

"I'm so not perfect, Sadie. I'm a wreck most days. I've done things I hate. I'm like this bowl." She looked down at the goopy, uneven object with a hole in the top.

"It's not finished yet, Fyn," I said.

She half-smiled, eyes still focused on the clay. "Right. Just like me." She wiped her hands on a rag, then pulled her knees up to her chest. "I spent some time…away from home recently…and I learned this passage from the Bible. I'm not a church girl or a good girl or a Bible know-it-all, but this one gets me. It's when Paul writes about how God has put light in our dark hearts so that we can know who Jesus is. Then he goes—get this, 'cause it rocks—'But we have this treasure in jars of clay to show that this all-surpassing power is from God and not from us.' And that's why I love sculpting so much. It's a metaphor for me. It helped me learn to feel again when everything was numb. It's how I talk to God—through my art." She looked down at the clay with soft, shiny eyes.

"I'm just a messy clay jar with a treasure inside. And the treasure makes all the difference."

This was a side of Fyn I didn't know existed. A softer,

quieter, more vulnerable side. And a reminder that people were complex, and everyone had their own set of issues.

"There's actually this quote I memorized that's really similar. It goes, 'We are only clay pots—common ones of clay—so that the splendid power may belong to God and not to us.'" She scrubbed at her cheek with the back of her hand. "I love it."

"I love it, too. Who said that?"

"This lady named Elisabeth Elliot."

I stopped mid-hairband adjustment. "Elliot? Like that man? Jim?"

Fyn nodded. "Yeah. They were married."

"They were missionaries in South America, right?"

Fyn tilted her head. "Look at you, knowing your Christian history."

I shrugged. "Hardly. Liz was just telling me about that Jim Elliot quote about being 'all there.'"

"Mm-hm. He definitely practiced what he preached."

I rested my weight against her work table. "What do you mean?"

"Jim Elliot went to tell a group of hostile people about God and how He loved them. He knew it could cost him everything, but he did it anyway. He was all there. And they killed him."

I exhaled. "Whoa."

"Yeah. Later, Elisabeth went back to those same people."

I didn't know what to say. I complained about staying in Seattle for a few months, but the Elliots gave everything they had to tell people about a God who loved them. "What would it be like to have faith like *that*?"

I didn't realize I'd verbalized that last part until Fyn said, "They were 'all there.' I've got a pretty good feeling they don't regret it."

I kept thinking about Fyn's words long after I left her house, went home and did a load of laundry, and crawled into bed hours earlier than I would've before Jesus started sanctifying me. I had so much to learn.

In the elevator, I ran my finger down the list of doctors until I found who I was looking for: *Dr. Terry Hart.* That name sounded friendly, right? Mel sent me some info that I'd need for my first appointment and included a list of doctors. I had no idea how she found all of this stuff. Dr. Hart was the first name on her list, and her name made me think of terry cloth. And hearts. So warm and fuzzy. Plus, my reason for visiting her was super personal, so I wanted a doctor like Dr. Summers in Georgia who would actually listen to me.

On floor six, the elevator dinged, and I followed a sign into the waiting room. At the desk, I grabbed a clipboard and went back to my seat to fill out my family's medical history, most of which I kind of guessed. I didn't know my dad's parents at all, and I barely knew my mom's parents. Who knew if they ever had heartburn? I mean, really.

Then I got to the part about substances. I'd never smoked or tried drugs, by the sheer grace of God, but the alcohol thing was another story. I counted on my fingers how long it'd been since I had a drink. It was in the middle of summer—the night I went to a party with a guy who I thought understood my junk but still wanted to be with me. Turns out, he was a player. And that night of one-too-many was the night I came home in a cop car, broke my aunt and uncle's trust, and resolved the painful—both physical and emotional—side effects of drinking just weren't worth it for me anymore.

"Sadie Franklin?" The nurse called my name nearly an hour later, right as I was in the middle of a super foods crossword puzzle. Which was fine, since I wasn't sure how to spell *quinoa* anyway.

I stood and followed the nurse into a room, where she took my weight and blood pressure and asked me the typical doctor questions.

"What's the date of your last period?" The nurse looked at me through a pair of tortoise shell glasses.

"Spring. My former gynecologist told me that's part of this condition, so we're still working on that."

She nodded. "Are you on any medications?"

"Birth control." Whoa, that was still a weird one. The medication was supposed to help balance out my hormones and remind my body that it belonged to a seventeen-year-old girl. Although it was good for making jokes that made my aunt uncomfortable.

"Take a break from Seattle boys, Sadie," Mel had told me the day before I left.

"What are you worried about? I'm on the pill."

She'd actually thrown a sofa pillow at me.

After a few more questions, the nurse left me sitting in an exam table, staring at medical posters that made even *me* uncomfortable. Instead of analyzing what I was looking at, I pulled out my phone and checked my texts. One from Becca: *Let me know how it goes today. I love you!* And one from Truitt: *So I ate a whole large pizza yesterday. Please make better choices than I do.*

I smiled to myself. I missed them like crazy, but it helped to know they were still there for me, even in the busyness of life. The door creaked, and I slid my phone into my pocket.

The nurse entered the room, followed by a man in a crisp white lab coat.

Wait...

"Miss Franklin? I'm Dr. Hart." He extended his hand and I just stared at it.

"Miss Franklin?" He asked again.

I finally broke the staring contest I had going on with his hand and shook it. Then I looked at his face. His young, just-out-of-med-school, tanned face with killer white teeth. I felt heat creep up my neck.

"Oh, um, yeah. I'm Miss Franklin. I mean, I'm Sadie Franklin. You're Dr. Terry Hart?"

"I am. But let's talk about you. Tell me about yourself. Fill me in on what you're dealing with."

Under any other circumstances, I'd love it if a guy who looked like *that* cared about what I was going through. But I'd totally thought Terry Hart was a girl's name. What the heck?

I swallowed and took a deep breath, then dove in and told my story.

"I'm a runner, but this summer I started getting really bad stomach cramps when I ran. And then it started happening when I ate different foods, too. Sometimes for what seemed to be no reason at all. And then right here—" I pressed a hand onto my lower abdomen—"it felt hard, like I'd pulled a muscle. So I went to the doctor back in Georgia, where I was staying, and she did some tests…" Even though I knew he was the doctor and had more of a handle on this kind of information than I did, I went on to explain what Dr. Summers had said about ovarian cysts and how my body didn't process insulin like it should and how that condition was called polycystic ovary syndrome—PCOS. I left out the part about how I'd learned your chances of having children were a lot slimmer with this condition, and how I'd learned my mom had it and hadn't thought I'd be possible and how she never expected to get pregnant with my dad so young. And how I'd been a twin, but my brother or sister died before we were born. At this point, I realized I was babbling, but I'd worked through all of that this summer, and it had been incredibly painful. I'd come a long way in healing, but it was still a tender spot on my heart.

Dr. Hart asked me a few more questions before he was satisfied.

"Well, Sadie," he said, leaning back against the wall and crossing his arms. The man had muscles. "It sounds like you're doing everything right, and your body is responding well to that. Hopefully we can get your cycle back on track soon. I would like you to try to keep track of what you eat and how it makes you feel, but other than that, keep doing what you're doing. Low carbs, low sugar, all that. If you start feeling kind of off, you can try cutting out dairy as well."

"Dairy, as in ice cream?" What was he, delusional? "That'll be my last dessert—I mean—*resort.*" He laughed and I blushed again. This was so awkward. What was next, nervous giggling? Aunt Mel was *so* going to hear about this.

———oOo———

Fyn opened the door with a flourish, so quickly I took a step back. "Sadie! Welcome!" She pulled me inside and shut the door. "You're the last one here."

I held up a bag of snacks. "Dark chocolate M&M's and popcorn."

Fyn held out her hand in the direction of the kitchen. "Perfect. Jen and Liz are already here, so you can set your stuff in the living room and join us in the kitchen."

I followed orders. Jen sat at the kitchen island and watched while Liz pulled chocolate cupcakes out of a box and arranged them on the counter.

I'd just sat down on a barstool, my eyes never leaving the cupcakes, when the doorbell rang. Fyn shot up out of her seat, yelling about pizza.

I turned to Liz and Jen. "We're not getting any sleep tonight, are we?"

Liz rolled her eyes. "You may not want to. The first time I slept over, she poured Pop Rocks in my mouth."

I grinned. "Sounds exciting."

Jen sighed, the first noise I'd heard from her since she told me hello. "She froze my bra."

I laughed so hard I choked. Girls actually did that?

Fyn came back into the kitchen, carrying the largest pizza box I'd ever seen.

"Whoa." I almost started drooling as the distinct smell of pepperoni, cheese, and garlic reached my nose.

Fyn grinned. "I got the biggest size. It's gonna be a long night, ladies."

She lifted the lid and I whipped my phone out of my back pocket to snap a picture. Truitt would die when he saw this.

Distributing plates, Fyn said, "Someone pray so we can inhale this."

"I'll go," Liz said, and we all closed our eyes. "God, thank you for friends. Thank you for fun and laughter and this pizza. Although I'm not sure if we should ask you to bless it or ask you for forgiveness for what we're putting into the bodies you gave us. Amen."

We all dug in. I instinctively wanted to go for the biggest slice. I knew my gut would hate me, so I settled for a half slice.

Fyn eyed me suspiciously. "What's wrong? Not a pizza person? Oh no, are you vegetarian?"

I shook my head. I didn't really want to talk about what was going on with me physically unless I had to because it was kind of personal. But what was a sleepover without sharing secrets?

I sighed. "I actually have this thing where I have to watch what I eat—I've gotta stick to low carbs and limited sugar and dairy. Basically all of the good stuff." I tried to laugh but it sounded pitiful. "It has to do with how I don't process insulin and stuff like I should."

The girls all watched me, waiting for me to go on. I shrugged. "But yeah, that's me."

Fyn, for once, didn't say anything. Instead, she walked over to the fridge, opened the door, and began pulling fruit and a giant salad out of the fridge. My eyes went wide.

It was her turn to shrug. "Gran was worried we'd die if we didn't have real food, even though I told her we were getting pizza. So this is for us, too. Or you, Sadie, because I'm so calling dibs on your slices."

I smiled to myself as I piled strawberries onto my plate. God was looking out for me, even in little ways. And for that, I was grateful.

After dinner, Gran returned from her evening neighborhood stroll with a neighbor. The Larcy parents were at some sort of medical convention in Oregon for the weekend, and Fig was at a friend's house.

Gran walked into the living room right as we were settling onto the sofas in our pajamas. Hanging out in Fyn's room was out of the question, since it basically looked like a FEMA project.

"Gran! What's up!" Fyn jumped up and led Gran over to a spot on the couch. "You're just in time for girl talk. Tell us about that time Bart Millard hit on you with a pick-up line about ham."

Gran chuckled, the deep wrinkles around her eyes doubling. "Oh, Bart." She leaned back on the sofa, somehow managing to keep her perfect posture. She folded her hands in her lap and her eyes took on a faraway look as she thought for a minute. "Well," she said, looking at the three of us. "I was serving New Year's Eve refreshments at the nursing home.

They do it up big each year, with a ball drop and everything. So it was a few minutes 'til the ball drop—"

"At eight thirty," Fyn muttered.

Gran swatted her. "Nine thirty, thank you." She winked at me. "So there I was, refilling the deli tray before I found my seat, and Bart comes up to me. He stabs a piece of ham with a serving fork and holds it up to me and says...'Marilyn, will you *meat* me for dinner tomorrow night?'"

Gran's eyes twinkled as she laughed softly.

"Tell them what you said!" Fyn bounced in her seat.

Gran shushed her with her hand. "Now, Bart's an older gentleman—he's ninety-five—and not really my type."

Wait, was this woman ninety or nineteen?

"So I take another fork and stab a slice of provolone and say..." She paused for a beat. "Now, Bart, that was too *cheesy*."

Fyn lost it and fell over onto Jen. Gran laughed with us, too, her laugh warbly and warm.

Then she yawned and slowly stood up. "You ladies have a fun night." She waved as she headed for the hallway. She paused when she reached the doorway and leveled her gaze on Fyn. "No bras in the freezer this time." And with that, she left us to our own devices.

"I can't get over how cool your grandmother is," Jen said. "I miss mine."

"Yeah, I don't know mine all that well," I added.

Fyn smiled, and something in addition to her agreement flickered in her eyes. Something that looked like a mix of sadness and pain. She blinked it away almost as soon as it appeared. "I definitely don't take her for granted."

After a movie and a few trips to the bathroom for each of us—since way too much coffee and pop was consumed—we all found ourselves on the floor of the living room, spread out on a pallet of quilts, blankets, and pillows. Fyn turned off all the lights, except for the flashlight on her phone, which she placed on the floor beside us.

"So," Liz said around a mouth full of popcorn as she plopped down onto an extra-long pillow. "Who's got a good guy story?"

Jen, Fyn, and I all shrugged.

"Sorry, Liz," Jen said softly. I was learning she was a force to be reckoned with when she had a mic in front of her on stage, but she was quiet like a mouse in regular conversations. "No juicy information here."

"Please," Liz said. "It's always the quiet ones you've gotta watch out for." Jen just smiled. Liz nudged me with her elbow. "Sadie?"

I sighed. Where did I begin? "Not really, no. I mean, I met a guy over the summer and we're still talking. But I'm not really sure what we are. We're kinda...volatile."

Three faces stared back at me in the glow of the phone light, waiting for me to explain. I pulled a blanket onto my lap and pulled my knees up to my chest. "I couldn't stand him when I met him. He seemed to have it all together. Everyone adored him. He loved to be everyone's hero, and that got on *all* of my nerves. For whatever reason, he decided he wanted to be my friend, even though I was a complete jerk to him. We ended up spending a lot of time together, and honestly, we fought more than we got along. But I got to know him, and he's got a big story of his own. Now..." I paused to choose my words. "Now it's like he gets me in a way no one else does. And one night, the night I became a Christian, actually, he kissed me."

My mind went back to that night in the hospital when my cousin was born. Truitt had been in Chicago on a mission trip and he, Becca, and my Uncle Kurt had hurried back for the emergency birth. I went out in the waiting room after Evie was born because Kurt said some people wanted to tell me congratulations. And there was Truitt. He ran to me, picked me up, spun me around, and kissed me. It was so unexpected, yet it felt like it was what I was waiting for all along.

The girls sighed at my story. "So then, what's the deal?" Liz asked. "It sounds like everything's right."

I shrugged. "We've never really had a conversation about it. Life got super busy and then I left a couple weeks later." *Plus, he and Becca say they're just friends, but I'm not so sure.* "So we'll see…" I trailed off, still not used to sharing so much of my life so candidly. "Okay, Fyn. Your turn."

"Super single," she said, although her eyes seemed to widen slightly in the dim lighting.

Liz said, "Amen, sister friend," then the conversation shifted to a discussion about dry shampoo.

Somewhere around 3:00 in the morning, Fyn and I found ourselves as the only two awake. I was exhausted from the hours of movies and chatting, and I didn't know if I was still up because of all the coffee I'd consumed or if it was because I really didn't want to experience icy underwear the next morning.

I followed Fyn up to her room for a couple more blankets, carefully stepping over Jen, who'd curled up like a cat right on the floor.

Fyn flipped on the light in her room, and we squinted. She recovered sooner than I did and snagged a gray quilt off her bed. She tossed it to me, and it hit me in the stomach. I still couldn't see.

My eyes adjusted after a second and I sat on the bed while Fyn fished a hoodie out of her closet.

"This has been fun," I yawned. "Thanks for inviting me."

Fyn emerged and pulled a navy sweatshirt over her head. "Of course. I've only known those two a little bit longer than I've known you, so it's good for me. My parents are all concerned about me making good friend choices." She rolled her eyes.

I could only dream of a parent who cared about my friendships. I'd told Dad I was spending the night at a friend's, and the only thing he'd asked was when I'd have the car back.

"So, seriously, no guys for you, huh?" I asked, still not quite ready to fall asleep.

She climbed onto the bed and scooted back to the pillows. "Not really."

I almost accepted her answer, until I noticed how her hands fidgeted with the drawstring on her hoodie. "Who is it?"

She sighed, reminding me of Jen. "There was a guy, but we're too different now."

"What happened?" I yawned again and flopped onto my stomach.

"He knows too much about my past to ever want me. So it's not even a discussion, really."

Something about her words seemed familiar, and I wracked my tired brain to remember. Slowly, a conversation came back to me—Fyn had said she'd avoided someone and his friendship because he knew her past.

"Owen," I whispered, even though there was no one else awake to hear us.

She nodded and continued to fidget with the hoodie. "It's painful, Sadie. To like someone so much who could pull your past into your present."

"Was he involved?" I still had no idea what she meant when she referenced her past.

"Oh, not at all," she said quickly. "But he saw it all go down. I'm working so hard to start over, and he could ruin that."

"But would he?" I flipped onto my back and stared at the

ceiling, which was covered in sketches done on sticky notes. "He seems so sweet."

Fyn shrugged. "I don't know. Probably not. But even if he wouldn't, I still feel too ashamed when I think about what he knows. It's just not meant to be."

We were quiet for a minute, each lost in our own thoughts about the situation.

Finally, I said, "Truitt knows all about me, and it didn't scare him away. And I've been in some pretty rough places. I'm not the best spokesperson for this, but you could talk to him and—"

"I'm just not there yet."

"Okay." That was really all I could say because I knew as well as anyone that heart stuff took a long time.

Fyn slid down onto her pillow and joined me in studying her ceiling. Somewhere in the middle of her explanation of a series of Bigfoot sketches she had tacked up there, I drifted off to sleep.

Chapter Eight

○◯○

I opened the door and took a deep breath, my party music blaring from the living room. I hadn't been in Dad's room in so long. It used to be my parents' room before Mom died, even though they didn't always sleep in the same space. Dad spent a lot of time on the couch because of the weird hours he worked. Or at least, that's the reason he gave me. I knew my parents had deep issues. Like the God thing, for starters. Mom had faith, and Dad had the sports network. But I had always considered their room Mom's space. It had made me angry that he took it over after Mom died. That's where I'd crawl into bed during a storm or for a story. That's where I'd tell her about my dreams and where I'd watch her get ready for church on Sunday mornings.

Thinking about all of that made anger threaten to rise in my throat. I had a thing for avoiding memories because even the good ones were tinged with pain and hurt. It didn't matter that Mom had been gone nearly nine years, or that I'd lived just as long without her as I had lived with her. What mattered was a little girl lost her mom in a horrific car accident, and her dad was more of a symbolic figure than a present parent.

I breathed a quick prayer and entered the man cave. The bed was made, which totally threw me for a loop. Mike Franklin wasn't much for housekeeping. I unmade his bed and tossed the sheets and pillowcases in the wash. Then I dusted the furniture, my eyes clouding at the pictures of Mom, of Mom and Dad, of all of us. The pictures of a whole family, no matter how loose the definition of family was. I then vacuumed the bedroom and set about scrubbing the bathroom. Gross. This was servant love.

After lunch, I pulled the warm sheets out of the dryer and took them into Dad's room. Everything looked so neat and clean and awesome, and it felt so good to be productive. Dad would be thrilled when he came home. I'd heard him leave early this morning, and I didn't know when he'd be back.

I dumped the sheets on the clean floor, then spread out the fitted one. I was kinda tempted to play parachute with it, but we were aiming for maturity these days. The sheets had been easy enough to pull off, but because one side of the bed was against the wall, I had to slide the bed out a little to tuck in the corner sheets. The frame was solid wood or something, so I ended up sitting on the floor, feet against the frame, wrestling the thing into submission. When that failed, I realized I could just slide the mattress. Duh.

I walked around the bed and the mattress slid effortlessly. Now I could see that a t-shirt had fallen down the crack at some point. I reached down and picked it up. Only, it wasn't a shirt.

I stared down dumbly at the camisole in my hands. Somehow it must've gotten tangled up from my laundry and into the load of sheets. But then I looked closer. No way was that mine. Sadie Franklin was not a lace kind of girl, and this thing looked more like straight-up fancy underwear than what I wore. And my mom's clothing couldn't still be there after all these years, right?

I tried to rationalize it all in my head for several minutes, holding the thing loosely in my grasp and staring at it. There was only one other explanation, and I refused to go there.

No. No way. That's not possible. No one else had been in the house. I was sure of that because I was always home. Surely...

On an impulse, I rushed into the bathroom and started flinging open the cabinets. I had no idea what I was looking for, but I didn't find anything.

I had just finished making the bed when the door opened. Would I never learn my own father's schedule? I finished fluffing the pillows and stuffed the cami back where I found it. I washed my hands and refused to think about it. And I refused to bring it up.

I met him in the kitchen.

"What's up, Dad?" My smile wobbled, and dark thoughts crowded into my mind. *Whose is that? Surely Dad isn't...doesn't... Mom.*

Everything came back to Mom. Our glue. Without her nothing made sense in this house, even though she'd been gone so long.

"Sadie," he said as he studied my face. That was weird. Dad didn't study my face. "You look a little green."

"Gee, thanks. I love a good confidence boost," I deadpanned. It just happened automatically, and it kind of freaked me out how quickly I could retort without even thinking about it.

Dad opened his mouth, probably to tell me to shut mine, but I interrupted. "I shouldn't have said that." Pride kept me from outright apologizing. "I've been cleaning. The chemicals must be messing with me." Then, quickly changing the subject, I added, "I cleaned your room today. Fresh sheets and all that."

Dad looked shocked. He slowly set down the bottle of beer he'd been sipping. "You cleaned my room?"

"Yeah."

"Why?"

I shrugged. "I didn't want to do homework all Saturday,

and I just wanted to help out. I know you work crazy hours and you're always tired."

He leaned against the kitchen counter, the lines around his eyes deeper than they should be for a man in his thirties. Sometimes I forgot how my dad was younger than my friends' parents, which was probably part of why he never really hung out with my friends' parents when I was growing up. My parents were just a little older than I was now when my mom got pregnant. It's possible I might've followed in their footsteps and ended up with a baby in high school if God hadn't gotten my attention. The thought made me shudder.

Dad looked at me a moment longer, tilting his head slightly to the side, his brown eyes blinking. "Well, thank you, Sadie. I appreciate that."

I shrugged again. "No problem."

Then it was his turn to shock me. As he walked past me into the living room, he patted me on the shoulder.

I wanted to give Dad the benefit of the doubt, but the longer that camisole sat in my mind, the harder it was to stay silent. Not that I'd ever greatly admired my father, but in a way, I could depend on him to be the same man he'd always been.

My only escape from all of the questions was to run, fast and hard. I was addicted to the feel of my shoes hitting the pavement, the air brushing sweat off my face, the fire in my calves. I loved gasping for breath because it meant I was pushing myself to do more, be more than I was before.

On Tuesday, I ran until the sun set. By the time I stepped into the house, everything hurt, especially my abdomen. My doctor had told me running wouldn't hurt my cysts, but that didn't mean my cysts didn't hurt me. I clenched my fist against my side and bent over, realizing I had overdone it.

Sweat dripped from my face. Some of it was from the run, but some of it was from the throbbing pinch in my gut. I popped a couple ibuprofen into my mouth and washed them down with a cup of water. I glanced at the clock on the stove. Apparently, Dad was working. He had the weirdest schedule. Maybe he was covering for someone else's shift at the hotel where he worked.

Leaving my shoes outside the bathroom door, I stepped inside the bathroom, turned on the shower, and began peeling off my sweat-drenched clothes.

As I scrubbed my face, I made a mental note to call my aunt and uncle. It had been a few days. I knew they were up to their chins with their kids, church, and everything else in their lives and they didn't have time to listen to me whine about my life. Truitt, too, had been so busy we'd only texted back and forth a handful of times over the past week. Becca wasn't one to have deep conversations through texting, and we hadn't had time to talk on the phone recently. She must be swamped, too.

Rather than feeling refreshed by my shower, I ended up feeling discouraged and alone. Kurt and Mel would be putting kids bed, so I knew it was a bad time to call. And Fyn declared at school that she was spending the evening locked in her studio because stress was getting to her.

A few hours later, I tucked my feet under a blanket on the couch and struggled through precalculus homework. This class would be the end of me.

Dad stepped into the house and tossed his keys in the little bowl on the table by the door.

"How was work?" I asked before I remembered he didn't usually wear jeans to work.

He stopped moving for a minute to take in the candle burning on the coffee table and the classical music streaming from the laptop. I admit it was very un-Sadie-like, but I read an article called "5 Ways You're Doing Homework Wrong," and it told me to light candles and listen to music that was good for my brain. Or something.

Dad fished his wallet out of his pocket and added it to the bowl. "I had dinner with a friend tonight, since I had some time off."

I resisted the urge to ask him why he wouldn't choose to have dinner with his kid and forced a smile. "That's awesome. Do I know him?"

Dad shook his head. "No, I don't think so. Is that cinnamon?" He scrunched his nose and pointed to the candle. It *was* a little strong.

"Autumn Abundance," I corrected. I stifled a yawn and went back to my homework. It was getting late, and that was enough niceness.

"Here," Dad said, and I noticed for the first time he held a cup in his hands.

My eyes teared up as he held out the coffee cup. "This is for me?"

He nodded. "My friend told me to try the spiced flat white, but I guess I'm not classy enough." He smiled and I smiled back as I took the cup from him. My fingers touched his, and my mind flashed back to when I would clasp his sturdy fingers with my little girl hand. Was it lame that I wished I could still do that?

"Thanks, Dad. Maybe this will keep me from drop-kicking this precalculus textbook straight up to Canada."

"Precalculus, huh?" Dad said. He walked around the coffee table and sat on the other end of the couch.

I sipped the lukewarm coffee, too lazy to actually get up and stick it in the microwave for a minute. "Yes. Remember how I barely scraped by in Algebra last year? This one's already kicking me. And I'm actually trying this time."

Dad reached for the textbook in my lap and flipped through a couple pages. What was going on? Who was this man?

"Hand me your notebook," he said, putting the textbook between us on the couch. I handed it over. "You know, I'm not too bad with numbers. . ."

True. Dad had managed to rise to a management position with only a partial business degree. When Mom got pregnant, he stopped going to school to get a full-time job.

I was scared to ruin this awkward but sweet moment, but I had to ask: "Do you think you maybe could help me with this? I've got a quiz in the morning and I had to spend most of the afternoon studying for the SAT."

Dad slipped off his shoes. Propping his feet on the coffee table, he placed the textbook on his lap. "Probably not, but let's give it a shot."

I watched in amazement as Dad spent a few minutes reading the textbook and working out some things on his phone's calculator. The light from the lamp created a soft, cozy feel in the living room, and the candle added even more warmth. It was all so unfamiliar, the warm feeling in my chest I got as my dad and I sat side-by-side, working through math problems. I glanced over at Dad as he searched the textbook glossary for a term neither of us knew. He really was handsome for a dad. He kept his hair short, but the ends frayed out just a little, giving him a youthful look. The lines that appeared on his brow as he focused were evidence he'd dealt with some serious stress in his life, but his strong jaw showed he could handle it. I imagined my mom falling for his rugged features and that self-confidence he always wore so naturally. I'd never really thought about my dad as a person apart from being a dad. I thought about asking if he wanted to run with me some time, but that was something sacred that was only mine, and I didn't want to share it.

Instead, I sipped my coffee as Dad read a paragraph about inverse functions. He stayed next to me while I worked through the assigned pages, nodding along and referring back to the book when a problem stumped us.

"So, Dad?" I ventured as we finally closed my textbook a few minutes before eleven thirty. "I'm taking the SAT next Saturday, and after that I'm gonna start job hunting. I need as much time as I can to save up a few hundred dollars for the plane tickets, and—"

"Plane tickets?" Dad stood from the couch, so tall. "Where are you going?"

"Well." I untucked my legs from beneath me and stretched them out the length of the couch. "To go ho—I mean, back to Pecan Creek over Christmas break. I need a few hundred dollars, at least."

"Seriously?" Dad asked, rubbing his neck.

"Well, yeah. I didn't want to ask you for money."

"No," he sighed and his expression cooled. "I mean, you've only been home a little while and you're already planning when you can leave again. It's like you can't wait to get away from me."

"It's not you, it's—"

"It's what, Sadie?" He used his knee to slide the textbook away from the edge of the coffee table.

I looked at him for a full minute, focusing on taking deep breaths so I wouldn't go off on my father. Finally, I whispered, "It's nothing."

He shook his head. "It's not nothing. How do you think I feel? You can't wait to escape your own family. You *hated* the idea of going to Pecan Creek, and you hated me for forcing you to go. You hated all of the structure and rules so much you rebelled and did your own thing anyway, like you were back home. But *that* is better than being where you belong?"

"I've been trying to tell you I've changed, but you won't listen. You only hear what you want to hear!" I yelled, surprising both him and me. I mumbled an apology, but my pounding heart drowned it out.

"Really? You've changed?" he said, crossing his arms over his chest. "Because it sounds to me like you're doing what you've always done. Distracting yourself from what's in front of you, not caring who you're hurting or inconveniencing in the process."

I put my feet on the floor and stood so he wasn't looking so far down at me. I crossed my arms. "Right, like getting me out of your hair is such an inconvenience." I knew I was winding up and it scared me, but I couldn't quit. "I thought you'd be thrilled I wanted to leave again. I thought you'd be counting down the days until I left so your problem child wouldn't be in your way, taking your money, begging to spend time with her own father. I thought you'd be *so* excited for me not to be here so you could invite your *girlfriend*—" I clamped a hand over my mouth, my eyes wide. I had *not* meant to say that. Why did that come out? I wasn't even sure.

I squeezed my eyes shut, cursing myself and not wanting to look at Dad. When I finally opened my eyes, he was staring at me, jaw slack.

"I found her camisole, Dad."

"Her what?"

"Camisole. It's a girl's undershirt, Dad. I found it the other day when I was cleaning your room."

His eyes narrowed. "Why were you cleaning my room...?"

"I already told you," I choked on my words and tried again. "I was *trying* to be *nice* to you because you're my *dad*, and

I know you work long hours and just wanna crash when you get home. I didn't know I'd find the underwear of some—"

"That's *enough!*" Dad yelled, kicking the coffee table. I knew he wouldn't actually hurt me, but who knew what he'd do to the table. He swore.

"Who. Is. She?" I asked, punctuating each word like it was its own, complete sentence.

I wanted him to deny it. *Needed* him to deny it, rather than just stand there looking at me. My dad had a woman over. In the bed he shared with my mom. His *wife*.

I stared at Dad through hot, angry tears, waiting on his answer. Begging him to say it was a mistake. It was one thing to have a girlfriend, but a whole other thing to have her over at night.

Oh, God, please let this be a nightmare I'll wake up from in the morning. Chin trembling, I whispered, "Please. Tell me I'm wrong. Tell me I've accused you of something horrible and I'm way wrong. Please tell me it's all a misunderstanding, Daddy."

I hadn't called him Daddy since I was very young, and looking at his face, I could tell he was aware of that.

"Sadie." He paused, ran a hand over his jaw, his eyes still intense. "She's a nice woman. I've been lonely, and—"

"So you're sleeping with Mom's replacement."

At the mention of my mom, his brow furrowed. "That's enough," he said slowly. "I don't need to explain my decisions to my kid. I'm not doing this with you right now." He turned and walked to the door, grabbing his keys and jacket on the way out. Leaving me standing in the living room, feeling like I'd been fooling myself to think my dad and I might actually build a relationship.

Chapter Nine

○○○

Dad spent even less time at home that week. Fyn was also taking the SAT on Saturday, but said she studied better under house arrest, so I saw little of her as well. After spending so much time together ever since we'd met, it felt weird only texting her while I studied in the evenings.

I took an SAT prep class over the summer, so by now my vocab index cards were pretty battered. I absolutely had to do better than the last time I took it while hungover from a friend's birthday party. I would not do so much as suck on a cough drop this time around.

I had no clue what I would do after I graduated in the spring. I assumed I'd get some kind of a job, since I had zero college money set aside. But I wanted to do well on this test for my aunt and uncle, who had invested so much in my education. And these tests weren't free either, which meant this could be my last shot.

By Thursday I was on the verge of crazy. I hadn't seen Dad at all, just heard him come in and out while I was in bed, and I'd only seen Fyn at school and Café Graffiti. I was so tired of being alone with my thoughts, thinking about where Dad was and what he was doing, like he was the teenager and I was the parent. It all made me sick, so I ran.

Even though the weather had cooled off, I still wore shorts, knowing once I got started the blood pumping through my body would warm me up. It was about a half hour before sunset, so I used the fading daylight to motivate me to go faster. I didn't want to be out after dark, when the clouds would hide the moon. I focused on breathing, on the sound of my shoes hitting the pavement, on the stretching of my leg muscles. When I got back to the house, I hopped the wire fence and went around to the backyard, since I'd left the back door unlocked. I noticed the grass was starting to look really shabby, and I guessed it would be up to me to mow it at some point. After the stress of the SAT was over, of course. Maybe I could call Truitt and he could give me some pointers...

A shrub by the back door rustled, and I froze. Raccoons were often an issue near the garbage cans, and woodland creatures creeped me out. If this was one of them, I'd scream.

It was almost completely dark now, so I turned on the flashlight on my phone. I made a wide arc around the bush so whatever it was couldn't jump out and maul me. Just a few more feet and I'd reach the door. Almost—

A head poked out from under the bush and I jumped back, dropping my phone. The light temporarily blinded me as I bent down to pick it up. Blinking away dark spots, I stared at a small dog. A puppy, actually. He looked like some sort of scruffy terrier, although I'd never spent much time around dogs. When I aimed my light on him, he yelped and retreated back under the bush.

It was supposed to be really chilly tonight, so I couldn't just leave him, especially if he had a collar letting me know where he belonged. I went inside and grabbed a piece of lunch meat from the fridge, then flipped on the back porch light as I slipped back outside.

The air smelled like rain, and chill bumps popped out on my legs as a breeze whispered past me.

"Come here," I called softly, my voice sing-songy. I prayed it wasn't really a rabid opossum. "Come to Sadie, little guy…"

I slowly held the meat out to the bush, imagining the neighbors sitting at their window, watching me feed a shrub.

Slowly, the puppy poked his head out from under the bush and sniffed the meat. When he inched out enough for me to reach him, I quickly scooped him into my arms. I was ready for a fight, but instead, he tucked his shivering little body as close to me as possible. He was wet and muddy, like he'd fallen into a puddle. He whimpered, and a wisp of compassion grew inside me.

"Come on," I cooed. "Let's get you inside."

We booked it straight for the bathroom, where I set him in the tub. In the light, I could tell he didn't have a collar or any other form of identification. I hoped I hadn't just brought a bag of fleas into the house.

"Let's get this mud off you, then we'll figure out how to find your family."

The dog blinked up at me. I turned on the faucet, and he scrambled to climb out of the tub, his nails clacking against the side. "Oh, no." I waved my finger at the dog, laughing. "I just shampooed the carpet. No way I'm gonna let you loose like this."

I ran the water until it was warm, then grabbed the dog with both hands and stuck him under the stream. He howled miserably. I didn't know if it was safe to use people soap on animals, but his hair smelled rotten and I couldn't deal.

"Just sit there and enjoy the spa, mutt." I lathered Sassy Berry shampoo into the matted hair, rinsed, and repeated. Then conditioned for good measure.

By the time I set the dog on the bath mat, he looked like a drowned rat. "Not your best look," I mumbled, reaching for the towel on the counter. The dog shot around me and took off running through the house, his little nails clicking across the floor.

"Stay away from the rug!" I yelled, running after the dog. I found the rat creature by the couch, lifting his leg and—

"Hey! Freak!" I yelled as I watched the dog pee all over the freshly-cleaned sofa. "What is your *issue?*" Deciding to handle one thing at a time, I grabbed the dog, holding him away from me, and marched back to the bathroom. I towel-dried him for a minute, then shut the door, humming to block out the wailing as I searched for my phone.

It rang for a minute before Fyn answered. "What's up, Sadie?"

"How do you get pee out of the sofa?"

"*What* did you do? Why would you pee on your sofa? That's barbaric!"

"Not me, Fyn! This, this—giant rat I found in my yard." The line was silent for a good ten seconds and I thought she might've hung up. "Um, Fyn?"

She sighed. "I'm super concerned about you right now. What have you been slipping into your coffee? You know what, don't answer. I'm on my way." And then she really did hang up.

I knew there was no point in calling her back, so while I waited on her to show up, I grabbed a roll of paper towels and soaked up as much puppy pee as I could, the little rat still wailing in agony from the bathroom.

Just under an hour later, Fyn knocked on the door.

"What's going on?" she asked, letting herself in. She looked at the paper towels piled on the floor. "Are you experiencing kidney issues? 'Cause there are meds for that and…"

"Fyn!" I grabbed her shoulders so she had to look at me. "Calm down. I did not pee on the couch. The dog did."

She brought her eyebrows together. "The dog…what is that noise?"

I released her and grabbed her wrist to lead her into the bathroom. Sometimes physically restraining Fyn was the only way to make her focus. I opened the bathroom door and the dog shot out and made a break for the living room. Again.

Fyn screamed and leaped onto the bathroom counter. "What is *that*?"

Leading her back to the living room, I launched into the story: "I was out running and when I came back he was in the bushes behind my house. He was all gross and shaky and sad, so I brought him in and gave him a bath, then he pulled a Houdini and ran into the living room and wet the couch, and I put him in the bathroom until you got here and now I really just want a strong coffee." Out of breath, I leaned against the wall. "So my question to you is how do I get pee out of the couch?"

For once, Fyn was speechless. Then she started laughing hysterically. She kept laughing until she had to sit on the floor and lean against the wall. Finally, she regrouped and asked me to point her to the cleaning supplies.

Within ten minutes, the house smelled like disinfectant and the puppy lay curled up in my lap in the recliner. Fyn surprised me by bringing in an overnight bag—she said she'd been greatly concerned about my mental well-being when she left her house, so she told her mom she was staying over.

The whole ordeal had been exhausting and I just wanted to sleep. "Fyn," I yawned, "We've gotta go door-to-door and find this mutant's family."

She looked up from the British literature anthology she was reading while she reclined on the couch. "Yes, but that'll have to wait. It's past courtesy hours to go knock on random people's doors."

"What am I supposed to do with this?" I poked the puppy

gently, and he rolled onto his back, stretching to take up my entire lap.

"You'll just have to keep him tonight and then go looking for his home tomorrow after school. Do you have a pen or something you can keep him in?"

"I've never had a pet before. Can't you take him to your house? You have pets."

Fyn rolled her eyes. "Fig has Walnut the hamster. This thing would swallow him whole and I'd never hear the end of it. Plus, I've never had a dog either. Maybe we can make him a nice little towel bed in the bathtub?"

"I'm not turning this place into a bed and breakfast for a dog. Besides, he's not even cute."

Fyn gasped and brought a hand to her chest. "That is so rude! He's so ugly he's cute."

I yawned again. "It's late and we've got school in the morning. Let's figure something out and go to bed. I probably should feed him first, though..." Tucking the puppy under my arm, I stood from the recliner. "Will you go get some towels out of the bathroom cabinet for his bed?"

Fyn grinned. "Not turning this place into a B&B, huh?" She headed down the hallway while I rummaged through the fridge for a leftover hamburger patty.

I stumbled into the bathroom early the next morning, feeling like I had a hangover. Fyn and I had slept a combined total of about three hours the night before. We'd never make it as parents.

At first, we'd put the puppy in the bathroom, but he wouldn't stop whining. So we grabbed him before he woke Dad up—if Dad was even home—and put him to bed with Fyn on the floor. Then there was the go-outside-and-sniff-around routine that happened what seemed like every half hour. Then he woke Fyn up by gnawing on her hair. The two on the floor had finally fallen asleep, so I decided to let them rest while I started getting ready for school. I took a hot shower, brushed my teeth, and dried my hair. I'd forgotten my clothes, since I was usually the only one moving around in the mornings, so I tiptoed back into my room and opened my jeans drawer.

I felt a tug on my towel and whipped around, snatching the towel out of the dog's tiny jaws. "Let go, you little pervert," I whispered, shutting my door behind me on the way out. After I dressed, I woke Fyn up and watched the dog in the kitchen while Fyn got ready for school.

I couldn't figure out where to put the dog so Dad wouldn't know about him. I finally decided to stick him back in the backyard with another hamburger. The yard was fenced, but apparently he'd found a way to get in. If he got out during the day, we could just assume he went home and not have to deal with it. If not, I'd start looking for his owner after school. I shook my head, wondering why I hadn't thought of that last night. I also wondered when I'd grown such compassion for taking in a stray dog.

"Sadie." I spun around at the sound of my name, my backpack swinging into a random student.

Everything else faded around me—that kid I'd just walloped and all of the noise and bustling of the school hallway. My jaw went slack, words froze in my mouth, and thoughts came to a halt in my brain. *Gavin.*

It was only a matter of time before he caught up to me. I knew that, but it didn't stop the anxiety from creeping in. I'd been so careful to stay glued to Fyn's side before and after class. So careful to avoid eye contact.

But now, Gavin stood in front of me, wanting to talk.

His curly, dark hair looked the same as always. So did his dark blue eyes. The only difference was he'd gotten a deep tan over the summer.

"It's been a while," he commented as he followed me in the direction of the cafeteria. He said it nonchalantly, like our last conversation hadn't been through a haze of blurred vision, sloshing red cups, and cop lights. And a bloodied nose. Come to think of it, his nose was slightly crooked now, reminding me of a crow.

Honestly, I was amazed he was talking to me like we didn't have such a dark history. He'd been furious to find out Reese and I were getting back together, which meant I was ending it with him. And he'd been even less thrilled about being restrained in my coat closet until the cops showed up.

"Yeah…" I started slowly, my eyes darting around in search of Fyn. "I got stuck up at the front of class, and you're all the way in the back." I clamped my jaw shut. Now he knew he'd been on my mind.

"At least we're together now." He shrugged.

"Well, fun running into you, but I've gotta—"

Gavin grabbed my arm and turned me toward him. My mouth froze in mid-protest. He pulled me off to the side near the stairwell.

"Sadie, wait. Let's catch up. At lunch, I'm sitting with Ruby and Sam…"

What was he even thinking? Those were the *last* people on the planet I wanted to be around. Just thinking about them made me forget to inhale. What was he up to, trying to pull me back into enemy territory?

"Look, Gavin," I said, backing away slowly. "We both know things didn't end well this summer. We're not pretending everything didn't happen, and we're not pretending you and everyone at that table doesn't hate my very existence. I'm meeting up with someone anyway."

I turned again, determined to escape to Fyn, Liz, or Jen. Where were they?

He grabbed me again, by the waist this time, and I jerked away so I wouldn't punch him. "Let go of me," I said between my teeth.

He didn't, just tightened his grip near my hips and said, "Don't worry about those other jerks who turned on you. Stick with me. I'll look out for you."

For a moment, I actually wished Reese was still at school. Gavin wouldn't dare come at me then. But Reese had graduated and gotten a new girlfriend as soon as I left town, and I wanted to throw up whenever I thought about all I'd thrown away by being with him.

"Gavin, no. I'm starting over."

He let go of my waist and reached out to hold my shoulders. Had he always been this touchy-feely? I blushed at the memories.

A couple of guys stopped next to us, lost in conversation. Bringing his mouth down toward my face, Gavin whispered, "Please, Sadie. At least start over with me. I still like you."

I couldn't help but look at his face, into those eyes that had practically worshipped me over Spring Break. Eyes that had seen more of Sadie's former life than anyone ever needed to know. He looked like he wanted to kiss me. I'd seen that look before and I'd given in. Heck, he'd seen *me* give that look before. But the mere thought repulsed me now. One week of weakness when Reese was out of town and now Gavin still thought I belonged to him.

I swallowed in a vain attempt to dislodge my heart beating wildly in my throat.

God, please help me...

I pulled myself away. "Get out of here." Somehow, my voice was firm.

"Wait. Just—"

"Sadie?" I released a breath as Fyn stepped up next to us.

I turned my back on Gavin and walked away quickly with Fyn, who looped her arm through mine. I slipped into the restroom, locked myself in a stall, and missed half of lunch. I was shaking and couldn't form the words to tell Fyn why while she waited on the other side of the door. I wasn't even sure why. I wasn't scared of what Gavin would do to me. I was scared of what *I* would do to me. One step backward and I'd be right back to who I used to be.

"Are you cool with talking about what went on at lunch today?"

I shrugged and shifted the dog to my other arm. He'd been curled up by the back door when I got home from school, so I'd called Fyn to help knock on neighbors' doors, promising dinner if we were successful.

"I just—he's—I mean, yeah." I took a deep breath and absentmindedly rubbed the dog's head. "He was one of those people from my summer I was telling you about."

"A boyfriend?" We walked up to the first door and knocked.

"Kinda. Not long-term. It was a mistake." *Just one of like a bajillion.*

After knocking again and getting no answer, Fyn and I walked to the next house.

"Do you guys have baggage or something? Sorry, I know that's personal, but did you…"

"We didn't go that far, if that's what you're asking. I've done more than I should've with more guys than I should've, but never that far." I didn't add the fact that I had to think really hard about that last night Reese and I were together to be sure I was telling the truth.

Fyn shrugged and rang the doorbell. "Well, that's a plus, right?"

An older woman opened the door just enough to peek out. "Yes?"

"Uh, yeah, hi," I said. "We're wondering if this dog is yours? I found him in my backyard."

She quickly closed the door. I turned to Fyn, who shrugged. We heard the chain slide off the door, then it opened again.

The petite—maybe five feet tall—lady had styled her short, curly, white hair in a classic grandma perm. Though she appeared to be about 95, she wore yoga pants and a tank top.

"Let me look." She slid a pair of purple-framed glasses from the top of her head to the bridge of her nose. She peered at the dog for a full minute. I glanced behind her, where a TV displayed a woman doing a downward facing dog pose.

The older woman shook her head. "Nope, not mine. Thank you for asking." She offered a smile and closed the door, cutting off the TV's loud instructions about breathing through sun salutations. The chain slid into place.

"Namaste," Fyn whispered, dipping her head in the direction of the door.

I covered my mouth in a failed attempt to cover a guffaw.

"That woman was bizarre," Fyn declared as we walked back to the sidewalk. "Like, is she missing a dog, but this one isn't it?"

"Or maybe she was trying to decide if she was missing a dog?" I asked.

"She's my new best friend," Fyn said, hopping over a crack in the sidewalk.

"She's you in a hundred and fifty years."

Fyn stuck her tongue out at me and fingered her silver-streaked hair. "She doesn't have near as much class as Fynnigan Larcy."

"How does your hair not fry and fall out with how often you color it?" I'd been curious ever since I met her, but figured we were just now getting to the level where I could ask that kind of personal information. Besides, she had just asked me if I'd slept with Gavin.

"Clip-ins, dear. They're a game changer."

The dog squirmed, so I set him on the ground. He immediately ran into the middle of the road.

"He is so deranged!" I yelled. I ran into the road and scooped him up, then met Fyn back on the sidewalk, where she held up her phone, documenting the event.

"Where next?" she asked, saving the video and slipping the phone back into her pocket.

"I think that's it." I wrapped my arms a little more tightly around the dog.

"How about that one? Right next to yours? I can't believe we didn't think to check with your next-door neighbors first!" She took off ahead of me.

"Fyn, wait!" I jogged to catch up with her. "Not that one."

She stopped and turned to face me. "Why not?"

My mind reeled. That house belonged to Carl and Judith Wade. They definitely knew who I was. They'd called the cops on that infamous party, after all. I hadn't seen them since the morning after the party when I collected cans and bottles from their front yard.

"Well," I said slowly, "We're not exactly on the best terms..."

Realization slowly dawned in her eyes. "Oh. Well, if this is their dog and you return it, that could be a really good thing for your relationship with them, yeah?"

Everything in me wanted to take the dog and run home, but I knew she was right. Mustering up a tiny seed of courage, I walked up to the front door and knocked. The dog whimpered in my arms, like he knew something was amiss. "Don't worry," I muttered, "You weren't the one who violated a public noise ordinance."

No one answered, and I turned to leave. Fyn grabbed my shoulders and turned me back toward the door. "Give them longer than ten seconds, Sadie."

The dog and I whined in unison. Fyn leaned around me to press the doorbell.

Finally, I heard footsteps coming toward the door. It opened, revealing a woman in her mid-sixties.

"Can I help you?" She peered at me, light blue eyes narrowed in suspicion. My throat closed up, and my heart beat so hard I just knew she could see it pounding through my shirt. I couldn't make words form. I broke out into a cold sweat and had a flashback to the school bathroom when I'd encountered Ruby.

"What do you need?" she asked again.

My mouth opened, but I couldn't say anything. Judith shifted, putting her weight on her right hip. "Um, is—" I stammered.

Fyn jabbed me in the back, snapping me back to attention. The dog whimpered, and I realized I was almost squeezing him in half. "Hi, Judith."

She sighed. "Hello, Sadie. How can I help you?"

"This dog. I found him in my yard. Is he yours?" There, that was at least slightly coherent. I pictured Fyn slow-clapping behind me.

Judith shook her head. "No."

"Do you know who he belongs to?"

Again, she shook her head. "But I can ask Carl."

"No, that's—"

"Carl! Get out here!"

Oh, no. If Judith was hard to face, Carl would be even worse. He'd banged on my front door countless times during my hostess career.

I felt like I was gonna throw up. I couldn't do it. I breathed rapid-fire prayers for deliverance. Prayed a sinkhole would open up and take me with it. Prayed Jesus would come back, like, right now. Prayed Fyn would stop poking me and actually help in my time of crisis.

Carl stepped up behind Judith. "What's going on? Who's the mutt?" I honestly couldn't tell if he was referring to me or the dog. Or both.

"Sadie's looking for its owner. You think it belongs to Morris?"

He squinted at the dog, who was now intent on licking the sweat off my face. "No, he has a beagle. I don't know who this one belongs to."

They both looked at me, and I looked back, the blood still pounding in my ears. I needed to end this encounter but didn't know how. My brain wouldn't formulate an escape. It just wanted to shiver.

Finally, Fyn piped up. "Thank you for your time. Let's go, Sadie." She grabbed my arm and pulled me backward down the front steps.

"Hey!" Carl called. Fyn stopped and turned. I was still facing the house.

"Yes?" she called back.

"You seem like a nice kid. I would think twice about spending time with this one. She's trouble."

He looked like he wanted to say more, but Fyn interrupted. "Okay, well, this has been a treat." She spun me around and pushed me back to my house.

We sat on the front steps, and I set the dog on the ground. Exhausted from trying to escape all day, he curled up at my feet.

"What on earth was that back there?" Fyn asked, turning to face me.

I dropped my head in my hands. "I don't know. I've never cared so much about what people think. Never freaked out so much as I have since being back in Seattle. And then Carl—"

"Stop it. You're trying to drag your past into your present. That's no way to live. God's forgiven you, and you're not who you used to be. That's more than enough reason to hold your head up."

I brushed my hair out of my face. "I know."

But did I really? Why did I nearly have a panic attack when I was just asking if the dog belonged to the Wades? Why did I lose it when I ran into Ruby at the beginning of the semester? Why had I nearly hit the floor in front of Gavin? I'd always prided myself on suppressing emotions for the reason I now understood: When you let yourself feel pain, it hurt. Badly.

I reached down and rubbed the dog's head, ready to break away from the heaviness of the conversation.

I sighed. "I just have no idea what to do with him. Do you know of a vet's office or something where I could put up a poster?"

Fyn glanced at me, then looked at the setting sun. "Yeah, but I can't."

The dog barked and took off chasing a bird.

"Can't what?" I asked over my shoulder as I darted back into the street and caught the dog. Holding him like a sack of potatoes under my arm, I stood in front of my friend.

"Owen works at the animal clinic where his dad is a vet. I guess you could ask him."

"That's awesome! Why didn't you say anything earlier? Oh, right, 'cause Owen."

"Don't be mad," she whined. "I just can't be around him."

"Whatever happened that he knows about anyway? How bad can it be?"

She shrugged. "Just stuff."

I watched her closely as she reached out and took the dog. I'd just shown all kinds of vulnerability in front of her, and she wouldn't tell me why she couldn't face Owen? A part of me wanted to be angry about that, but a bigger part of me knew how hard it was to open up. Fyn must have some big demons in her past.

We watched the sun continue to go down together, then I went inside with the puppy and she went back to her home and the secrets she held so tightly.

Chapter Ten

ooo

My alarm went off at 5:30 Saturday morning. I literally rolled out of bed and landed on the floor, wrapped in my blankets like an angsty teenage burrito. I trudged into the bathroom and got ready for the day, spending a little extra time on my hair and makeup. Not that I was trying to woo the SAT proctor, but I'd heard something about "dress well, test well." I'd wear a prom dress and smoky eyes if it meant I'd score better than last time.

I choked down a banana and a couple strips of microwave bacon, then stepped into my shoes and grabbed my bag. When I pulled into the school parking lot, my phone buzzed, and I grabbed it off the passenger seat. Truitt and Becca smiled back at me—his endearing chin dimple on display and her kind eyes warm and welcoming. Their faces were close together to fit in the picture, and his arm circled her shoulders. "We're cheering you on!" Their text said. "You've got this!"

I turned off my phone and slipped it in my bag. Pre-test jitters were replaced with a brick in my gut. They weren't telling me something, I knew it. Over the summer, I'd watched the easy, familiar way the two of them interacted. I'd outright asked Becca if they had feelings for each other, and she'd quickly denied it, claiming they were just really good, longtime friends. But I'd seen the movies. The rugged, heroic guy and the quiet good girl equaled a sweet romance.

It was only a matter of time. My presence helped Truitt get honest about his life, and my absence created a perfect space for her to fit into his world. And could I blame them? Truitt and I weren't officially anything, and Becca deserved a prince.

But as I climbed out of the car and slung my bag over my shoulder, I decided I'd blame them anyway.

———— ○○○ ————

When Dad came home early that evening, I knew life was about to get interesting. He found me stretched out on the sofa napping after that grueling SAT. Thankfully, the dog was in the backyard because Dad still didn't know about him. I'd picked up a bag of actual dog food on the way home earlier, and I hoped the kibble would keep him quiet.

"Hey, Dad," I yawned.

"Hey. How was the SAT?"

I sat up and redid my ponytail I'd made the minute I left the school building. "Exhausting. How was work?"

Dad didn't say anything, just walked into the kitchen. I heard him open the fridge and a drawer. He came back into the living room, holding a brown bottle, and dropped into his recliner.

I took a deep breath and released it. "Dad, listen, I wanted to say I'm sorry for the other day. It was awful, I was awful, and I'm sorry. I shouldn't have said any of that." *Even if it's true...*

Dad looked at me over the rim of his bottle. "Maybe it's best if you do get a job."

"To ship me off quicker?" Man, I needed to work on using a filter.

But Dad didn't comment on my smart mouth. "A job will be good for you. You can start saving some money, and I could really use some help paying for stuff you need, like your prescriptions and snacks and gas for the car."

Was he serious? Me, the *kid* paying for gas for *his* car? He had a job, and although we'd never had a lot of extra money, we weren't poor. My dad worked hard and long hours at his job, and I didn't eat like a horse or anything.

I took a deep breath, held it for a few seconds, then slowly released it, wishing it was that easy to get rid of the tension. I reached up and felt a knot forming at the base of my neck. "Um, okay. I can look, but I don't know if I'll make enough for groceries. Did you take a pay cut at work?"

For a second—so brief I would've missed it if I'd blinked—a look of shame passed over my dad's face. But then it was gone.

"What's going on at your job, Dad?"

He looked at the TV, the wall, the floor, the ceiling. Everywhere but at his daughter. His own flesh and blood. The human being he made seventeen years ago. His little girl.

"Dad. What?" I asked again, my voice barely above a whisper.

"There is no job, Sadie. I got laid off."

I felt the blood drain from my face. "What? Why?"

"I—"

A bark sounded at the back door and we both froze, turning our heads in unison.

"What was that?" Dad asked, standing.

"Sounded like a dog," I said, technically not lying because it *did* sound like a dog. "But tell me. When did they let you go?"

Dad walked toward the back door as the dog barked again, me following behind like the dog whenever he trailed after me. "Three weeks ago."

I stopped walking, reached out and grabbed my dad's arm. The movement startled us both. "You haven't had a job in almost a *month*? What happened? What have you been doing? Why have you been—?"

"Sadie!" Dad yelled, silencing me. "I don't answer to my *daughter*. There was a miscommunication, and things got messed up. They canned me. I get some severance and I'm looking for work somewhere else, but in case you hadn't heard, it's not easy getting a good job without a college degree. The last thing I need is for you to harass me about what I choose to do in my own time."

Through all of this, my mouth hung open. Dad was unemployed. Who knew where he'd been spending his evenings if he wasn't on the clock at work. The possibilities nauseated me.

"Anyway, that's why I think you should get a job," he said, his voice still firm but lowering in volume with each syllable. "Since it might take some time before I find another good job."

That annoying dog barked again, and I bit my tongue so I wouldn't shout nasty accusations about him spending time at bars and out with that woman and other things I'd regret. *Please, God, help me!* Shaking, I said, "Okay."

Dad opened the back door, and the dog ran in.

"What the—"

A puppy yelp cut off Dad's colorful word choice. The dog took off into the living room and hid behind the recliner. Something outside must have scared him.

I slid behind the recliner and scooped up the dog. His paws were muddy, and he'd left prints all over the rug.

"Do you know this dog?" Dad asked, a look of utter puzzlement on his face.

"Actually, kind of. See, he was trapped in the backyard last week and…"

"You've been sneaking a dog around the house for a

week?" The puzzlement was gone and it was back to anger. What a yo-yo.

"I've been asking neighbors who he belongs to, and I'm gonna put a flyer at the vet's office. I can't leave him out there, Dad."

"Animal shelter."

"Dad, no!"

"Sadie..."

I sat on the floor, the dog still in my arms. Now he was growling at my father. Perfect.

"I get so lonely here, Dad. And this dog, it's like he gets me." Wanderer, always in trouble, scruffy and rough around the edges. Wow, were we similar. Why I was drawn to him in the first place was starting to click. "Let me keep him safe until I find his home. I'll pay for everything."

Dad's brow furrowed. I could almost hear the *No, Sadie* on repeat in his brain. His cell dinged at an incoming text just then and he fished it out of his pocket. Reading it, he started backing toward the door.

"Dad?"

"Yeah, sure, whatever. But if I see *any* evidence of that dog left around the house...if I step in *any* pile of—"

"Yes. Got it. Thanks."

He waved and went out the door. I sat on the floor, hugging the gross dog, and felt like crying.

Monday after school I went home to get the dog and the flyers Fyn helped me make. We included a picture of the dog, along with my number. Fyn insisted on sketching him, too. The pieces of paper looked like pages in the dog's modeling portfolio. I loaded the flyers into the backseat of the car and wrangled the dog into the passenger side floorboard before navigating to the vet's office.

When I arrived, I tucked the dog under one arm and grabbed a poster I'd made with the other hand. I opened the door and Owen greeted me at the front desk.

"Sadie, good to see you!" He smiled and set an obese cat on the ground from where it had been lounging on the computer keyboard. The dog scratched aggressively behind his ears, scratching me in the process.

"Ouch, you mutant!" I hissed.

Owen stepped out from around the desk. He smiled again, his light blue scrubs making his skin look tanner than it was.

"What can I do for you?"

"Fyn told me you might let me put up some missing pet posters? This dog got stuck in my yard and I've been asking around the neighborhood, but nobody knows him." The dog started chewing at his hind leg, and I set him on the floor, holding on to his leash.

"Is that a jump rope...?" Owen cocked an eyebrow.

"The Franklins aren't exactly animal people."

"Ah."

The dog continued chewing on his leg.

"Cool it, Dracula," Owen said, reaching down to pick up the dog. "You're drawing blood."

I shrugged and watched Owen gently massage the dog's leg. "I guess he might have fleas."

Owen motioned for me to sit in the waiting area and sat beside me. His knee bumped into mine as he adjusted the dog on his lap. He began gently separating patches of hair on the dog to look at his skin.

"What did you bathe him with?"

I shrugged. "I don't know. Just some shampoo. I'd rather have him smell like Sassy Berry than garbage."

"Okay." Owen looked at the dog for another minute. "I'm not a vet, but I think he's having an allergic reaction to the shampoo. You didn't condition too, did you?"

"Actually…" I stopped when I noticed his grin. "You're messing with me."

"Let me go ask and see what I can find you. You can pin that poster to the board over there." He motioned behind me and plopped the dog back in my lap, then disappeared behind a door.

He came back a few minutes later with a small white envelope. "Here. It's basically Benadryl, but they told me this much won't knock him out. Dad wrote the dosage instructions on the package."

"You rock, Owen," I tucked the package into the back pocket of my jeans. "How much do I owe you?"

He shrugged, "It's a gift. Any friend of Fyn's is a friend of mine."

It was a weird thing to say, but I didn't ask questions. Besides, I couldn't afford to spend money on a mutt, especially now that Dad was unemployed.

"Well, thank you, Owen. I'll let Fyn know."

Owen stepped back behind the desk. "Although, I'd like to give you something, too."

That made no sense. "What do you mean?"

"How about I buy you dinner sometime? I won't be offended if you order a burger."

Oh. Snap. He was asking me out? Would Fyn be cool with that? Would *I* be cool with that? My mind immediately jumped to Truitt. Yeah, we fought all the time and yeah, Owen was nothing but kindness. But Truitt and I…what were we? A missed chance? The last stop before he found happiness with Becca?

What would it hurt if I went out with Owen, let him pay

for my food? But my heart was too confused by my closest girl friend and the boy I loved to hate and hated to love.

I swallowed. "That's really nice of you, Owen, but just letting me have this medicine for the dog and letting me hang a poster is plenty of kindness. Really. Just let me know if someone asks about the dog?"

Please don't ask me again. Please don't ask me again. Please don't ask me again.

Because I would say yes.

Owen smiled, ever the gentleman. "You got it. See ya, Sadie."

"Can you tell me how to housebreak this mutant?" I dropped my head into my hands and let my phone drop onto the sofa beside me. I picked it back up and cradled it between my shoulder and ear.

"Well, I'm not an expert..." Becca said humbly.

"You at least have a dog."

"I was little when we got Pudding. My parents did most of her training."

I didn't interact much with Becca's chocolate lab when I was in Georgia, but I'd been around her enough to know she was a sweetheart...and super well-behaved. Just like Becca.

The dog jumped up from where he slept under the coffee table and ran down the hallway. I followed suit, jumping up and chasing him into my bedroom, where he'd already found a pair of jeans to gnaw on.

"Any tips would be awesome," I panted.

Becca thought for a moment. "I guess you just start taking him out all the time until he gets the idea. And if he pees in the house, I think you're supposed to stick his nose in it?"

I scooped the dog under my arms like a football and marched back to the living room. "That's gross."

"I think that's the point. I'll talk to my mom and see if she knows of some websites that might give some good tips. What does your dad think of the puppy?"

"What puppy?"

Becca groaned. "Sadie…"

"He knows. He's just not exactly throwing a welcome party for him." I switched the phone to speaker and put it on the coffee table so I could hold onto the dog with both hands. He squirmed until I scratched behind his scruffy ears. "Dad wants me to take him to the animal shelter. Like, *now* he decides to be my boss."

"I won't tell you what to do…"

"Thank you."

"Even though I want to. But—"

"Becca?" I waited a few seconds until Becca came back on the line.

"Sorry, Sadie. Truitt texted. I was seeing if he needed me."

Did he? I wanted to ask. Instead I said, "Oh, neat."

"Are you feeling okay?" Becca asked.

The dog grabbed my finger between his little needle teeth, and I glared at him. "Yeah, I'm fine."

She sighed. "Good. Hey, I've gotta run. Truitt'll be here any second, and I need to go get the laundry off the couch before he shows up. I'll send you some dog training articles."

Why was Truitt going to the Shepherds' house? Why would he text Becca if he was just mowing their yard? What was happening? I ended the call with Becca, put the dog in the backyard, and changed clothes to go for a run. I needed to breathe.

○○○

Fyn sat across from me in the living room Thursday after classes, her homework spread out on the coffee table and the dog barking out the window at a man walking down the street.

"Oh. My—"

"Now, Sadie…" Fyn said. "I know he's obnoxious, but he's in a brand new life. He's probably perpetually freaked."

Yeah, like me.

The dog bolted to the window on the other side of the room to continue watching the walking man. On his way, he bumped against the coffee table, knocking my mug to the floor, coffee spilling all over my homework assignment.

"That's *it!*" I yelled. I grabbed the jump rope and tied him to the sofa leg. "I swear, he's like a moose in a china shop!"

"A *what?*" Fyn started laughing uncontrollably. "Sadie, that's *bull.*"

"Excuse me?"

"Bull." She wiped her eyes on her sleeve. "The expression is 'like a *bull* in a china shop.'"

"Oh." I blinked.

"You know you totally have to name him Moose now."

I stared at the dog currently trying to chew his way through the rope. He was small and wiry and had hair sticking out everywhere. And no antlers. The only thing that could possibly resemble a moose was his dark coloring. And yet, in some bizarre way, it seemed to fit. And how bad could it be to give him a name?

Until his owner contacted me, we were buddies.

"Hey," Fyn said. "Let's go get tacos."

I looked at the dog—Moose—and considered it. "To be honest, Fyn, I don't know if I need to spend money on eating out right now."

Fyn didn't pause. "Fill up on free chips and salsa then

take a burrito home. That's two meals for the price of one, practically BOGO. Besides, it'll be my treat."

I knew Fyn's family was loaded with money, but I didn't want to feel like a charity case. People had been helping me so much recently. "No, that's okay. I can swing a taco. Let's go. I'm starved."

―――――― oOo ――――――

"No, he did *not* say that!" Fyn said, waving her fork in the air.

"I'm telling the truth! Owen said, 'Any friend of Fyn's is a friend of mine.' When are you actually going to explain what the deal is with you two?"

Fyn stabbed a bite of steak fajita and popped it in her mouth. I waited for her to chew and swallow before she responded. "It's not a big deal. That was nice of him, though."

I stabbed a forkful of taco salad and casually added, "I hope it also wasn't a big deal that he asked me out."

Fyn's fork clattered to the table. "What? No!"

"I'm sorry?"

She stared at me, mouth gaping. "He asked you out?"

"I told him no."

"You did?"

"Yeah. I know you like him."

She slowly picked her fork back up and blinked a few times. "Okay, then."

What was her issue? Was she afraid Owen would tell me all of her secrets about her past? At least then maybe someone would enlighten me.

"What's up, sisters?"

I looked up from my food. Liz stood over us, her hair doing its usual purposefully mussed thing.

"Liz, hi!" Fyn said around a mouthful of rice, the previous

weird conversation seemingly forgotten. "Did you eat yet? Come sit!"

I scooted over in the booth so Liz could slide in, fully aware of the way Fyn was once again avoiding a topic. "I was on a pity date with Dale. He's been asking me out since June, so I decided to take advantage of some free guac. Most unexciting hour of my life. I saw you guys and sent him home. Thankfully I drove my own car here. What are we talking about?"

"I was telling Fyn how O—*ow!*"

Fyn kicked my shin under the table. "Nope! We're going to dissect this date of yours, Liz."

Liz began to tell us a tale of poor Dale and his khaki pants. We spent the next twenty minutes laughing so hard our drinks tingled in our noses and our eyes burned.

"He did *not* ask if you could practice a goodnight kiss at the table!" I blurted, sending Liz into her own laughing spasm.

Fyn's cell phone rang, and she put a hand to her ear so she could answer.

Liz wiped her eye, where dark eyeliner was smeared. "I was like, 'Not in front of the refried beans!'"

We dissolved into cackles again. Suddenly, Liz froze, and I followed the direction of her stare. Fyn's face had gone white, and the hand she had pressed to her mouth trembled. She stared, unblinking, straight ahead.

"No. Oh, no. No," she mumbled. She ended the call and quickly slid out of the booth, knocking over the basket of chips in the process.

"Fyn…" I started.

She frantically pulled some money out of her bag and dropped it on the table. "I've gotta go."

"But I'm riding with you! What's going on?" I realized my voice was raised and a few people at nearby tables were staring, so I brought it back to normal volume. "Fyn?"

"Oh." Fyn stood, paralyzed, like she couldn't make a decision.

I grabbed her by the shoulders. "Fynnigan Larcy," I said, ignoring my usually large personal bubble by bringing my face close to hers so she had no choice but to look at me. "Tell me what's going on."

With a voice barely above a whisper, and so wobbly I could barely make out her words, she said, "It's Gran."

Chapter Eleven

I drove, not trusting Fyn behind the wheel. She still stared straight ahead, mumbling, "No, no, no, no," over and over.

I promised to update Liz once I dropped Fyn off at the hospital.

We pulled up outside the ER entrance. "Oh, no," I said. "I forgot I'm in your car. Um, maybe Liz can help me get it back to you."

"Stay with me," Fyn whispered, her eyes wide and glassy.

"Okay."

I pulled into the parking garage and wove up a few levels until we found a spot.

I got out and went around to open Fyn's door when I noticed she wasn't moving. "Why was Gran unconscious? Why wouldn't she wake up when Dad found her? This isn't happening, Sadie. Tell me it's not happening."

"I have no idea what's going on, Fyn," I said. "Let's pray?" It came out as a question. I wasn't used to praying for people or offering to pray for them.

Fyn nodded and we sank to the cold curb. I looped my arm through hers and pulled her close. We bowed our heads together.

"God," I said, my voice echoing through the concrete parking garage. "Fyn's scared. We're not sure what we're gonna see when we go in there, but please be with us. Help Fyn to not be afraid and to trust You because we know You have a purpose. Amen."

Fyn clutched my hand as we silently walked into the ER waiting room, where Fyn's mom and little brother stood waiting for us.

"It was a heart attack, Fyn. She isn't in any pain now..." Aubrey Larcy took her daughter in her arms.

I felt the color drain from my face. Gran was *gone?* Just like that? The tiny, spicy lady who taught exercise classes at a nursing home? The room felt very small and claustrophobic. I took a step back to let them have a moment and to remind myself to breathe. The last time I was in a hospital, we were celebrating life when my cousin was born. This time, we were mourning the loss of a life.

"Where's Glenna?" Fyn asked, her head on Aubrey's shoulder.

"I'm not sure. I left a message on her phone," Aubrey said.

I opened my mouth to ask about this mystery person, but Fig interrupted.

"There she is!" Fig pointed to the door where a tall, slim woman slipped in, her black hair pulled up in a stylish ponytail. She looked like she was somewhere near the end of her twenties.

"Hey, Aubrey."

"Hi, Glenna." She gave the woman a loose hug.

I awkwardly backed toward the door. "Sadie, wait," Fyn said.

For the first time, Aubrey seemed to notice my presence. "Oh, Sadie. Thank you for bringing Fyn. Have you met Glenna?"

I shook my head and stepped into their circle.

"I'm the other Larcy," Glenna said, turning and smiling softly at me. "It's nice to meet you."

I shook her hand, confused. Fyn had an older sister?

"Okay, someone fill me in," Glenna said. Aubrey led her over to some chairs in the corner and they sat, whispering with their heads together. Poor Fig joined them and started playing a game on his phone.

Fyn turned to me. "Mom told me we could go see her. To say goodbye, even though she's already gone. My dad's in there waiting on us. I don't want to go, Sadie. I can't."

My only experience with death was when my mom died. My last view was of her in the driver's seat, glass and blood and an exploded airbag everywhere. I didn't know it then, but she was already gone. Never saw her again. A part of me wished her casket had been open at the funeral. I'd give anything for a chance to see her beautiful face cleaned off and peaceful after the trauma of the accident. I know now, nearly a decade later, that her soul wasn't even in that casket. She was already with God, more alive than she'd ever been.

"Sadie." Fyn's uttering of my name brought me back to the present.

"This is it, Fyn. Go tell her goodbye. Go be with your family."

"Come with me."

There was no way I wanted to do that. I didn't want to see death because just thinking about it made me feel and see too much.

"This is a family thing. But I promise to be right here." As soon as I said that, I regretted it. I didn't know what all was involved in that promise.

So while the Larcys went to go see their grandmother, I curled up in a corner chair, under a TV announcing the latest news. I connected to Wi-Fi on my phone and started reading an article for my political science class. Anything to distract my mind.

Sometime later, I looked up as Fyn, Fig, and Glenna filed silently back into the waiting room.

Glenna waved to me as she ushered Fig out the door.

"I told her you'd take me home," Fyn said. "Mom and Dad are staying for a little while to take care of some things." Her eyes were dry but it was as if she wasn't actually focused on anything.

"Of course." I stood and slid my phone back into my pocket. "Are you ready?"

Fyn's face crumbled, and she fell against me, nearly knocking me to the floor. I put my arms around her and eased us into the chairs. "I'm not ready. I'll never be ready. Why did this happen, Sadie?" I held onto her while she cried on my shoulder. I'd never seen Fyn cry, even though I knew she had enough emotion for at least five people. I'd just never seen her broken. "She was my best friend, Sadie. She was there for me when even my own parents didn't trust me. She saved me, Sadie."

I awkwardly rubbed her back "I know, Fyn."

She pulled back, makeup running, and swiped her nose on her sleeve. "No, you don't. You don't know my story!"

"I'm sorry," I muttered.

"No." Fyn took a deep, shuddering breath. "I am. Do you know what I did, Sadie? Do you know?"

"Fyn, you don't have to tell me."

"Yes, I do. But not here. Can we go to your house? I need to tell you who Fynnigan Larcy is."

―――――oOo―――――

Moose curled up in Fyn's lap, sleeping. She absently stroked his head, her bloodshot eyes focused on him, while

I sat on the other side of the couch, leaning against a throw pillow.

"I've always been kind of…emotional."

I almost rolled my eyes and said, "No, really?" but caught myself just in time. Her grandmother had just died, after all. I nodded for her to go on. It was getting late, but Fyn needed me.

"I've dealt with anxiety and depression my whole life. And I'm hyperactive, but you probably couldn't tell." She gave me a sad smile, and I smiled back before she dropped her eyes back down to Moose. "I've always taken meds for those. I couldn't fit in at school, either, which didn't help. I was the rich girl with the weird personality, and nobody wanted to be near that. So I got in with the wrong crowd." She sniffed. "I got into drugs, Sadie. I'd trade my pills for theirs. And then, when I needed more, I'd…. I'd steal from Dad's office." She brought a hand in front of her eyes. "I got busted at school. I was an addict. I didn't know what to do. I was supposed to be a good Christian, but I failed. I couldn't keep it up anymore and the mess I'd made was too, too big.

"During all of this, I'd been so ashamed of myself. I hated myself, but it's like I was so distant from Fyn Larcy that I couldn't do anything to stop." She shuddered and bit her lip. "At first I tried to channel everything into my art. I've burned those pieces because if I tried to look at them now, I'd throw up. The paintings and drawings were so dark and hopeless."

She slid the puppy onto the couch beside her and slid herself next to me. She slowly pulled up the sleeve of her shirt. Scars lined her pale arms, like a tiger had grabbed her and scraped his claws across them. How had I not noticed these before? "I did this to me. And not just here, but on my thigh, my stomach. They're the worst on my stomach. I was trying to release all of the agony, trying to channel the pain and focus on something other than the pills. I told no one about anything. Then, after the secret about the drugs was out, I tried to overdose with them. It almost worked, but Gran found me. She literally saved my life." She slid back to her side of the couch, like she'd given up so much of her soul she needed to hold onto anything she could—even if it was just a foot of space.

"They admitted me to the hospital on suicide watch. When my parents saw the scars, Mom fainted. Dad cried. I got expelled because of swapping drugs at school, of course. Then I spent the whole summer in rehab, and reentry back into the real world happened just a couple of weeks before school started back." She stroked the puppy's head again, and he stretched but didn't wake up. There was a chance I'd accidentally given him a little extra Benadryl for his rash, but Owen had assured me I couldn't hurt him.

"Jesus got a hold of my life at rehab, Sadie. He stripped away literally everything about who I was. Fynnigan Larcy's way had to die so He could live in me. He gave me a second chance to live. I changed schools, my family switched churches, I got a counselor, and I went back to my art."

She stopped talking. Silent tears fell from her eyes. "And Gran was there through all of it. She was the only one I felt like I could cry in front of because it felt too weird being around my parents and the way they'd look at me, like they were afraid I'd jump out the window every time I went upstairs. But Gran didn't judge me or scold me. She prayed over me and loved me so much. We talked every night. We talked last night. She told me she was so proud of me for how far I've come. I still have such a long way to go to be healthy. And now she's not here and she never will be again and..." Fyn broke down again, and I didn't know what to do so I went into the kitchen and fixed a pot of decaf coffee. After pouring the coffee into a mug, I went back into the living room, where Fyn still sat. "I'm so sorry for unloading this on you." She dropped her head onto my shoulder. "You wish I hadn't, I know. This is why I don't let anyone see who I really am because it's disgusting."

"No, Fyn, I'm glad you felt safe enough to tell me."

"I've done some bad things, Sadie."

"I have, too, Fyn. I've lied, cursed, snuck out, gotten way too involved with guys, and I'm really good at nursing a hangover. I thought God would never want someone as messed up as me."

"But He does want you because He loves you."

"And He loves you."

"You're the only person other than my family I've ever told this to, but I felt like I could trust you. Owen already knows most of this because we were friends at school. I'm too ashamed to have anything to do with him, and we used to be best friends."

I handed her the cup and she lifted her head.

She took a cautious sip, then sagged against me.

"Of course you can trust me, Fyn. I know what it's like to run away from pain and lose everything you thought was important to you. I know what it's like to be caught by God and forgiven. And I know what it feels like to have someone know you—really know you—and still be there for you. It's awesome. I want you to have that, too."

"Did we really just meet each other this fall?" she asked, "Because I feel like we've been friends forever. Is that weird?"

I shook my head. "Not when you've got grace in common."

We sat in the silence for a while, soaking up the sadness and loss and pain, and feeling the power of having a person who really knows you—mess and all. Fyn stood from the couch. "I need to get home, I guess. I hate the thought of going home and…and her not being there. But I need to get home. I feel like I'm in shock, and it hasn't really hit me yet."

"I'll drive you."

"No, that's okay. I think I just need to be with my family. Besides, I've got my car. I'll text you when I get home, okay?"

I hugged her tightly, whispered a prayer, then waved as she went out the front door. I had no idea what it was like to truly be a friend to someone—to be there for them through hard times without offering alcohol to help numb the pain. I felt emotionally exhausted.

And very alone. Rather than put Moose outside in a box I'd made for a bed, I brought him to my bed and crawled in without even changing clothes. Tucking the sleepy puppy up next to me, I brought my forehead to my knees and cried myself to sleep.

Chapter Twelve

A bell jingled when I opened the door to the salon after school the next day. The funeral was tomorrow, and my hair was in desperate need of a trim.

I walked into a room filled with the smell of hair products and walked up to the front desk, which stood in front of a waterfall backdrop.

To the left was a small waiting area with chairs, a coffee table, and fashion magazines. Beyond the waterfall, I could see all of the hair stuff on the left, and manicure and pedicure stations on the right. Pop music poured through the speakers.

"Welcome!" A girl said when I stepped up to the front desk. I was dressed in what I'd worn to school, but I might as well have been in gym clothes for how fancy this place was. I didn't know how much it cost, but it was a new place near Goldfinch's, and it welcomed walk-ins. I figured if I ended up with a nightmare of a haircut, I could at least drown my sorrows in espresso.

I offered the receptionist a smile and told her why I was there. My ends were so split they could file for divorce, and my hair was its natural dirty blonde. And my nails? Oh, man.

The receptionist led me to the seating area and told me a stylist would be with me momentarily.

A few minutes later, a woman appeared, tying an apron around her waist. I set down my tabloid and looked up.

"Glenna?"

The woman smiled, but her eyes looked hollow and tired. I couldn't imagine showing up at work so soon after what happened. Even Fyn hadn't come to school. "Hi, Sadie. What can I do for you?"

I stood. "I'm just hoping for a trim." I flopped my long ponytail over my shoulder. "I'm so sorry about your grandmother. I plan to be at the service tomorrow."

"Thank you, Sadie. That means a lot. I decided work would at least help me take my mind off things, but it has been a really, really long day." She reached out and ran a hand through my ponytail, inspecting the ends. Releasing my hair, she attempted a smile. "Now let's get to work."

She offered a complimentary wash because I was a first-timer and a friend of Fyn's, and I sighed with happiness as she gently massaged my scalp. I needed to relax more often.

While she snipped my dead ends and added long layers to my hair, she asked basic questions about my life. What grade was I in? What did I like to do for fun? What were my plans after graduation? That last one almost made me jump up and leave with my hair half-clipped.

Then she asked me if I had an afterschool job.

"Actually, I'm looking for one. Heard of anything?"

Glenna thought for a second while she pulled the ends of my hair together to meet below my chin. "You could work here," she finally said. "They're looking for someone to do janitor-type stuff. It's not glamorous, but it's money." She waited for my response.

I smiled and breathed a prayer of thanks to God. Glenna may have just solved my problems. "Yeah, that would be great!"

After Glenna finished drying my hair, she sent me to the front desk to pay and speak with the manager. After a minute, the manager appeared from the back of the shop.

"Can I help you?" She extended her manicured hand to

shake. This felt so grown-up. I'd need to go watch a Disney movie later to remind myself I was still a kid.

"Um, yes. I was hoping you're hiring. I can't cut hair or do nails, but I can clean…" *Just don't look at my bedroom floor…* "And answer phones, I guess. And I can, like, make coffee runs and…" I stopped talking when I caught myself rambling. So long, salon job.

"Are you in school?"

"I'm a high school senior. I was hoping to work maybe some afternoons or on the weekends."

"Do you have a resume?" What would even be on my resume at this point in my life? High school party host?

"I don't, I'm sorry."

The manager studied me for a minute. "I can't give you much, but you could come in after school and sweep, clean bathrooms, all that fun stuff. I'm sorry it'd just be for a couple hours a week. Would that work?"

It wasn't as much as I wanted, but it was better than nothing. I nodded enthusiastically. A little too excited. Kind of like Moose. "Yes! Thank you!" Then, feeling like *quite* the grown up, I extended my hand and initiated a handshake.

I honestly thought I'd have a panic attack as I slipped on a black dress and curled my blonde hair which still fell halfway down my back, even after the trim. I reminded myself to breathe and pray. *You can do this, Sadie. God's not gonna drop you. Oh, God, help me not freak out!*

I slipped a pair of flats on my feet and grabbed my purse. I barely recognized my reflection in the mirror. *What would Kurt say if he saw this?* I laughed to myself. *His niece has turned into a church girl.*

That reminded me I needed to call the Elliots. I'd

texted back and forth with Mel, letting her know about Fyn's grandmother and sending the kids pictures of Moose, but that's it. She'd been so busy homeschooling the two older kids, potty-training Cooper, and caring for newborn baby Evie that I'd felt bad about taking too much time. Besides, I could honestly assure her I had everything under control. I was doing well in Seattle. Not necessarily thriving, but I was handling the whole clean-up-my-life, be-a-good-Christian thing. Except for some of the things I told Moose every time he peed on the carpet. So my mouth could still use some scrubbing, but I was working on it.

I checked the time on my phone before slipping it into my bag. The funeral was going to be held at an old Presbyterian church downtown, where Fyn's grandmother had been a member since before she married her late husband, Fynnigan Larcy (the guy Fyn was named after), and then the graveside service would be just outside of the city at a cemetery. The anxiety started to rise in my throat again. I told myself to just focus on one thing at a time.

"Sadie!" Fyn said when I stepped into the building. I'd had to wait in a line of people to greet the family, but when I got to Fyn, she pulled me out of line next to her. "Oh, Sadie. You came. And you're pretty!" Holding my hands, she took in my hair and dress. "I mean, you always are, but your hair looks so good down."

Leaning next to my ear, she whispered, "I've been hugged at least a thousand times already. Someone needs to tell old ladies to lay off the perfume. I mean, seriously."

"I'm gonna go find a seat," My breath quickened as an organ started to play. Plus, the smell of perfume *was* a little potent. Fyn nodded and braced herself for another hug.

Instead of entering the sanctuary, I slipped over to a bathroom. I locked myself in a stall, letting my purse hit the floor. I brushed a few Moose hairs off my dress and leaned against the door. I wrapped my arms tightly around my middle and closed my eyes, a cold sweat breaking out on my forehead. *You can do this, Sadie. Pull yourself together for Fyn. You can lose it later.* Giving myself permission to freak out later brought some relief, until I realized how scary that could get. Instinctively, I craved a drink.

At the front of the sanctuary, a spray of pink carnations adorned the closed casket. My stomach churned at the display, and I averted my eyes. The room was packed with people, most of them in their seventies, eighties, and maybe even nineties. And then the lady who sat next to me had to have been at least 108. We were told to stand and turn to a hymn number in our hymnals. I had never used one of those. When the organ started again, I panicked. Everyone began to sing the first verse of "Great is Thy Faithfulness." My mom's favorite song. I couldn't do it. I had to get out.

"Excuse me," I whispered to the old woman next to me, but she didn't hear me, so I slid by anyway. I retreated back to the bathroom, where I stayed until I heard the organ play again, signaling the end of the service. Fyn found me waiting around the corner where I couldn't see the pallbearers carry out the casket. Her eyes were red and swollen, and she clutched a handful of shredded tissues. "Thank you for coming, Sadie," she said, grief dripping from her words. "Are you coming to the graveside?"

I knew if I couldn't even handle sitting through a funeral there was no way on earth I could handle going to that place.

"I've actually got to leave. Please tell your dad I'm so sorry about Gran."

Fyn nodded. "Yes, sure. I should go find Fig and Glenna. We get to ride in a limo," she smiled sadly.

"Hey, Fyn? I know this is a weird time, but can you explain

Glenna to me?" I really wanted to know, and I figured it might be a good opportunity to give Fyn a brief distraction.

"I wish I could…"

"No, I mean, who is she?"

"Oh." Fyn and I stepped over to the side, by a daisy wreath on a stand. "Glenna's my sister. Well, technically, my half-sister. My dad was married once before he met Mom. Glenna's kind of the black sheep of the family. We don't see much of her, so it's like a miracle she's here. Dad is thrilled."

I nodded. That made sense. She did have eyes similar to Fyn's, and for all I knew, they could have the same hair color, it was just hard to tell what color Fyn's hair actually was. I almost opened my mouth to tell her how helpful Glenna had been in helping me land a small job, but Fig came over and dragged her away before I had the chance.

I decided I desperately needed coffee.

"What can I get you?" The barista asked as I stepped up to the counter at Goldfinch's. Though it was autumn and we were in a climate known for being overcast, the guy was tan. When he smiled, his white teeth were so white I could almost hear them gleam. I ordered The Forest—a strong, earthy brew with nutmeg and cinnamon.

"Do you know if you guys are hiring?" Man, I loved this place. If I could work at the salon during the week and at Goldfinch's on the weekends, Dad should be thrilled. I could earn that plane ticket in no time.

The barista brushed his blonde hair out of his eyes and grabbed a cup off the stack. "Not that I know of," he replied. "But the owner is in today. Let me go ask him." He handed me my order, then slipped through a door.

The owner came out of the back, hand extended. "Bill Muller. How can I help you?"

I set my coffee on the counter. I felt like I was meeting a celebrity. "My name is Sadie Franklin. I'm a high school senior, and I'm looking for a job to work on weekends."

Bill watched me. "Do you have a resume?"

"No, sir." Boom. Southern manners for the win.

"I'm sorry, but we're covered right now. But we will have some holiday season openings when my college students leave for the break." He motioned toward Mr. Sun and Surf. "You could check back then?"

Discouraged, I grabbed my cup and adjusted my purse on my shoulder. "I appreciate it, but I really need to find something now. Thank you, though."

I headed toward the door.

"Sadie?"

"Yes?" I turned back around.

"It's not coffee, but my nephew owns an indoor inflatables place across town. Go over there and tell them Bill recommends you."

"I-I-thank you. Seriously. But you don't even know me."

"I know you have good taste in coffee, and that speaks volumes. And you dressed up to job hunt. Shows you're willing to put in some effort." He grabbed a napkin off the counter and scribbled an address with a stubby pencil. "Good luck, Sadie."

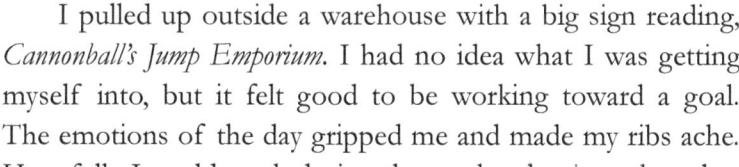

I pulled up outside a warehouse with a big sign reading, *Cannonball's Jump Emporium*. I had no idea what I was getting myself into, but it felt good to be working toward a goal. The emotions of the day gripped me and made my ribs ache. Hopefully I could work during the weekends, since the salon couldn't give me Saturday hours. Taking a deep breath, I unclicked my seatbelt and dragged myself inside.

One time, I was standing on the side of the road near some train tracks, waiting for a friend to bring me some gas for dad's car. A train passed by and the horn went off right as it passed me. That was so loud. But it was nothing in comparison to all the yelling and shrieking happening inside Cannonball's. At least fifty elementary-age kids ran back and forth between inflatable bounce houses, slides, and obstacle courses. Mothers sat in chairs scattered around the large room, talking to each other or scrolling through something on their phones while the banshees played. I involuntarily shivered.

"Welcome to Cannonball's! I'm Grrrreg! *Arrrr* you ready for adventure?" A deep voice cut through the shrill squeals.

I stared at the husky thirty-something guy wearing a tie-dye t-shirt and a smeared beard drawn on his face with a brown marker.

"Shoot me," I mumbled.

"What's that?" He kept on grinning.

"Nothing, sorry. I'm Sadie Franklin. I was hoping to fill out a job application. I can only work weekends, but anything you can give me would be great. Bill at Goldfinch's sent me."

"Old Uncle Bill! Sure!" Greg brandished a form from under the desk.

He grabbed a pen and used it to point to the chaos over his shoulder. "I'm mainly looking for Friday and Saturday help. That's when we get the big crowds. You up for that?"

I nodded, grateful Friday was the only day I'd have to talk to the salon people about.

"Good. There are some picnic tables over that way where you can sit to fill it out. I've got a party starting in about five minutes, so I've gotta go suit up. Just leave it on the desk when you're done, and I'll be back in a half hour if you've got more questions."

I already had more questions, but took the form and the pen and wove around small children to get to the tables.

I did my best on the application, then stepped over to the desk to wait on Greg to come back.

"Alllllrighty!" I jumped at the muffled voice behind me. An overweight unicorn stepped around me and behind the desk.

"Let's see what we've got!" The unicorn took his head off, and I whispered something four letters long before I caught myself. Old habits die hard.

Greg's head poked out of the unicorn's neck. "Sorry. No rest for Cannonball!"

"Cannonball's a unicorn…?" I shook my head. "Never mind. Is there anything else I need to fill out? Can I meet the manager?"

"You're looking at him! Manager and owner!" Greg patted his fuzzy belly, where I could practically hear the stretched threads of the unicorn suit screaming for mercy.

I shook his hoof, thanked him, and walked out of Cannonball's Jump Emporium.

Greg called later that night and told me I'd gotten the job. I wanted to cry, and I wasn't sure whether I was relieved, elated, or scared out of my mind.

"What did your dad say about you having two jobs?" Becca asked, her face filling up my phone screen.

"I don't know. I can never really tell with that man," I sighed and sipped my decaf coffee.

"Well, I'm proud of you. And proud you haven't intentionally backed over that dog yet with the car."

"Becca! Watch your mouth!" I clamped my hands over the sleeping puppy's ears.

"I have nothing against dogs. I love mine. You're the one who's anti-animals."

I sighed and studied my cuticles. "You're right. I guess we just kind of get each other, in a weird way. It's like this vibe. We're both kind of loners, trying to fit into a new life."

"You're such a poet." Becca smiled. I heard a faint cry, and she held up a finger before slipping out of view. She returned a minute later, cradling Evie in her arms. The baby was still small, but she was starting to get some serious cheeks.

Becca kissed the baby's forehead, and I was hit with a pang of jealousy. I wanted to hang out with my cousins while my aunt and uncle had a date night. I wanted to be able to hold Evie, feel her fuzzy hair, watch her grow up. She was named after me, after all. Or at least, her middle name. I watched Evelyn Grey be born, but I had to leave soon after she got here. When she had to spend an extra week in the hospital, I'd visited her as much as I could. We had a bond. Evie whimpered, and Becca gently bounced her on her shoulder.

"I wish I were there," I whispered.

"I know," Becca said, surprising me that she'd heard my soft comment. "And I wish you'd been able to call before I put the other kids to bed so you could talk to them. They miss ya like crazy."

I nodded. "Yeah. Me, too."

Becca promised to tell Kurt and Mel I said hi when they returned, and I promised to update Becca about the job situation. We ended the call then. It was a chilly night, so I brought Moose's box into my room and prayed super hard he wouldn't destroy the house while I slept. Then I crawled into bed feeling homesick.

Chapter Thirteen

I started at the salon Monday afternoon. After filling out some paperwork, I learned Glenna would be showing me the ropes. Apparently, she'd had my job back when she was still in cosmetology school. I'd yet to figure out what was so weird about the relationship between Glenna Larcy and her family. Yes, she had this intriguing shoulder tattoo I had to force myself not to stare at—was that a flower or a cabbage?—but she seemed normal enough.

"So you hang out with Fyn a lot?" she asked after she'd given me the grand tour of the cleaning supply closet. This job didn't seem too stressful, even if the waterfall behind the counter did send me to the bathroom every ten minutes.

"Yeah, Fyn's awesome." I inspected a picture in my magazine, trying to decide how much my aunt would freak if I shaved half my head. "I think God knew we needed each other." I still surprised myself when God-talk popped out of my mouth.

The phone rang and Glenna put her hand on it but said to me before she answered it, "For the record, Fyn thinks you're awesome, too."

The knowledge of that kept me smiling through sweeping clumps of hair off the floor after closing time.

"We have some news." Melina's face wobbled as she propped her phone on the kitchen table in front of her.

"You're pregnant?"

She leveled me with her glare. Yikes, she could be fierce. "Sadie, I have a newborn. Don't even joke."

"Well, you already have four of them and what're you, like, thirty?"

"We'll go with that."

"I'm just saying you seem really good at the whole producing-kids thing." I shrugged.

Was extremely-frank, always-speak-her-mind Melina *blushing*? "Child, don't test me."

Kurt's face popped up on the screen behind Melina. He put his arms around her shoulders and leaned forward. "What's up, kid? What are we discussing?"

Mel turned her head to kiss his cheek. "Sadie thinks procreating is our talent."

Kurt raised his eyebrows and tilted his head. "Practice makes perfect."

Now *I* was the one with heat shooting to my face. "I'm hanging up now."

They both laughed, unconcerned with how much they disturbed their seventeen-year-old niece.

"Our news is that we took Cooper in for allergy tests. We always thought he was allergic to dyes or something, but turns out, it's more than that. We started noticing he would puke after eating different kinds of things, even when they weren't necessarily dyed colors."

"What's he got?"

Kurt moved around the chair and took Melina's seat. She perched on his lap so they were both in the camera view. "Well," Kurt said, "We're waiting on results. They're thinking he may have a problem processing sugar."

"Welcome to the club, Coop," I muttered. "What does that mean?"

"It means I'm suddenly doubting he's my kid," Melina said. "I mean, *my* child not eating sugar?"

Kurt rolled his eyes. "Mel does like her sweets."

"Dang right. Anyway, Sadie, it mainly means our usually calm, orderly life is slightly more chaotic right now." I caught the sarcasm in her tired voice. The Elliot home was always anything but peaceful, but somehow the chaos was comforting.

"Man. I'm sorry, you guys. I'm glad you're getting some answers, though."

Mel leaned against Kurt's chest. "We're thankful God showed us we needed to get help when He did."

I nodded. "I'm learning He's kind of good at that."

Kurt ran a hand through his curly, bright-red-like-Trissy's hair. "Always remember that, kid."

Homesickness filled my throat, and I tried to swallow it back. Now was not the time to start feeling emotions.

"You okay?" Mel asked, tilting her head to the side until her dark, short hair brushed her face.

"Yeah, I'm fine. Just thinking about the times God has shown up right when I needed Him most, even when I didn't realize it." I felt my cheeks warm as I thought about the last party I'd thrown before going to Georgia. While I hadn't officially given it all away that night, I'd come scary close. Closer than any other time. I tried not to let my mind drift back because shame would rush in. If the police hadn't shown up at that party at my house when they did… if someone hadn't banged on the bedroom door to let us know what was happening…

My stomach turned at the thought of it. I knew that nothing I told Melina about my life or past choices would faze her. Kurt was a squeaky-clean good guy when Mel married him, but she had a past like mine. And Kurt was a youth pastor and high school counselor. Not much surprised him. But it was still hard to admit how misguided I had been, even when they already knew it all.

I sighed. "He's shown up right on time when I didn't even know He was on the way."

Kurt adjusted Mel's phone. "Except now you know there's really no showing up about it. He's *always* with you. And remembering that changes everything."

———oOo———

When I arrived for my first day of work at Cannonball's on Saturday morning, Grrrreg gave me a bag containing a couple tie-dye t-shirts with the pirate unicorn thing on the front, a pack of temporary tattoos, tax forms, and a box of sour candy. He went over some details about answering the phones and checking in kids, which basically involved their parents signing away their lives.

Then there were wristbands and tokens and concessions and prizes to hand out. And retrieving kids who were too scared to go down the inflatable slide they'd climbed up. Turns out, Greg was a little short-staffed. The hardest part of the job, by a long shot, was the volume. The roar of the fans from the inflatables was one thing, but the squeals of kids and the music pumping through the sound system were loud enough to drown out all of that. By the time Liz showed up with her two younger cousins that afternoon, I was ready to take a nap right there on the concessions counter.

"How's the job going?" she asked as I attached a band to the wrist of one of the chunkiest eight-year-olds I'd ever seen.

"I'm exhausted. The owner is a little short on help, so I've been doing a lot." To prove my point, I pulled a piece of popcorn out of my hair.

Liz swatted at her cousin, who bounced off toward the giant pirate ship inflatable. "Think he'd hire me?"

I laughed. Tough Liz? The one who read poetry and intimidated people as hobbies? Working with kids? She just blinked at me.

"Oh, you're serious?"

A nod.

"I'll go find Greg."

――――― ○○○ ―――――

The days blended together in a strand of homework, housework, and real work. My days were full, and my tiny pockets of free time were spent trying to housetrain Moose and comfort Fyn. She constantly apologized for being clingy, but honestly, it felt good to have someone depend on me and trust me. It was a pretty new feeling for me. And Glenna turned out to be pretty fun, too. After closing the salon in the evenings, she would hang around for customers who couldn't make it during regular business hours. We chatted or listened to music while she waited and I cleaned. Even with all of the busyness and the horrible situation at home, this was one area of my life that was working out. I felt peace inside.

Glenna invited me to grab dinner with her after work one evening. I was more than a little surprised, especially since Fyn made her sound the opposite of friendly, but I was glad for the opportunity to get to know her better. At the restaurant, I chose a teriyaki pineapple burger with lettuce in place of a bun, and I substituted sweet potato fries for the regular ones. In Pecan Creek, that option probably wouldn't even be on the menu—those people liked their fried carbs and starches—but on the West Coast, it wasn't uncommon to make choices that let you live longer. That was one positive thing about being back in Seattle. It was easier for my special diet to blend in.

Glenna went with a turkey burger, and while we waited on our food, we chatted about what my high school experience looked like compared to when she was in high school a decade earlier. When our food arrived, I instinctively dipped my head to pray. I felt Glenna's eyes on me, and sat up straight, my cheeks warming. Somehow, praying before a meal had ingrained itself in my routine.

"Sorry," I mumbled to Glenna and God.

She shrugged and speared a bite of her side salad. "It's fine. We all have a right to our own truths, so why would I try to convince you otherwise?"

I chewed on a sweet potato fry and thought through that.

"The main thing," she continued, "is that you believe something because *you* want to believe it, not because someone has convinced you to adopt their truth, you know?"

I swallowed the fry. "That makes sense," I responded slowly. And it really did. But I knew I wasn't a Christian because my family had forced me into religion. God had chased after me until I realized I didn't want to keep living my own, self-destructive way. Or my own "truth." I started to share that with Glenna, but she shook her head. "It's totally fine, Sadie. What's right for you may not be right for me, and that's okay. As long as we love ourselves and accept others, that's what matters." She took a bite of her turkey burger, ending that part of the conversation. "So tell me about Southern fried culture."

She smiled at me over her burger, and I was glad for the chance to share about life in the South.

But as I got ready for bed, I couldn't stop thinking through our conversation. Glenna said what mattered most was that we "love ourselves and accept others." That seemed right on the surface. After all, my friends and family in Georgia were content in who they were and definitely accepted me as I was, even though I was a disaster.

But they didn't leave it at that. They cared enough to encourage me to choose a different path. They told me about Jesus and insisted I had a purpose, and pointed out all of the pieces God had worked together to bring me to that summer night when I gave my heart and life to Jesus, the Father who would never let me down.

Was anything else even love? Was allowing someone you cared about to make scary life choices without showing them you cared even love? And how did that fit in when it came to my dad and how I disagreed with him?

Glenna's philosophy seemed watered down somehow.

As I crawled into bed, I pulled my Bible off my nightstand. Under the glow of my lamp, I flipped to the back of the book and searched for the word "love." I was overwhelmed by how many times the word showed up. I didn't have the mental energy to go on a scavenger hunt right then.

I yawned and set my Bible back on the nightstand. That was a lot of information at once, and I had no idea where to begin. So I did the only thing I knew to do: I told all of that to God.

Sunday morning at church, my mind was cloudy from a 10-hour shift manning the bounce houses at Cannonball's. But those thoughts about love had been running through my mind the whole time. I decided to find Jordan after the service and ask him to point me to more verses.

He and his wife, Claire, had tried to reach out to me ever since I'd started going to Raining Grace, but I'd been so busy I hadn't taken them up on any coffee offers yet.

But maybe that could change.

Jordan and Claire invited me over to their apartment for lunch that afternoon. I suddenly understood why they never had the group over to their house; the place was a tiny, one-bedroom apartment. It made Fyn's house look like a palace.

But Jordan and Claire didn't seem to mind the space. In fact, it was kind of cozy. A blanket was draped over one arm of the sofa, and a basket sat in the corner with more blankets. The shelves of the TV stand were filled with games, and a tall bookshelf was packed with books. More books were piled on top of the shelf until the stack nearly reached the ceiling.

As soon as Claire entered the apartment, she lit a candle that sat on the small coffee table. Then she invited me into the kitchen while Jordan went to change clothes.

"I'm so glad you could come hang out with us, Sadie!" Claire smiled as she walked over to a Crock-Pot on the counter. If I had to guess, I'd say she was around Glenna's age. Somewhere in her mid-to-late twenties.

"Thank you for inviting me," I smiled back. They were pretty much strangers to me. Other than saying hi at church each Sunday and seeing them at Café Graffiti, I didn't know them well. But I got the impression they were the same people they seemed like at church.

We got to know each other over giant bowls of chili. They listened intently as I told them about Georgia and about how I became a Christian. The conversation was the opposite of the talk I'd had with Glenna. With Jordan and Claire, I felt free to talk about how I believed in one truth and real love.

After lunch, Jordan cleaned up the table while Claire and I took mugs of coffee and bowls of fruit into the living room.

Claire laughed when she saw me staring at Jordan, who filled up the sink with hot, soapy water.

I shook my head. "I'm sorry, it's just unusual..."

"To see the guy do all the dishes?" She laughed again. "I know. But he wants to help, and I don't trust him with the cooking. Besides, he'll put in his earbuds and listen to music and be in his own world for a while."

I tucked my legs beneath me on the couch and gently blew on the piping hot hazelnut brew. "I think it's cool how you guys get along. My aunt and uncle are crazy about each other to the point where it gets kinda nauseating." Until the summer, I'd never seen many examples of good marriages. My parents were married because they had me in common, but that's about it. I never remembered seeing much affection between them.

Claire carefully sipped her coffee. "That's sweet. I don't think we hear enough about good marriages. We hear plenty of the bad stuff. But the good stuff is really good, and it's worth celebrating. I hope I get the chance to meet your aunt and uncle one day. Plus," she added candidly, "we're not that far into it yet. Jordan and I will take all the role models we can get."

I nodded. It would be fun to introduce one youth pastor and his wife to another, although I couldn't imagine that ever happening.

We chatted for a while until Jordan joined us with his own cup of coffee.

I still needed to ask about what had been in my head for so many days. I had told them I lived with just my dad, and I'd mentioned our relationship wasn't super awesome, but I hadn't gone into much detail about how stressful it really was.

Setting my empty mug on a woodgrain coaster, I dove in. "I was talking with a coworker the other day"—I paused here to bask in how mature that sounded—"and she mentioned how our main goal in life is to 'love ourselves and accept others.' That doesn't sound completely right to me, but I'm still so new at all of this. My conversation with her reminded me of what you and Pastor Theo have been talking about, Jordan. So

I wanted to look for some verses to help everything click for me. I was hoping you guys could maybe help?"

I picked up my empty mug, just to have something to do while I waited. Vulnerability was an even newer idea to me than the Bible.

Jordan leaned forward in the chair he sat in on the other side of the coffee table, his elbows on his knees. "Of course, Sadie. But what if we did this: Want to learn how to find the answer?"

When I nodded, he reached over to the bookshelf and grabbed his Bible.

Handing it to me, he said, "Flip to the back. There's a concordance."

"Yeah. I tried that on my own, but got overwhelmed by the options. I was hoping you'd just give me the right answer."

Jordan grinned. "Yeah, but what would help you more: me telling you what you're supposed to believe, or you discovering the truth for yourself?"

I pretended to roll my eyes. "Fine." He and Kurt would get along *so* well. I opened the big, worn Bible to the back and found the love verses. "Okay, I'm there," I said.

Jordan stood and crossed the room in two steps, then sat beside me on the couch. Sandwiched between Jordan and Claire, I felt strong and able to learn everything.

"Next to prayer," Jordan said, "the key to Bible study is to have patience. It takes time and commitment, but that's how we grow. There may be a faster way to find what you want, but the process is where it's at. That's how we leave room for God to speak to us and teach us."

Starting at the top of the list, I read the little snippets of verses containing the word *love*.

I scanned the page until I found a verse that started with, "This is how we know what love is…"

That seemed like it was sure to give me a definition. I flipped to the front of the Bible where all of the books were listed out. I still didn't know where all of the books in the Bible were, but Jordan and Claire didn't seem fazed. Nor did they try to hurry me. I never even saw them take out their phones or anything. They just sat with me.

I finally found 1 John 3:16 and whispered its words into the silence, "This is how we know what love is: Jesus Christ laid down his life for us. And we ought to lay down our lives for our brothers and sisters."

I leaned back on the couch to process that. It reminded me of what Jordan had been teaching on at Café Graffiti, about how we're supposed to love others even when we're not feeling it because Jesus loves us so much.

"It's just like what you talk about," I said, turning to Jordan.

He nodded. "Jesus showed us what real love is when He died in our place. And because He gave everything for us, we're supposed to do that for others to show them His love."

I knew that was the right answer, but it still caused me to stiffen. That meant I needed to show Dad love by giving, even when it wasn't easy. I kept reading the next verse: "If anyone has material possessions and sees a brother or sister in need but has no pity on them, how can the love of God be in that person? Dear children, let us not love with words or speech but with actions and in truth."

I sat there, reading the verses over and over. I didn't want to comment, because that might open up the wounds in front of Jordan and Claire, even though I got the feeling they wouldn't care.

Somehow, they seemed to know my thoughts anyway. "We're not promised it's going to be easy loving others," Claire said. "But we're promised we're not alone as we do it."

Okay, so my dad didn't need material stuff. I didn't need

to go out and buy him new socks or anything. But he did need some hope. He was so caught up in his own truths, that he didn't know the Truth I knew. Maybe it was my job to share it with him.

"Yeah." I kept my eyes on the page. "I think God is showing me what I need to do."

"I think He might be too, Sadie," Jordan said. "Can we pray with you?"

Chapter Fourteen

○○○

I left Jordan and Claire's home feeling warm and newly resolved to show love to my dad in whatever ways I could. But I still wasn't looking forward to re-entering the fray after my calm, stress-free afternoon, so when Fyn texted and asked if I could come help her with something, I drove straight from the tiny apartment to the Larcys' architectural masterpiece.

I shifted in my seat and stretched, my back cracking from fatigue. Fyn told me to check my posture, and I straightened. I'd been sitting at her little round window, obeying her orders to keep an angsty expression on my face, for nearly an hour. Fyn wanted to improve her people-sketching skills while she avoided sinking into depression, and I didn't want to be home, so I was her subject.

"Why doesn't your brother or sister model for you?" I asked during the first twenty minutes of the process.

"I'm pretty sure Fig is Ritalin-resistant, and Glenna doesn't live with us. Besides, she's weird."

"She's nice to me at work, and it was really cool of her to go have dinner with me."

"She's an actress."

I'd tilted my head to see Fyn, only to have her shoot me an icy glare. "Really? What's she been in?"

Fyn rolled her eyes so hard I thought they would pop out of her head. "I meant she's good at pretending, genius."

"Hey," I said. "Don't prey on weakness."

Fyn laughed, then turned serious again, focusing on her sketch. "She's got a cosmetology license, and she's awesome at what she does, I'll give her that. But other than her job, she's twenty-seven and hasn't got a clue. She's spoiled and ungrateful and only visits when it's convenient for her. The night she showed up at the hospital, I thought my whole family would pass out from shock. Dad has done everything for her. Too much, really. Paying to put her through school, getting her a car, all of that. And Mom took her in as her own child."

"That's rough, Fyn."

"Yeah." Fyn shook her head. "Hence the lack of warm, fuzzy feelings. Let's talk about your drama instead. So what all do you know about your dad's lover?"

"Fynnigan Unita Larcy..."

"It's *Louise*. Fynnigan *Louise* Larcy. And sorry. But what do you know?"

"I know he's not out pounding the pavement looking for jobs when he's out at one in the morning, because who is holding interviews in the middle of the night?" I felt the warmth of the afternoon threaten to boil in my veins. "He's with *her*—I just know it. The whole thing is just disgusting."

From her easel, Fyn nodded sympathetically. "That is gross, but hold still."

"That...that...*she-bear*," I mumbled.

"What did you call her?"

I sighed deeply. "It's the only thing I could think of that would keep this conversation PG." I squirmed, *really* needing to go to the bathroom. "I hate knowing she's slept over."

Fyn's mouth dropped. "Again?"

"No, not since I've been back. I think me being here is

super inconvenient for Dad, because he can't play house when his kid is around."

Fyn considered this. "Your dad's probably lonely."

"That doesn't justify having an affair."

Fyn set down her pencil and opened her mouth to speak, but I interrupted her. "Yes, I know my mom is gone, so it's not like he's technically cheating on her. But it still feels like he's cheating on her memory—on our family." I grit my teeth, refusing to cry in front of Fyn.

Fyn scratched her nose, and I envied that freedom. My hand was asleep pressed against the window.

"And also, it's like we've traded roles. Like I'm the parent, and he's the teenager. He sent me away because I was too into drinking and partying and guys, and now he's the one with alcohol on the premises and crazy-late nights and this girlfriend."

Fyn didn't say anything for a moment, just tilted her head and studied her masterpiece.

"I'm done!" she declared. "Come and see!"

I stood, rolling my cricked neck and stepping around the easel. I froze. "Fyn!"

"I don't mean to brag, but I think this may be some of my best work."

"*Fyn!*"

"What? Speechless?" She asked.

I opened and closed my mouth, not sure of what to say. "You…it's…that's…my *hand!* An hour of holding perfectly still for a drawing of my *hand?*"

"Well, I wouldn't say you were *perfectly* still."

"What was with all the death threats when I tilted my head? And I thought you were gonna have a coronary when I sneezed earlier."

Fyn crossed her arms over her chest. "I didn't want the

image compromised. Didn't it turn out so...*hand*somely?" She fell back on her bed and doubled over, cackling like a lunatic.

I shook my head but couldn't stop the laughter that bubbled out of my mouth. Fyn was many things, and I understood exactly none of them. But she also got me, and we'd become crucial to each other's survival.

I humored her by *oohing* and *aahing* over her hand portrait for an appropriate amount of time before I couldn't avoid going home any longer.

"Hey," Fyn looped her arm through mine as she walked me to the door. "My family has its share of issues. All families have their faults. But at the end of the day, they're the ones who stick with you when the world walks out. I got to learn that one the hard way last year. I know your dad's not all that easy to love right now, and I know the whole situation is a nightmare. I really do. But the two of you are Team Franklin. You need each other, even though you may not think so right now." She shrugged. "Besides, count your blessings. At least Glenna's not in *your* family."

That coaxed an eye roll and a smile out of me, and on the way home, I promised God I'd make an extra effort to keep Team Franklin intact.

───── ○○○ ─────

When Dad came home one night that week, I sat on the couch with Moose, looking through career options on the laptop. I had a meeting with the guidance counselor soon, and she wanted me to be ready to discuss how I saw myself in ten years. I figured she wanted more than "alive."

Dad went into his room and shut the door, and I went back to googling, "What should I be when I grow up?"

I heard the shower running, then his door opening about fifteen minutes later.

"I'll be back later."

I opened my mouth to comment, but he put his hand up. "Yes, I'm going to see her. She makes me happy, Sadie, and we both know it's been a while since I've been truly happy. At least I'm not bringing her home." He glanced out the window.

"Don't go." My words were calm but so unexpected, Moose jumped off the couch and ran to my room.

Dad looked at me. "What?"

"Don't go." My voice was eerily calm, but my hands trembled. I shoved them under my legs. "Let's hang out. Watch something. I'll pop popcorn, make hot chocolate."

It wasn't so much that I wanted to spend time with my dad—I did, even though I really needed to buckle down on homework—but if he was with me, he wouldn't be with *her*. Bratty? Maybe. Desperate? Oh, yeah.

"Maybe next weekend, Sadie. I'm exhausted from job hunting all day and just need some down time."

Biting back reminders that *I* was the one who was a full-time high school senior who had just worked most of the weekend at her job and could really use some down time, I said, "Relax here, at the house. The Chinese takeout place doesn't close until 10:00. We could get some of that awesome lo mein…"

"Not tonight. I already have plans."

"But Dad! *I'm* your family, not her!"

Dad put his hand on the doorknob. "Don't even go there with me right now. I'm under a lot of stress, and—"

"*You* don't even go there with me right now, Dad!" So much for biting my tongue. "I'm the one trying to start my life over. I'm the one in my last year of high school who is now busting my neck at two jobs to buy stuff for myself since my dad stopped showing up for work and got fired! I'm the one cleaning the house and cooking meals! I'm the one cleaning up my act who hasn't touched alcohol in months and who hasn't so much as hung out with the opposite sex all semester! Sometimes I wonder if I'm not the real parent around here!"

That did it. Dad hit the door with the palm of his hand. "I am finished with your self-righteous attitude, Sadie! I don't know what lies those people in Georgia filled your head with, making you think you can really have a new life and that there's actually a God who cares, but I regret sending you to them. And I'm starting to regret letting them send you back."

"You tried to keep me away?" I clenched my jaw so hard my teeth grit together.

"I've never known what to do with you."

"You know what? I'm sorry I'm such a problem!" I stood, the laptop falling off my lap and hitting that awful rug. I cursed a string of words that would make a sailor tremble, and my dad flung open the door.

"Don't wait up!" he shouted before slamming the door hard enough to knock my kindergarten picture off the wall. The glass shattered.

I shouted at nothing in particular and stomped into the kitchen where I flung open the fridge. The beer bottles filled the vegetable drawer, and I grabbed one. I found the bottle opener in the drawer by the sink and popped it open. My heart throbbed in my throat and I panted like I'd just run a marathon. All I needed to calm down was a night with my old friend. I could get so drunk nothing else would matter. I could forget about all of it.

Leaning against the counter, I raised the bottle to my lips. I could smell it. Almost taste it. I tipped it back, the cool beverage filling my mouth and—

I know the plans I have for you...

I spewed the beer into the sink. Where had that come

from? Wasn't that a Bible verse? Why was that running through my mind now, of all times? I tipped the bottle back again.

Plans to prosper you and not to harm you...to give you a hope and a future.

My hand let go of the bottle, and it crashed to the floor. What had I almost done? I'd almost ruined everything in one moment. I slid against the cabinets down to the floor, not even caring I was sitting in a puddle of beer and glass shards. I dropped my head into my hands and sobbed.

"I'm sorry. I'm sorry. I'm so sorry." I cried over and over, my arms tucked around my legs, my head dropped to my knees, rocking back and forth.

My tears of frustration ran off my chin and onto my jeans. Glass poked at my legs through the denim, but I didn't even care.

How had it come to this? I'd just cussed out my dad and turned to alcohol to numb the pain. I was a *Christian!* What was I thinking?

I continued rocking back and forth until no more tears came, and Moose barked at the back door to be let outside.

I was just so angry. I clipped a leash on Moose and took off running down the street, never minding the fact that it was nearly 10:00 at night and I didn't live in the best neighborhood. As I ran, sirens blared in the distance, signaling some sort of emergency. *Might as well be my life...*

I ran until my abdomen throbbed in pain and my lungs burned for more oxygen. Little Moose gave up and I had to carry him home. I pulled the house key out of my sports bra and let Moose inside, then I collapsed on the couch, breathless. My phone rang, and I reached over to where I'd left it on the coffee table earlier. I answered without even checking the caller ID, desperately needing something to distract me from my anger and the beer in the fridge.

"Hello?" I panted.

"Sadie?"

"Um, yeah."

"It's Glenna."

What in the world...? "What's up?" I slowly sat up on the couch, running a hand across my dripping forehead.

"It's your dad. He's been in a wreck. Apparently the paramedics found his phone and dialed the most recent number and it was mine. You need to get to the hospital."

Thoughts swirled in my brain, ranging from *Why on earth would dad call you?* To *How does he even know you?* To *Wait, Dad was in a wreck? No way he was in a wreck—I just saw him.* And back to *How do you know my dad?* But I somehow managed to voice the most important question: "Is he okay?"

Glenna sounded panicked. "I don't even know if he's still alive! Just come to the hospital."

I ended the call, and the phone dropped to the floor. Spots danced in front of my eyes while Moose tried to lick the sweat off my face. I felt numb. So numb. But somehow I managed to jump up, stick Moose in the backyard, grab my keys, and go outside.

When I realized Dad had been driving our car.

I paced back and forth for a minute, frantically trying to figure out what to do. My first thought was to call Fyn. I continued pacing outside my house until she pulled into my driveway a little while later.

She didn't even wait for me to open the car door before she called out the open window. "What's going on? Spill it."

I did. I doubled over and threw up in the bushes.

Fyn's mouth dropped open and she eyed me warily as I climbed into the car, spots dancing in front of my eyes. I knew I was dehydrated from the run, and the taste of beer still lingering in my mouth didn't help.

"Are you...what happened?"

Praying she didn't smell the alcohol on my breath, I dropped my head in my hands and muttered the name of the hospital. My mind raced, and I couldn't slow it down.

My dad might be dead.

Chapter Fifteen

○○○

I left Fyn in the parking lot and raced into the ER to figure out what was going on.

"I'm looking for Mike Franklin." I ran into the desk, catching myself with my palms so I didn't sail over the top. "I'm his daughter."

The nurse looked up, and her eyes widened slightly. I guess she was caught off guard by the hair plastered to my makeup-free forehead and my bloodshot eyes. And probably my puke breath because that had just happened again in the parking lot. But she recovered quickly and nodded. "They brought him in a little while ago. Please have a seat, and we'll keep you updated."

"Can you at least tell me if he's…alive?"

"As far as I know—"

"But what—?"

"Sadie." I felt a hand on my shoulder, and I jerked around. Glenna stood behind me. "Come sit. They've promised to update us as soon as they know something."

Nothing made sense about this situation at all. Why was Glenna…?

Oh, please God, no.

The color drained from my face. "You're…Dad's…*her*."

"What?" She furrowed her perfect eyebrows, and her forehead didn't even wrinkle in the process. She reached out to touch my shoulder again.

"Don't touch me!" I whispered, my defenses coming alive as the pieces began falling into place and one of the worst nights of my existence began to take shape. "You've been *lying* to me at work!" I said, my voice escalating too loud for so late at night.

"Lying to you?"

"About dating my dad." I forced my voice to a quieter volume. Now it was more like a growl.

Glenna put a hand out, like she was afraid I'd pounce. "I didn't know you were his daughter right away. I just knew you had the same last name. Then I started noticing how you favored him. You have the same nose." She offered a smile, like the fact I'd inherited my dad's facial features would someone make everything okay. Ludicrous.

I narrowed my eyes.

"But your dad mentioned you were hostile to the situation and, well, we both thought it was for the best to keep it quiet for a while."

We. She was referring to herself and my father as a unit. As a pair. As a couple. I wanted to barf again, this time out of pure disgust.

But then I remembered Fyn. Without another word, I turned and marched out of the hospital. I found Fyn getting out of her car.

"How could you keep this from me?" I said through gritted teeth as I approached her.

She looked at me under the parking lot light, confused. "What are you talking about? How is your dad?"

"You knew, didn't you? But you didn't tell me."

"Sadie!" Fyn backed against the car. "Know *what?* I have no idea what you're—?"

"Your freak sister is dating my dad!" I yelled, clenching my fists at my side so I wouldn't shake her.

Fyn's jaw dropped. "Oh, no. No, no, no..." She stuttered. "I had no idea, Sadie."

"You seriously had no idea?" I unclenched my fists, but my breathing was still strong.

She shook her head. "I wasn't a hundred percent..."

"So you honestly didn't know your sister was such a—?"

"Don't!" She yelled back, overlapping my choice of words.

"How can you even defend her right now?" I asked, "When she not only seduced my *father* like some tramp, but lied and kept it hidden around me?"

"Sadie, that's enough!" Fyn yelled back. "That is my *sister!* You don't mess with my sister!" She shoved me. Wrong move, Fyn.

"You hate your sister!" I shoved her just hard enough to make her stumble back against the car.

"I never said I hated my sister. I disagree with her, but she's still family. I will not stand here and let you bulldoze Glenna."

"She deserves much worse." I crossed my arms against the cold night air and the icy conversation.

"Yeah? Well, you're no better than her! You said yourself you've used guys to get what you want!"

"And you're an addict!"

I wasn't entirely sure of what she said next because we dissolved into an all-out argument, complete with more yelling and rough words from both of us. A security car came around the corner, headlights in our direction. I'd had more than my share of running into the law, and I wasn't about to add an arrest to whatever this night was about to become. I stepped away from Fyn, creating space and silence.

She looked at me through blurred vision. "Opening up to this friendship was a mistake."

"At least we agree on one thing." Hot, angry tears pricked my own eyes. "Please leave so I can turn around and go get an update on my injured father without worrying you'll stab me in the back again."

Fyn slammed the car door and peeled out of the parking lot. I was too worked up to think clearly. Fuming too hard. I paced back and forth until I saw Glenna leave the building, talking on her phone, crying loudly.

Then I sunk down to the curb and sat, shaking. My father could be dead right now. If my father was dead—I shuddered—I'd be an orphan.

———— oOo ————

They wouldn't let me see my dad. Around three in the morning, I'd fallen into an exhausted sleep on a stiff, squeaky waiting room chair in the intensive care unit. Nothing else mattered—not the piles of homework, not the girlfriend, not the Fyn catastrophe, not even the class I was supposed to show up for in a few hours.

"Sadie Franklin?"

I slowly peeled open my swollen eyes at the sound of a deep, male voice. "Yeah?" I looked around for Glenna, then remembered she'd gone home after checking in again. A small mercy.

"I'm Dr. Denver. You're Michael Franklin's daughter, correct?"

"Yeah…" I slowly sat up in the chair, every part of me aching and cramped from sleeping in the chair. "Is he…?"

"We didn't know if he'd pull through the night, but he's still with us."

"Oh, thank you God," I breathed. "Can I go see him?"

I stood, but Dr. Denver reached out and put a gentle, yet firm hand on my shoulder. "Yes, but I need to prepare you for what's in there. Do you know the details of the car accident?"

I shook my head.

"Your father ran a stop light. A car t-boned him and spun his vehicle, flipping it and sending it across the road. He has a concussion, and we're watching for swelling on the brain, which we thankfully haven't seen yet. He has two broken ribs with a punctured lung, a dislocated shoulder, a broken arm and leg, and several lacerations. We operated on his lung last night, and we're waiting to stabilize him a bit more before we go back in to do surgery on his leg. The arm was a clean break, so we didn't have to operate on it."

While Dr. Denver talked, I felt myself sinking back down into the chair. I didn't know if I could do this. I didn't *want* to do this. But I knew I had to.

Whispering a prayer for strength, I slowly stood and adjusted my ponytail. "Okay, I'm ready." It was the biggest lie I'd ever told.

The cold, stark white hallway smelled like bleach and fear. The lights overhead made my weary eyes burn, and I rubbed them with the back of my hand. Dr. Denver pointed me to Dad's room, and I took a deep breath before opening the door.

Then the rest of my breath left me.

There were so many wires and monitors and IVs. That's the first stuff I saw. Then I focused and saw a man lying in the bed. I couldn't even tell if he was Mike Franklin. My tall, self-assured dad looked so small and broken. Very broken.

I swallowed a wave of nausea and walked over to the bed. The doctor told me he was on some pretty strong meds, so he wouldn't be awake for a while. I stood over him, my mind racing.

He left in a hurry because I made him angry. If I hadn't been so selfish, he wouldn't be lying here, half-dead. What if he doesn't make it? What if he dies? Dad doesn't believe in Jesus. God wouldn't really let my dad go to hell, would He?

My chest tightened, and I struggled to breathe. I gripped the bed rail, closed my eyes, and focused on breathing.

Oh, God. Please, God. Please.

It was all I could pray. I didn't have words. I didn't know how I could be so angry at someone and yet so full of regrets for myself at the same time.

I knew I didn't have long in the room, so I leaned down and gently kissed the one part of my dad's face that wasn't scraped or bruised or bandaged. Then, stifling a sob, I slipped out of the room.

I didn't want to leave the hospital, but there was so much to do at home. The only problem was, I just didn't know how to get there. I also didn't have the mental or emotional strength to explain my need for a ride to anyone. Fully expecting her not to respond, I texted Fyn.

Even though she texted back to say she would come, I was shocked when she actually pulled up outside the hospital.

"Hey," I said climbing into her little car. "Thanks for coming."

She shrugged. "I seriously almost ignored your text, but Mom was reading over my shoulder and made me come."

Ouch. We rode in silence, and she waited in the car while I went into the house. I cleaned up the broken glass before taking some food outside for Moose. I sat with him for a minute, letting the dog lick the dried tears off my face. Usually, I would be grossed out by that, but I was too tired to care. After refilling his water bowl, I gathered clean clothes and stepped into the shower. I wanted to stand there and let the hot water burn away all of the stress and anxiety, but I didn't have time.

After that, I collected the bottle glass and mopped the kitchen floor where the beer had turned sticky. Then I cleaned up the shattered picture frame in the living room. So much broken glass. So many shards. So much brokenness and hurt. How had this become my life?

Why wasn't God helping me out? I was trying so hard to be good, and yet everything kept breaking. No one told me faith would be easy, but I never knew it would be this hard.

I packed an overnight bag, grabbed an apple off the counter, and filled a bottle with water before opening the front door. To my surprise, Fyn had indeed waited for me. I climbed back into Fyn's car wordlessly. The only sound for the drive back to the hospital was me crunching my apple.

When we got there, she still hadn't looked at me. She finally said, "I don't think I can do this, Sadie."

I wrapped my apple core in a napkin. "I don't get why you're the one who's so upset. What if your dad was secretly dating your coworker who was your friend's sister and you didn't say anything?"

"My dad is married."

"So was mine."

"Yeah, but he's not anymore, Sadie. You sure as heck don't want anyone telling you how to live your life, so why are you so set on micro-managing his?"

Prickles crept up the back of my neck. "Stop it."

Her eyes flashed. "Get over yourself."

I opened the door and climbed out. "Thanks for the ride, Fyn. Sorry to be such a burden."

"I'm sorry, too," she said quietly. I ducked down so I could see her and hear the rest of her apology more clearly.

"Yeah?"

"Yeah. I'm sorry I ever got so close to you. Too close. I hope your dad is okay, seriously. But I need space."

I watched her drive away, feeling anger and hurt and so many other emotions I couldn't even begin to identify. If I weren't so exhausted and overwhelmed, I would've gone for a run. As it was, I felt like a zombie. Numb and detached.

Dad had surgery later that day, then they moved him out of the ICU and into a regular room.

I sat in the chair next to his bed, slipping in and out of sleep.

"What happened?" Dad's gravelly voice broke through the fog.

I used my elbows to sit up straighter in the chair. "Do you remember the wreck?"

"Yes. But me." His words were slow and slurred from the pain medication. "What happened to me? I feel like death."

I sniffed. "You almost experienced it. I'll have to let the doc explain it to you. You took a beating, though. Something about your shoulder, broken ribs, a punctured lung, broken arm, broken leg…they just operated on that. Some bumps and scrapes. Apparently, it's a miracle you survived."

He moaned in response.

"Do you want me to call the nurse?" I asked, but there was no response. I pulled my legs under me and stretched to see Dad had drifted back into sleep.

I yawned and scrubbed my eyes with my hands. My head lolled to the side, and I slipped into sleep.

"Hi, Sadie." My head jerked up. Glenna leaned around the doorframe, waiting for me to acknowledge her.

"He's sleeping," I mouthed.

She motioned for me to follow her. I shook my head.

Dad shifted in his bed. I gave up, not wanting Dad to know she was there.

"What?" I pulled Dad's door closed behind me.

"Can I talk to you?" She wore her hair in a professional-looking ponytail, and her makeup was virtually perfect. Meanwhile, my hair was sliding out of its band, and my face hadn't seen makeup since I'd cried it off.

Reluctantly, I followed Glenna to the waiting area.

She motioned for me to sit, but I honestly felt like I might explode if I tried to stay still.

"Let's go grab a coffee, my treat."

"No, thanks." I crossed my arms.

"But we love hanging out together. That hasn't changed." Glenna twisted the end of her ponytail and let it go.

"Are you even being serious right now?" I moved my hands to my hips. "Absolutely *everything* has changed. I liked hanging out with you *before* I knew you were secretly dating my dad and—No, I can't even go there with you, Glenna. You lied to me. Your sister was right about one thing. I never should've trusted you."

She turned her eyes to the ceiling and stared at it, then looked back at me. "I don't understand why you're so set on making Mike miserable."

I opened my mouth to respond, but words wouldn't come. I had nothing. Finally, I said, "I'm not a monster. I want my dad to be happy."

"Are you sure?" She crossed her own arms. "Because from what he's told me, you're always nagging him to change his life, even though you have your own reputation to deal with. And you're always talking about leaving town the next chance you get. I make him happy and help him forget about his kid and her issues. And even though your mom has been gone for over—"

"Don't drag my mom into this!" I snapped. I could feel adrenaline coursing through my veins. I may have been exhausted, but I would speak up for my mom's memory with all

I had left. "And don't even start with me about my reputation. You're one to talk."

She fished her keys out of her coat pocket. "Will you tell Mike I stopped by and I'll call him later?"

I shrugged. "I don't know."

Glenna left and I paced the hallway so I wouldn't punch something.

"I don't know if I handled that in the right way or not, God," I prayed as tears burned my cheeks. "But I'm just so *mad*. At everyone. What are you *doing*, God?" I stopped there because I was afraid of how I would start accusing God if I kept going. The last thing I needed was a wedge between the two of us. I slipped into the restroom and locked myself in a stall. I leaned against the wall and dropped my head into my hands. "I'm sorry," I whispered. "I just don't know where You're at in all of this. Help me trust You because without You, I'm not gonna make it."

———— ○○○ ————

I didn't go to Raining Grace on Sunday. I spent a sleepless night curled up in the chair in Dad's hospital room. The thought of telling everyone what had happened and seeing Fyn was just too much. The thought made me feel exhausted and nauseated.

Later that afternoon, Claire texted me: *Missed you this morning! Everything okay?*

I absently tapped my phone against my knee. I didn't want to tell her. It felt too vulnerable, and I'd never liked letting people see too much of my heart. Because then they'd see how broken I really was.

But that was supposed to be the past, right? This summer, I'd learned the importance of letting people in. If I hadn't spilled my guts to Melina, I never would've started to heal from the pain of my past and the shame of my decisions.

I drew in a deep breath and glanced over at my dad, helpless in a hospital bed. "Okay, God. I hear You."

I set down my textbook and tip-toed out of the room. Old Sadie would've run the other way, but New Sadie—the Sadie who had to believe God loved her and had a plan for her life—stepped into vulnerability.

After I asked Claire if we could talk, she told me to meet her at the hospital's front doors in an hour. When she showed up, she told me to get in the car. I was too tired to protest.

"I'm sorry it took me so long to get here," she said. "Cramps have tried to kill me today, so I'm moving more slowly."

My hand went to my own abdomen, which ached from lack of healthy food. I made a mental note to be more aware of what I ate. "You should be home right now if you don't feel good, Claire. Seriously, it's fine."

She shook her head. "Of course not. I'm here for you because I want to be. Buckle up."

"Where are we going?" I yawned.

"First, I'm taking you home to get a shower."

"Am I that ripe?"

She rolled her eyes and pulled the car out onto the main road. "Of course not. You just look like you could use some hot water."

"And then?"

"And then I'm taking you to coffee and I want you to tell me everything."

I looked down at my hands in my lap. What had I gotten myself into? "Okay."

An hour later, Claire listened to the awkward silence between us in our corner of Goldfinch's while I absentmindedly swirled my coffee around in the mug. My goal was to stay quiet so that she'd eventually start talking and forget why we were there.

But Claire, as I was learning, had all the time in the world when she had her mind set on something. So I caved.

I filled her in on my fight with Dad, how I'd almost taken up drinking again, and the wreck. I wanted to stop there, but keeping the rest to myself felt like the loneliest thing in all the world. So I told her about Glenna. And Fyn. And then I collapsed against the back of the chair and took my turn to wait.

"Wow," she exhaled. "Sadie, that is a ton of stuff. I am so sorry."

I dipped my chin and sniffed. If I started crying now, I might never stop.

She reached across the table and tilted my chin so I was looking at her. The gesture reminded me of my aunt. "Here's what we're going to do," she said slowly. "We're going to pray, and then you are going to promise me you will let Jordan and me help you with all of this."

I nodded because I was too tired to argue, but the last thing I felt like doing was letting other people in. Though it felt like relief in the moment, a part of me regretted bringing Claire into the mess. Trust had never been my strong point, and I felt like if I tried to juggle one more relationship right now, I'd drop everything.

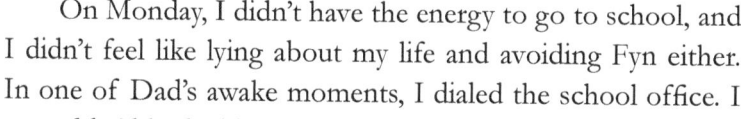

On Monday, I didn't have the energy to go to school, and I didn't feel like lying about my life and avoiding Fyn either. In one of Dad's awake moments, I dialed the school office. I prayed he'd be lucid enough to explain my absence and that I wouldn't get in trouble for being truant or something. My high school career wasn't exactly marked by perfect attendance.

In the hospital cafeteria, I braced myself for one other important call, although it was the one thing I didn't want to do: Call Georgia. Kurt and Mel had enough going on without worrying about me, Becca and Truitt were obviously too busy already, and I was doubting I could get through half a conversation without losing it. But I needed them to pray.

"Sadie! Hey!" Melina answered on the first ring, and the sound of her voice made me choke on a sob.

"Mel..." I pulled the phone away from my face and took a deep, trembling breath.

"What's wrong, Sadie Grey?" Mel's words were slow and careful, like she was working hard to sound calm.

In one breath, I filled her in on everything that was happening, ending with: "So I have no idea what's going to happen, but I just need you guys to pray."

"Absolutely. But how are *you*?"

I sighed. "I honestly don't know how I am right now."

"Kurt can come! I'll get him a flight and—"

"No! No, don't do that!" I shook my head vigorously before I remembered she couldn't see me. "You need him there. I'll be fine here." And I knew they couldn't afford the flight or the time Kurt would have to take off work. After all, he was not only a youth pastor but a high school counselor during the school year.

"You're sure? I guess you do have Fyn and her family. That's a blessing."

"Actually..."

Melina groaned. "Sadie..."

"We're in a rough spot right now. But Jordan and Claire are here for me. I can always call them if I need anything." *Like transportation...* "I'll be fine. Really."

"You're such a strong girl, Sadie Grey," Melina's voice sounded watery. "Just remember you're not meant to handle everything on your own. I'm gonna demand updates on Mike as soon as you get them, along with updates on how you're holding up, okay?"

I smiled through my tears. Good ol' Mel, always in charge. "I promise."

Twenty minutes later, I was up to my neck in writing a political science paper when I got a text from Becca:

> *Heard you're in the middle of a nightmare. Please, please, please let me know if there's anything at all I can do. Praying always!*

Then, while I was texting a response, my phone dinged with a text from Truitt: *How can I help?*

Man, word traveled fast in a small town.

I replied: *Praying would be awesome.*

Truitt: *Are you holding up okay?*

Me: *Yeah, I'm fine. Getting some homework done while he sleeps.*

Truitt: *Good girl. I miss you, Franklin. December can't come soon enough.*

Me: *Back at you.*

I slid my phone into my bag and went back to my paper.

An hour later, a rustling noise woke me up. I'd fallen asleep bent over my laptop, twenty pages of gibberish at the end of my paper courtesy of my forehead. I looked over at Dad. His eyes were open, and he was wincing.

"My leg…" he moaned.

"Dad." I stood over him so he could see me. "Are you hurting?"

He nodded slightly, so I pushed a button and called a nurse.

When she showed up, she handed me a cup of ice chips.

"Your dad's mouth probably feels like sandpaper. You can give him these if he asks." She finished taking care of Dad and left the room.

"Here, Dad." I stirred the ice chips with a plastic spoon. "They brought you ice cream, minus the cream." *And it probably costs about $500 dollars...* "Do you need help?" Dad closed his eyes and nodded. I gingerly sat on the bed beside him, and scooped a few chips out of the cup.

"Open up. Here comes the choo-choo train!" I meant to laugh but ended up exhaling a sob. I put the spoon in the cup and turned away so Dad couldn't see me cry. I'd never seen my dad so helpless. So weak. He had been a successful manager at a hotel and casino place before he lost his job. He had a natural head for business, and he was used to directing people. But when it came to me, he'd always been at a loss. Now I was the one at a loss.

I finally got it together and scooped a few ice chips onto the spoon. Dad's lips were dry and split, and a small cut from glass was on his upper lip. "Okay, here we go..." I said, my voice sing-songy. I slid the spoon between his lips and a tear dripped from my cheek to his. I carefully dabbed it off his face with my finger. "Sorry," I whispered, that one word encompassing our entire relationship.

He didn't take his eyes off me throughout the whole process, even once the cup was empty and I tossed it in the trash. I stood to go back to my chair, but I turned at the sound of his voice.

"Where's Glenna?" I bristled at the mention of her name, even though it hurt me to tell him the truth.

"I don't know, Dad. I saw her when they brought you here, but that's it."

"Will you call her for me?"

I felt my jaw drop. *Uh, no?*

Noticing the look on my face, he closed his eyes again. "Never mind." He didn't open his eyes this time, already asleep.

Jordan and Claire showed up at the hospital Monday afternoon with the biggest cup of coffee I'd ever seen. "Have you had any coffee recently?" Claire asked when my eyes filled with tears.

"Just hospital coffee."

Jordan shook his head. "That stuff is tar. Drink up. And take this." He dropped a car key into my palm.

"What's this?" I searched his face.

"It's my grandfather's car. He's in a retirement home and doesn't drive anymore. I want you to use it until you find a replacement."

"Jordan, I couldn't—"

"Yes, you can. With all you have going on, you don't need to have to arrange rides."

Jordan had helped me figure out car insurance stuff last night, and I'd learned just enough to know we could get a rental car, but then I learned I wasn't old enough to legally drive one and I wasn't up for a run-in with the law. This car was a huge deal.

I swallowed my pride and tucked the key into my pocket. "I honestly don't know how to thank you right now."

Claire pulled me into a hug. "No need. Just promise you'll reach out to us if you need us, okay? Come crash on our couch if you don't want to be home alone." I nodded against her shoulder.

Jordan put his hand on my shoulder. "We're here for you, Sadie. And when they let your dad out, I'll help you get him home."

I stared down at my cup of coffee. "You might not be so

willing to be there for me if you knew what a mess my life has always been."

Claire tilted her head. "Sister, you are loved. By God and by us. That's what matters. Now go take a nap."

"Over there," the mechanic said, motioning to a pile of metal. I stepped over to Dad's car, ready to collect anything important that might be inside.

"Oh…" I sucked in a sharp breath, and the ground shifted beneath my shoes.

The front was completely smashed in, like an accordion, as was the driver's side door. The glass was knocked out of the windshield and front windows, and cracked on the back windows. I held my breath and fought back nausea as I stepped up to the car. The airbags were deployed, and the driver's side airbag was covered in blood. A mix of glass and blood was also splattered across the other airbag and the seats. Brokenness and spilled life. So much of it. Inside, there was no leg room left, and I marveled at how only one of Dad's legs had been crushed, rather than both.

At the sight of all the blood, I turned away, slowly sinking to the ground so I could spend a minute with my head on my knees.

"Oh, God. He should be dead right now," I whispered. And yet Dad wasn't dead. He was lying helpless in a hospital bed, but he wasn't hopeless. He still had blood and bones and breath and life. *And purpose.*

The word *purpose* rang in my ears. That word was my saving grace last summer. Mel had told me that, as long as my heart was still beating, I wasn't done; I still had a purpose.

My dad's heart was still beating. He wasn't done. He still had a purpose, and God still had a plan for his life.

The realization that God clearly had a purpose for Dad's life hit me hard and fast. He was still here for a reason. A car wreck claimed my mom's life, and she was with God now. But Dad didn't know God. He'd been given another chance to choose real life and real Truth.

As I drove back to the hospital with Dad's wallet and phone, I couldn't stop thanking God for one more chance. Not just for my own second chance, but for Dad's.

We may have been at the start of one of the toughest seasons of our lives, but there was a purpose in it. I had no choice but to hold on to that as the week dragged on.

I was completely swamped with school and catching up on homework. When I wasn't stressing over homework, I was camped out in my chair at the hospital, helping Dad eat, taking notes from the doctor, and trying to figure out what in the world medical deductibles were and what I was supposed to do about them. I needed to have another conversation with Jordan.

Owen offered to watch Moose, which meant I was able to spend the nights at the hospital in case Dad needed me.

We finally heard from Glenna a few days later when she called Dad's phone. I was distracted by precalculus and too sleep-deprived to realize it was her when I answered. But Dad was awake, so I gave him the phone and put my earbuds in, pretending to listen to music on my phone whose battery had died an hour ago.

I couldn't understand what was happening in the conversation, but I did hear Dad slowly raise his good hand to his face and say, "Maybe that would be best right now. I'm glad you caught me up, at least." He ended the call a few minutes later.

Chapter Sixteen

"Right here...watch the door." I directed Jordan and Pastor Theo as they half carried, half guided Dad into the living room. "Good. No, bad. That was the coffee table. Yes, this way." Dad moaned and winced throughout the process, and I could tell he was trying his very hardest not to curse in front of the church people. Made me proud.

They settled him into the recliner, and he yelped like Moose whenever I stepped on his tail. The sound hurt, a reminder of how weak he was. I'd never looked up to my dad or even respected him all that much, but he was my *dad*. He was supposed to be unbreakable.

Claire and Theo's wife, Laura, showed up with enough meals to fill up the freezer. My eyes watered at the sight of so many tinfoil pans. These people barely knew me, and yet they'd recruited friends to make food for us.

We stuck a chicken pie into the oven, and I offered to make sweet tea for everyone, which earned me a room full of stares. After lunch, everyone left and made me promise to call the minute I needed anything. I thanked them, then collapsed on the couch. I was so exhausted, but I had homework to do before school the next day. Beginning tomorrow morning, a physical therapist would stop by for an hour or two while I was at school.

"Welcome home, Dad," I whispered to the ceiling before drifting off to sleep.

That night, I went by the vet to pick up my dog. Owen and Moose were waiting for me outside when I pulled up. Moose barked like a maniac, struggling to get out of Owen's grip.

"Hey, buddy! Come here, I missed you!" I took the dog in my arms. "Oh, hey, Owen." We still hadn't broached the topic of him asking me out again. Too much weirdness going on as it was.

"How's your dad?"

"Still sleeping, hopefully. He'll start physical therapy tomorrow morning while I'm at school."

"What about while you work?"

"I'll drug Dad and he'll sleep the whole time."

Owen missed the sarcasm and furrowed his brow. "That's dangerous…"

"I'm kidding. It'll only be for a couple hours a day and I can keep my phone on me in case of an emergency. I've got this."

"If you're sure."

"I am."

We stood in silence, except for the slurping sound of Moose licking my neck. I knew we both wanted to ask each other about Fyn, but my anger toward her wouldn't let me go there.

Dad was awake when I got back, and he didn't sleep at all that first night at home. I accidentally gave him his pain medicine late, so he was hurting like crazy, then I accidentally gave him regular coffee and the caffeine kept him up.

One thing I hadn't thought of was how to help my dad get to the bathroom. But the coffee gave us plenty of practice.

The first time, he was determined to go on his own, but he couldn't even get out of the chair.

"Sadie, can you help me?" he asked, and I knew that was a huge deal for him.

I looked up from my homework assignment. "Oh, sure." I dropped the recliner's foot rest, and he moaned. "Sorry," I whispered.

I went over to his good side, although it was still pretty bruised, and slowly lifted his arm over my shoulder. I counted to three and he slowly stood, hissing something profane under his breath.

"Does it hurt?"

"Like fire, it hurts."

We slowly made our way down the hall, into his bedroom, and into the bathroom, since it was bigger than the one I used in the hall.

We stopped in the doorway, neither of us knowing what to do.

"Um, can you take it from here?" I asked, my face turning red. I didn't embarrass easily, but this was my *father*.

"I hope so." He braced himself against the wall, trying to stand on his own, and wobbled.

I slipped out of the bathroom, pulling the door behind me, and waited. Moose trotted over to me and pawed at my leg, wanting to be petted.

"How are we gonna do this, Moose?" I whispered. "What about when he needs a shower or needs to change clothes? We can't help him with that!"

The toilet flushed, and the sink turned on a few moments later.

"Sadie!" Dad's voice drifted into the room. I slowly opened the door.

"Can you get me back to my chair? Everything's fuzzy."

The physical therapist arrived Monday morning as I was heading out the door for school. I guess I'd been expecting a frail little old lady or something, so I was relieved to see they'd sent a man. Roger was big and buff and probably in his mid-forties. He'd have no problems helping Dad move around. I quickly showed him around the house, Moose yapping in one arm and my coffee cup in my other hand.

Even though I was already running late, when I was finally able to slip out the door and into my car, I took a minute to just breathe in the silence and peace before heading to the chaos that was high school. That calm feeling lasted for about thirty seconds into the commute, because I spent the rest of the drive to school dreading another Fyn encounter. She was already there when I slipped into my seat, but she totally ignored me. A small mercy.

At lunch I found a seat with some girls from British literature, facing away from the table I used to sit at with Fyn, Liz, and Jen. Liz stopped by the table right as I was stuffing my mouth full of leftover chicken pie.

"Are you finished eating?"

I swallowed, obviously still in the middle of my meal. "Not quite."

"Hurry up. We need to talk."

The other girls at the table didn't know Liz, and from the looks on their faces, they thought I was about to be in serious trouble. Liz had that effect on people who didn't know her. I finished stuffing my face with her watching, then followed her into the bathroom.

"What the heck happened between you and Fyn?" she demanded in a loud whisper.

I totally did not feel like getting into all of that. "It's complicated. We're not friends anymore."

Liz rolled her eyes. "You're actually bailing on each other?

You do know Fyn hasn't opened up to another person since she got out of rehab, right? Not even to me and Jen. She always has a wall. But you, somehow, broke through that."

I shrugged. "We have some things in common."

"Yeah? Well, why don't you fix it?"

I sighed and stepped to the side so a girl could get to the sink. "It's not that simple. Besides, the ball's in her court now. She's the one not speaking to me."

I thought Liz might sound off at me again, but instead she folded her arms across her chest and leaned against the sink. "What did she do?" she asked softly.

"What do you mean?"

Liz started to speak, but shook her head. "Nothing. I'm just trying to figure out what caused this. She's in a mood."

"We just had an argument the night of Dad's accident. It got extremely ugly. We both just kind of lost it."

Liz headed toward the door to go to class. "Well, whatever you lost, I hope you find it." She grabbed the door handle. "Oh, by the way. Cannonball's? I called to apply for a job, but Greg said he'd just hired someone else to work with you."

I raised my eyebrows. That was news to me. "Oh. Okay. Thanks, Liz."

She opened the door and the noise of the hallway swallowed whatever she said next before disappearing into the mob.

Since Roger stopped by the house earlier in the day, I ran home long enough to make sure Dad didn't need anything before heading back out the door to work, praying he'd be okay on his own.

I also prayed I'd be okay on my own. If I didn't go back to work at the salon, I'd lose my job there. The manager had graciously given me time off while I figured everything out with Dad, but now I needed to go back. Except, Glenna was there and I now knew she'd hidden the fact that she was in a relationship with my own father. I felt nauseated whenever I thought of how nice she'd been to me, knowing all along she was trying to butter me up. And Dad must have known she knew me, too.

It was all such a mess.

That afternoon, I did homework at the front desk between customers and phone calls, then busied myself in the storage room, organizing the supplies after closing time. I accidentally caught Glenna's eye a couple of times but tried to make it clear I would not be speaking to her again. Like, ever.

But I knew the distance wouldn't—couldn't—last. We'd have to communicate at some point. I could only pray I didn't channel the Old Sadie when that happened. As it was, I felt like putting bleach in her shampoo bottles.

When I got back home a few hours later, I fixed another casserole for Dad and fixed a salad for myself. The stress of the past few days meant I hadn't eaten as healthy as I should, and now I was paying for it with strong pains in my abdomen.

While we ate, I happened to look at Dad's phone and noticed a voicemail. The doctor's office wanted to confirm Dad's post-op appointment the next week. Great. I'd have to miss work at the salon. I made a note on my own phone to call tomorrow to confirm the appointment. It was late, and there was a wet chill in the autumn air, but I refilled Dad's cup of water and grabbed Moose for a run.

While I ran, I tried to figure out how I was going to juggle it all. I went to school early each morning, and then went to work as soon as school was over. Then I went straight home to fix a late dinner and look after Dad. That left just a little bit of time for homework, but after just one day of this new routine,

I was already exhausted. I didn't even have time for this run, but if I didn't escape and breathe for a minute, I'd go insane.

"How am I going to do this?" I whispered to the sky, unsure if I was asking myself or God.

---◦O◦---

I showed up at Cannonball's Friday afternoon to work until closing. Greg stood at the counter, training the new employee Liz had mentioned. They looked up, and the blood drained from my face.

"Sadie!" Greg beamed and pushed his pirate bandana further back on his forehead. "Meet your new coworker!"

I honestly didn't know what to do. Apparently, neither did Alyssa.

She nodded once to acknowledge me, then went back to filling out her paperwork. I mumbled something about needing to change into my uniform, then bolted for the bathroom. By the time I locked myself in the staff bathroom, I was seeing spots. My mouth was dry, and my hands were shaking. How could this be happening? I thought she'd gone off to college... but now she was here?

My first thought after my mind finally stopped racing was to quit. Just walk out there and tell Greg I was done. But although I wasn't exactly rolling in the cash, this job paid a little better than the salon, and Dad and I desperately needed the money for medical bills.

My next thought was to call Fyn—to pour out all of my anxiety and ask her what I should do. I'd actually reached for my phone when it hit me that I couldn't do that. No one else would understand.

Greg met me in the staff room when I'd finally changed into my tie-dye t-shirt and gym shorts. "I'm working with Alyssa up front, so I've got you on inflatables tonight. Cool?"

I quickly agreed to that and slipped out of the staff room. Inflatables duty was usually the very worst. I didn't like the stress of refereeing the kids, rescuing them from the top of slides, and making sure no one was running. But I'd take anything over working with Alyssa.

Cannonball's was one large room, but thankfully it was big enough that once I was immersed in the world of the inflatables, I didn't have to interact with the front counter.

But that was short-lived. I showed up again on Saturday morning to work a full day. Roger wasn't at my house, so I promised Dad I would keep an eye on my phone. I talked Greg into an extended lunch break, and Jordan planned to hang out for a few hours at my house that afternoon.

Alyssa and I were set to both work the counter. I was on concessions, and she handled signing people in and cashing in prize tickets.

"Excuse me," I said, slipping past her to get to the popcorn machine.

"If I had any idea you worked here..." she said under her breath.

"Yeah. Back at you."

I grabbed the bag of popcorn kernels from the cabinet and filled the popper.

"Just don't even talk to me, okay?" she said.

"Gladly."

I grabbed a measuring cup and the jug of oil and began measuring out the right amount for the day's first round of popcorn. Alyssa bumped into me, knocking the oil out of my hand and spilling it all over the floor.

"Oops," she said lightly as she grabbed a plastic Cannonball's cup.

I glared at the back of her head. How dare she...

Alyssa filled the cup with Dr. Pepper and took a long drink.

"I don't know if Greg told you yet, but we actually have staff cups, so we don't have to use these more expensive ones."

She rolled her eyes. "I'm sure Greg will get over it."

"Did you know Greg before you got this job?" I hadn't mean to engage in conversation with her, it just happened.

"Yeah, I've known Greg." She didn't elaborate, but the way she said that still made me shiver.

I mopped up the greasy mess as best I could, actually relieved when a big group of kids stormed into the building.

Chapter Seventeen

○○○

I asked Mrs. Zurich if I could trade partners for our midterm project, but before I could finish talking, she said, "No, Sadie. Remember what I said at the beginning of the year? If I let you pick your partners, I would not let you re-pick. Besides, you should be nearly finished with your project by now anyway."

It was all I could do not to stomp my foot. "Some things... came up." *To put it mildly.* "And I can't work with Fyn anymore."

"All I know is Fynnigan already asked to trade partners, and I told her the same thing I'm telling you." Mrs. Zurich tightened her graying ponytail. "I'm not doubting there is drama going on between you two. You're in high school, after all. But I do know this is an opportunity to prepare you for life outside the familiarity of school where you get to pick your partners."

"I doubt that." I clamped my mouth shut. The last thing I needed was for Mrs. Zurich to bust me for getting sassy.

My teacher shrugged, and her eyes softened the tiniest bit. "I'm sorry, Sadie. But I can't trade you out with anyone, and the assignment can't be completed on your own. If you feel like you absolutely can't work with her alone, the two of you can work in here while I grade during your lunch period. That's the best I can do."

That didn't go liked I'd hoped, but I decided I should take her up on her offer to serve as a buffer between Fyn and me.

I texted Fyn and told her the plan, then shut off my phone so I wouldn't have to see a reply. At lunch, I brought my chicken salad to Mrs. Zurich's room. Fyn was already in there, and it took every ounce of my strength to keep my feet moving forward.

I'd always written people off when they hurt me in the past. Always blacklisted them or sought revenge or pretended they didn't exist. It was easier to run from pain and emotions. Easier to avoid than process. I knew this about myself. After all, I'd had plenty of practice.

But for some reason, the roles were reversed this time. As furious as I was, I was also deeply hurt. I wanted things to go back to like they were. I didn't want to forgive her, but I didn't want to make her life miserable, either.

"Hey," I said. I felt like I had one mini-Sadie on my left shoulder telling me to be angry and act out of spite and another mini-Sadie on my right shoulder telling me I should just wallow in the hurt. Regular-size Sadie didn't know how to feel.

"Hi," Fyn said, her eyes cool but searching.

I glanced down at my lunch. I'd be sick if I took a bite. Shoving it back into my backpack, I slid into the desk.

I glanced over at Mrs. Zurich, who was lost in the world of grading book reviews, her red pen practically creating sparks.

"We better get started. We don't have long," Fyn said. If this project wasn't such a big part of my grade, I'd take a zero.

I stifled a sigh. "Okay. What do you have?"

Fyn reached into her bag. She pulled out an old Monopoly board, now completely repainted.

"Wow," I couldn't help but whisper.

Different writers from the Romantic Period and images from their most famous works were represented in abstract, yet recognizable mini paintings. Ruins of an old building, which I assumed to be Tintern Abbey, stood in one corner, wildflowers surrounding it. In another corner, a man stood on a wooden ship, a giant bird hanging from his neck. *The Rime of the Ancient Mariner*. Nice. A Grecian Urn took up space on another part of the board, and the fourth corner featured a tiger and a lamb. Each space on the board had one of four categories: Poet, Quote, Culture, and Wild Card.

I sat in silence, marveling at Fyn's masterpiece.

"When did you have time to do all of this?" I asked quietly.

She shrugged and avoided making eye contact. "When you're hurting, you run. When I'm hurting, I create."

I ran a hand over the board, feeling the texture of the paints. "I thought you sculpted."

She dropped a plastic sandwich bag in front of me.

I reached in and pulled out little clay figurines of the images painted on the board. A little Abbey, urn, albatross, and tiger. And then two small, clay dice.

"I made two because everyone's always losing the dice."

Fyn had definitely done more than her share of work. I reached into my bag and pulled out the index cards I'd been working on.

Fyn raised an eyebrow. "Are these the trivia questions?"

"Yes. I'm gonna type them up and have them printed and laminated."

I slid them across the board toward her, and she thumbed through them.

"Cool."

That's all she had to say? I'd spent hours researching these poems I didn't even understand. I could recite more about Don Juan than I ever wanted to know.

I swallowed back a sharp retort and instead asked, "What's next?"

She slid the cards back to me, and our eyes met for the first time. "The presentation."

I fished the rubric out of the bottom of my bag to refresh on the requirements. We had to give a ten-minute presentation of our topic—Poets of the Romantic Period—and then explain the game and why we chose to teach the material that way.

Fyn took her turn looking over at Mrs. Zurich, who still couldn't be bothered to pay us any attention. Carefully putting the clay pieces back into the bag, she said, "You handle the historical background part and I'll take care of the poets and explaining the game. Fair?"

Absolutely nothing about my life was fair. I felt anxiety begin to grip my chest as Fyn kept her eyes on me. I nodded and stood. "Okay. Let's do a run-through during Thanksgiving break."

"Whatever." Fyn turned to leave, and that's when I'd had enough.

"What?"

She turned back around. "I said *whatever*, Sadie. We'll get it done."

"This project is important to me, Fyn. I need to get a good grade in this class."

Fyn rolled her eyes. "Right, like *I* haven't put any effort into this thing. Did you *see* that gameboard?"

I opened my mouth to say something smart, but Mrs. Zurich chose that moment to interrupt. "That's enough for today, girls. Go to your next class."

Fyn narrowed her eyes and glared at me. "Yes. You've done more than enough lately."

I mumbled something un-holy under my breath. "Me? *You're* the one who lied to me about your—"

"Girls! Go. To. Class." Mrs. Zurich stood and pointed at

the door. "Or you'll find yourself in detention spending even more quality time together."

Without another word to either of them, I spun on my heel and bee-lined for the bathroom to calm down before my next class, scared of what I might do if I spent another second in Fyn's presence.

Life settled into a hectic rhythm. Rhythm wasn't even the right word because, although everything was scheduled, it was somehow still chaos. Fyn had completely shut me out whenever I tried to talk to her, which meant I ended up retorting with some unkind comment before storming off or sitting back down in my desk at school.

While talking to Mel one night, she said, "When it's hard to be nice to her, love her."

"But she keeps hurting me."

"I believe you. But Sadie Grey, I'm sure she's hurting, too."

Evie whimpered in Mel's arms, and Mel whispered something sweet to the baby to soothe her.

"I don't want to. Besides, I don't even know how."

"You'll get there," she said softly, gently, in that motherly tone that made me want to curl up next to her on the couch and just feel protected and loved and safe. "In the meantime, just start with kindness."

"So cussing her out is not an option...?"

"Child." Mel gave me her sternest look and it made me laugh.

I sighed dramatically. "I'll try."

"Good girl."

My next obvious opportunity to spend some time working on things with Fyn happened on Halloween night the next week. Café Graffiti hosted a costume party as a fun way to invite friends to church and also keep kids off the streets.

I had the afternoon off of work since I was supposed to take Dad to his appointment, which was rescheduled due to overbooking, so I ran by the store for a bag of chips and headed over to Raining Grace to help set up for the party. A part of me hoped Fyn would be there and we could begin to work through our issues.

"Sadie! Good to see you!" Jordan hugged me like the older, wiser brother he was becoming. "How's your dad? Some of us guys were wanting to stop by one day next week to check in on him. And Claire's got a couple homemade pizzas for your freezer." My mouth watered at the thought, even though pizza was the last thing I should be eating.

"That would be awesome—all of that," I said. "And we should be able to give your car back—"

"No time to talk about that. We've got too much to do." He winked and took off for the food table before I could protest.

For the first time, I took in my surroundings. The walls were covered with sheets of black plastic, with neon orange graffiti spray-painted all over the place. How had I missed *that* sign-up sheet? But it was so well done, I immediately knew who was in charge.

The chairs had all been removed, and long empty tables waiting for food lined one side of the room, draped in black table cloths with silver confetti in the shapes of spiders and pumpkins sprinkled all over it. The stage was set up for the band, and a guy at the tech board played around with different colored lights. This party was going to be *awesome*.

I set the chips on one table and looked around for something to do.

"Sadie, give me a hand?"

I walked over to where Liz attempted to carry in several boxes of cupcakes and took the top two boxes from her. I could instantly smell them. "Oh, my…"

"Right? I literally just finished frosting them."

"You baked these?" I turned to look at my friend, who currently sported varying shades of green stripes in her hair.

"Part of my costume for tonight," she explained when she noticed my stare. "But yes, I bake. I had to have something to keep me off the streets. Figured buttercream was better for you than pot."

We set the containers on the table, and I opened the lid. Each cupcake was frosted in lime green, deep purple, or orange with silver, glittery spider webs piped on top and little chocolate piped spiders. It matched the rest of the décor perfectly.

"Liz, you amaze me."

"Just wait 'til you taste them. Devil's food cake." But of course.

"You guys sure love the whole spider theme," I noted.

"Well, the elders weren't going for witches, ghosts, or fake blood. Because church."

"Ah."

It felt so good to be talking to her. I'd been so afraid I'd lost her friendship when the bottom fell out with Fyn. But if Liz was affected by the fact Fyn and I still weren't speaking, she didn't let on. I breathed a silent prayer of thanks. But speaking of…

"Hey, Liz?"

"What's up?"

"Have you seen Fyn?"

She shook her head as she pulled a plastic cupcake stand out of her shoulder bag and began assembling it. "Nope. But earlier she said once she finished the graffiti she was going home to finish her costume. She'll be back when it all starts." She said this so casually, but she studied me the whole time.

I opened my mouth to say something—defend myself—but she stuck up a hand. "I've been caught in the middle of too many things in my seventeen years. I'm staying out of this one."

She offered a sympathetic smile, then went back to assembling the cupcake stand.

Chapter Eighteen

○○○

I surveyed myself in the mirror one last time. I hadn't had the time, money, or energy to design an epic costume, but I was proud of myself for what I'd come up with.

My phone dinged as I stuck one more bobby pin in my hair. A text from Melina.

It was a picture of the kids. Cooper sat in a wagon, while Jackson stood beside him and Trissy held Evie. The kids were dressed in purple with green beanies on their heads and green felt collars on their shirts. A bunch of grapes. Attached to the image was the message: *On our way to the church carnival. Miss you BUNCHES!* Clever, Mel, Clever.

Becca sent a picture of the youth group in costumes, ready to host the games at the carnival. She was a pretty hula girl with a hot pink hibiscus flower tucked behind her ear, her brunette hair flowing in soft waves down her back.

Truitt was dressed in his rec league baseball uniform, and I laughed remembering Becca's vented frustration over the phone about how he refused to dress up. I was proud of him for this much effort.

I arrived back at Raining Grace after making sure Dad would be fine for a couple of hours. When I entered the building, the lights were dim and blacklights made Fyn's neon graffiti pop off the walls.

I shuffled over to where Liz stood, dressed as a... Christmas tree?

"I think you've got your holidays mixed up there, Liz..." I said, taking in the tree skirt she wore around her waist over her black jeans, with little gifts hot glued to it, her green shirt with little flashing lights, the gold tinsel wrapped around her, and a star on top of her headband.

"Well, see, I had this idea that—" Liz couldn't finish, instead dissolving into laughter. "You look *awesome*. Owen, come here!" She called over her shoulder, "You've *got* to see this!" Owen moseyed over, dressed as a cowboy, and grinned.

"Nice," he said.

"You kids and your secular music! Turn that racket down!" I yelled, only to have them laugh harder.

"Wait..." Liz leaned closer, "What's in that cup?"

I shifted my stuffed cat to my other arm and held the cup closer to her so she could see it in the dim lighting. "That's my teeth."

She howled again, and I shook my head, the flour falling from my hair sending me into a sneezing fit. I wiped my eyes on the sleeve of my housecoat and shuffled my slipper-clad feet over to the snack table right as the band ended their song. Jordan took the mike and welcomed everyone to the party.

"Hey, guys! If I could have your attention for just a second." The packed warehouse gradually quieted down as the house lights came on. "I just wanted to welcome you all here. You could be anywhere tonight, but you chose to be here. And I want you to know you've made the right choice."

While he talked, I watched him over the rim of my wire-frame glasses and sipped a cup of punch, careful not to smudge my bright red lipstick.

"I don't need to tell you there's a lot of darkness in the world. I think you guys get that already," Jordan said. "Every time you log into social media, catch a news report, or even just walk down the halls at school, darkness is so evident. But on a night that's usually devoted to celebrating darkness, we're here to celebrate light. But not just any light—*The* Light."

Out of the corner of my eye, I saw a mime slip into the room behind a Bigfoot. The mime wore all black, with a face painted white and lips stained red. A black beret sat on top of her head, and the only other color on her was a sheer red scarf tied around her neck. Something was so familiar about the way she walked into the room.

"John 1:5," Jordan continued, "says that 'The light shines in the darkness, and the darkness has not overcome it.' Jesus is that light. He is the light that overcomes the darkness. Cut the lights."

Everything went black except for the exit signs, causing me to lose sight of the mime, who had to be Fyn. I had no choice but to focus on the stage, where Jordan still stood, now holding a lit candle. "As long as there is one spark of light," he said, "total darkness is impossible. So in a world that seems hopeless, remember the Light of Hope is still shining. The Savior is still saving. And He wants you to share the light, too. Will you add your little flame? Let's pray together."

By the time the prayer was finished and the lights came back on, I'd lost sight of Fyn. I didn't see her again until after the band started back up, this time playing fun dance music.

"Excuse me," she said, reaching around me to spoon some queso on her plate of chips.

"Fyn?"

She looked up at me and squinted, a confused expression on her face.

Did she really not recognize me, or was she pretending so she didn't have to talk to me?

"Fyn, listen. I think we need to talk..." I trailed off when she didn't say anything. She was really working this whole mime thing. Which was so opposite of who she was. I tried again. "Can we talk for a sec? Maybe in the bathroom where it's quieter?" More silence. This was *Fyn* of all people. The girl who talked a thousand miles a minute!

She didn't say no, so I grabbed my teeth off the table, tucked my stuffed cat under my arm, and led her into the restroom.

My heart beat in my throat when it was finally just us in the restroom, away from the pounding bass and crush of costumed teenagers. This wasn't something I wanted to do, but at the same time, it's what I knew I needed to do. This was my act of kindness toward Fyn. My attempt to shine Light.

I didn't know what would happen next.

"I just wanted to tell you…" I stopped for a minute, not wanting to say what I was never good at saying. "I'm sorry. For the words I said about you and your sister." I still couldn't bring myself to say her name. "And about how I said it. I was so stressed and freaked out and didn't know how bad off Dad was, but that's no excuse."

I waited. For what, I wasn't sure. An apology? An offer of forgiveness? Certainly not the cool, silent stare of a mime.

"Oh come on, Fyn, break character for one second. Talk to me!"

She gave no sign to let me know she'd even heard me, and I wanted to shake her. Finally, she said, "Thank you, Sadie. I accept your apology. But I don't think we should hang out right now. I think we're toxic." She looked at me for another minute, and I tried to imagine the situation from her perspective, looking into the face of an old lady with gray hair and a beauty mark.

"What about all of the 'I've got your back' and 'I'll always stand beside you no matter what' stuff? Where is *that* Fyn?"

"She's been hurt."

"*I've* been hurt. You broke my trust." I put my head in my hands. I'd known a friendship this good couldn't last. I'd wanted to be positive, but I *knew* it. I was so good at messing up relationships. It was only a matter of time before I messed up the next one.

But the thing was, this time we were both at fault. I'd apologized, but she hadn't. Where did that leave us?

I heard her say, "See you later, Sadie," heard her compliment my costume, and heard the door shut behind her on her way out of the restroom, but all I could think about was how my first piece of sanity in Seattle didn't think I was worth it anymore.

We'd been drawn together out of desperation and loneliness—both starting over in a place where we'd always lived. Both needing just one person to not judge, to understand, and to push us to be a better person. Miraculously, we'd found that in each other. She was wild and artistic and felt emotions deeply, while I was stressed and new at faith and had a bad habit of trying to avoid what hurt.

Her past vice had been prescription meds; mine was alcohol and guys. She'd tried to run from the pain with self-harm. I'd tried to literally run from the pain.

But we both had a deep need to be truly known and accepted, despite our flaws and mistakes. We both needed someone to take on this crazy life alongside, and we'd found it in each other. Unlikely, yes. But an answer to prayer.

Only now, as I slipped back out of the restroom, it seemed God had other plans for His answer.

My guidance counselor was seriously pressuring me to consider different career options after yet another meeting in which I told her flipping burgers might not be such a bad gig after all. Like I had time to deal with all of that. But after finishing homework and helping Dad at night, I'd sit at the kitchen table researching careers. My guidance counselor had suggested social work.

At first, I'd balked at the idea. Me? Doing a job that involved lots of legal stuff and children? But the more I thought about it, the harder it was to shake the idea. I mean, I'd never been in foster care or in an abusive home. But I knew what it was like to come from a very broken family, to experience tragedy, to feel like you weren't at home in your own house. And now that I'd tasted healthy family with the Elliots, I craved that for not just myself, but other kids. I wanted justice, and maybe that's how I could help. It was a starting point, at least.

And although I didn't think college would be an option between my not-so-great grades and my struggling bank account, I at least wanted to dream a little and come up with an answer.

I craved family even more as Thanksgiving approached. Usually, Thanksgiving was pretty much like any other day. Dad and I would do our own thing, with me camping out in front of the TV to watch the parade and combing through the Black Friday adds in the newspaper. We'd usually order takeout that night, and the next day I'd get up early to go shopping with friends.

But this year, I wanted more for us. Even if it didn't mean much to Dad, this was my first Thanksgiving knowing God, and I had a second chance to be thankful for that. Plus, Thanksgiving would give me an opportunity to serve my dad. Cooking for him had to be a good start. I prayed about a way for Thanksgiving to be about more than just another day.

The more I thought about it, though, the sadder I pictured it: Dad and me on Thanksgiving, sitting in front of the TV—

him in the recliner, me at the coffee table. In the same space, but miles apart. Eating dry turkey and slimy canned cranberry sauce.

On Sunday, I showed up at Raining Grace with these thoughts heavy on my mind.

"Hi, Sadie!" Claire hugged me. "How are you?"

"I'm fine. Just trying to figure out what to do for Thanksgiving with my dad."

She nodded, thoughtful. "What do you have so far?"

I sighed. "Store-bought pumpkin pie? I just wish…"

She waited for me to finish as an idea formed in my head.

"…that…"

She nodded, inviting me to continue. The idea ignited, sending sparks swirling around my brain.

"Can I host Thanksgiving dinner at my house for the kids here who don't have family celebrations of their own going on? Would that be okay?"

She smiled widely. "I think that would be awesome!"

I smiled back, the idea coming together more fully in my head. "Can I clear it with my dad, then maybe announce it Wednesday at Café Graffiti?" I was so excited, I was practically bouncing now, and it had nothing to do with the espresso I'd drunk to stay awake during the service.

"Absolutely. I'll talk it over with Jordan, too. I'm sure he'd love to help however he can."

This time I initiated the hug before sliding into a seat next to Liz. I couldn't focus on what Pastor Theo's sermon was about, but by the time I left Raining Grace that afternoon, I had a ton of notes on my phone for Thanksgiving.

Old Sadie had a reputation for throwing the best parties. Now it was New Sadie's turn.

Praying for a Thanksgiving miracle, I rushed home from church to fix lunch, and pitched the idea to Dad over our bowls of chili.

"So, Dad, what do you think about doing something special for Thanksgiving dinner this year?"

"What kind of special?" he asked, his eyes on the football game on TV. He had a bad case of cabin fever at this point, and he was restless. I didn't blame him because being stuck in the house, practically immobile for so long, sounded awful. Other than the occasional visits to the doctor, he was a shut-in. And it made him grizzly. I knew I needed to tread carefully, so I breathed a silent prayer for the right words to say.

"Well, I know we don't usually do much, and I know you're probably ready for a change of pace, so I thought it might be nice to have some people over. I have some friends who don't have a lot going on at their houses either, so I figured we could all be thankful together."

Dad was silent, but he had turned his head to look at me. That was something.

"I don't know, Sadie," he said slowly. "We don't have money for that, and I'm not feeling all that thankful these days." He used his good arm to gesture to his injuries. When I was little, I'd imagined the tons of signatures I'd have on my cast if I ever broke a bone. It was kind of fun to think about, in a weird way. But the cast on Dad's arm was just as blank and blue as it'd been the day he'd had it plastered on. And something about that was tragic to me.

I tried to be sympathetic and gentle in my response for once. After all, I'd been in the trenches too, but somehow I still had hope.

"You're alive, Dad," I said slowly, cautiously. "It's a miracle you're even sitting here right now. I think that's something to be thankful for."

He grunted. "I'm an invalid."

"For *now*," I sighed. "And I think it might be fun to be around people."

"You remember what happened the last time you had a party here...?"

I winced at his accusing tone and the memories that came rushing back, still haunting me.

"I have regrets. But this will be different. It's friends from church, and Jordan and Claire said they'd be happy to be involved."

He shifted, groaning, to readjust in his chair. "You talked to them about it before coming to me?"

Man, it was like walking around landmines in this house. I bristled.

"I didn't commit to anything yet because I wanted to check with you first. If you say no, I won't host Thanksgiving dinner. I'll respect your decision."

That word *respect* made him pause. He rubbed the scruffy chin that made him rugged and handsome in a rough-around-the-edges way. My bowl of chili sat untouched on the coffee table, and I scooped Moose into my arms when he started sniffing at it.

Finally, Dad spoke, "I guess it'll be okay. If it doesn't go too late and if there will be other adults here to help."

I jumped up, dropping Moose on the couch and forgetting the whole maturity thing. "Really? Dad, thank you!" I hopped over to his chair and kissed his cheek, surprising both of us. He blushed, not used to father-daughter affection.

He focused on finishing his bowl of chili. "Just no booze or new holes in the wall, okay?" He shot a sly smile in my direction.

I grinned. "Got it."

Two weeks before Thanksgiving and the party I was actually looking forward to, I anxiously drove to my doctor's office for my scheduled appointment. The ache in my abdomen had turned into a pinched feeling, like my insides were being prodded with a pencil. The rain pelted my car as I drove, and I reminded myself to breathe.

My one consolation in all of this was that, as medical bills began to arrive, Dad had told me he'd taken out a health insurance policy right after he'd lost his job. He said something about how he didn't know how many visits to the doctor I would need while I figured out life with PCOS, so he wanted to be prepared. Neither of us had any way of knowing Dad would be the one racking up the medical bills. I wasn't super clear on what it meant when he said we had high premiums and deductibles, but I couldn't deny God had nudged Dad to make sure we were covered.

Dr. Hart assured me I hadn't messed anything up, but that I most likely felt bad due to stress and not watching what I ate as closely. He encouraged me to rest when I could and stay mindful of how many carbs I ate.

On the way home, I decided that was the final straw in working at the salon. If I wanted to manage my health, something had to go from my schedule. Since I couldn't control most of the craziness in my life, I needed to let go of one of the more stress-inducing parts of my schedule. I just couldn't do it anymore without losing the rest of my sanity and making another barely passing grade, so I had to walk away. Although I'd miss the money, not having to see Glenna everyday was priceless.

Unless she came over while I was at school, Dad hadn't spent any time with her since the wreck. If I had to guess, he still texted her. The thought still made my blood burn, but I knew if I let myself go too deeply into those thoughts, I'd spontaneously combust. Nobody had time for that.

After checking on Dad after my appointment, I quickly changed clothes and ran out the door to Cannonball's, already late. The doctor's appointment wasn't supposed to take that long, so I hadn't run the extra time it took by Greg.

On the way there, I got bogged down in regular Friday evening traffic, then got stopped by a train. I tried to call Greg while waiting for the train to go by but didn't get an answer. By the time I rolled into the parking lot, I was more than an hour late.

"I'm here! Sorry!" I called as I finally flung open the doors and rushed behind the counter, only to bump into a disgruntled Greg.

"Greg! I'm so sorry! I was at the doctor, and then I got caught in traffic and tried to call and—"

Greg hung up the phone I hadn't noticed him talking on and turned to face me, his washable marker pirate beard tinted blue and smeared around his mouth. He'd had a blue raspberry Icee while on the job again. "I know I'm not a strict boss, Sadie, but I do ask that my employees take their work seriously."

I nodded vigorously. "Yes, I understand. But I—"

"You were caught in traffic. I get it. But I'm talking about other stuff, too."

He tilted his head in the direction of the prize station, where I noticed Alyssa casually leaning against the glass display counter, no doubt eavesdropping on our conversation.

I glared at her. "What other stuff?"

"I've had customers tell me my two counter girls have argued in front of the kids."

My mouth dropped open. The only times we'd argued

had been when Alyssa provoked it—like when she made me spill popcorn oil, not just once, but three times. Or when she refused to take a turn cleaning the bathrooms.

"But—"

"And Alyssa tells me she's felt attacked by you. Like you're forcing her to do more than her share of work."

"Now that's just—"

"I know you have a lot going on right now, so maybe Cannonball's isn't where you should be. Maybe you should focus on other stuff right now?"

I wanted to cry angry tears, and I shook my head so I wouldn't. That jerk at the prize counter was *lying* about me? How low could she get?

I opened and closed my mouth, trying to figure out how to respond in a way that was respectable and mature.

"I *need* this job! Please! Put me on inflatables, I don't care. Just please let me stay here!" Begging. Close enough to mature.

Greg rubbed his chin, smearing his beard even more. Alyssa was practically lying on the counter at this point in her attempt to be as close as possible without actually walking over to us.

He sighed. "Fine. You have been good for Cannonball's. You and your friend over there just need to learn to get along at work."

"I wouldn't call her my friend," I said under my breath.

Ignoring me, he went on. "But I think some space might be good so we avoid any future cat fights in front of our guests." He glanced at the clock on the wall. "We've got a birthday at seven. Go suit up."

I froze, my feet refusing to move. "Suit up?"

"Kids love the unicorn," he said as he walked away.

I heard a *thud* behind me and turned to find Alyssa sprawled out on the ground; she'd slid off the counter because she'd not been paying attention to anything but her eavesdropping. I stepped over her on my way to the costume closet.

Chapter Nineteen

○ ○ ○

"You look awful." Truitt's eyebrows angled down toward his nose as he scrutinized my face through the phone screen.

"Wow, thanks, Adonis." I took in the hair plastered to his forehead by sweat and the smudge of dirt streaked across his cheek.

"You know what I mean, Franklin. How are you really doing?"

I pulled in a deep breath. "I'm tired, but I'll survive. Dad tried to do too much for himself while I was at work Saturday, and now he's in a lot of pain and needs help moving around. I've just gotta make it to Christmas break and everything will be awesome again."

"But that's over a month away," Truitt said as he tried to scrub the dirt off his face with the back of his hand.

I meant to reply with reassurance that I was doing just fine, that I was juggling school and work and taking care of Dad and Moose and everything, but it all came out as a sob.

Truitt listened as I broke down, not able to say anything coherent, just "I can't, I can't" over and over again. Then I spilled everything about Glenna and the Fyn fallout and everything associated with that.

He waited for me to calm down, but I didn't know if it was because he was so patient or because he was freaked out by my outburst and didn't know how to respond. But then, he'd listened one night this summer when he'd rescued me from a fight at a party I wasn't supposed to be at, even though I had been absolutely awful to him. He'd held me and smoothed my lake-soaked hair until I'd sobbed out my whole story.

When I finally stopped for air, he just said, "Oh, Sadie."

"I had to quit my salon job, Truitt," I exhaled. "It was either that or quit school. And Dad doesn't sleep well at night, so I don't either. I haven't slept in my own bed since before the accident because I need to be on the couch for when Dad needs me and…and I'm sorry I'm unloading this on you. I know you're max-stressed already with school and work and your mom."

Truitt waved like he was erasing my words. "I'm thankful for your honesty."

"But seriously, I'll be okay. I think I just needed to vent. Please don't tell Kurt and Mel. I know they've got too much going on already too. Let's talk about something else."

Truitt didn't look convinced by my reassurances, but he nodded anyway. "Okay. Let's talk SEC football."

When I groaned, he winked, and a genuine smile split my face for the first time in weeks.

The grin was long gone by the next day. First, I got a bad grade on a political science test. Then, Fyn told me she was leaving town for Thanksgiving, so I rushed to finish my part of the project so we could have a rocky run-through. And finally, I came home to find Moose had eaten one of Dad's shoelaces and vomited all over the living room. The smell had me gagging and Dad yelling while I cleaned it up.

The following day, Moose threw up again while I was at school. By the time I checked my phone when I got in my car, Dad had left me a string of increasingly annoyed text messages. I went home, cleaned up, and promptly took Moose to see Owen.

The dog was so weak and felt a lot lighter. He probably didn't have anything left in him, not even the energy to move around. It freaked me out. I couldn't lose my ally. We were in this literal mess together.

The vet wanted to admit Moose and give him IV fluids since he was so dehydrated, but that wasn't exactly in the budget. I wrapped him in a blanket to take him home and pray for the best.

"Sadie, wait up," Owen said as I stepped out the door.

"Yeah?"

He slipped around the counter and followed me out. "What did you find out?"

I rested my chin on the dog's scruffy head. "He's dehydrated. I guess there was a piece of the shoelace stuck in his throat or something so he puked until he got it out. I was supposed to leave him overnight for some fluids, but I can't pay for that."

Owen sighed, genuinely sad for me. Instinctively, I stepped closer to him. He pulled Moose and me into a gentle hug and I felt myself sag against him.

"I'd help if I could, Sadie," he said.

"I know. You've done more than enough already."

He rubbed my back. "Are you doing all right with everything else?"

I shook my head against his shoulder, refusing to cry. "Not really."

He let go of me so he could look at my face. "Can I at least take you out to dinner to feed you and give you a little break? Maybe tomorrow night?"

That look. The one he had in his eyes that said he really, truly cared about me.

"That's really sweet, Owen. But I have a—"

A what? Truitt was nearly three thousand miles away, and I had no idea where we stood. Yeah, we'd kissed that one time when we were both deliriously sleep-deprived. And yeah, we talked as much as possible and understood each other in a way no one else really could. But whenever we were together, we fought more than we got along. And we'd both agreed neither of us were in a good place for a relationship—with anybody.

Except that he might've even been changing his mind about that last part. I didn't have the energy to think about him and Becca.

But Owen stood in front of me. Present and attentive and kind. My heart wanted to be wanted. In a way, that scared me, because I'd always sought affirmation from guys, always turned to them when I needed to feel better about myself. Like I was desirable. Was I doing that now? Or was this different? Was it really wrong to want to know someone had your back? And Owen had proven he wasn't like other guys. He was respectful and polite and asked nothing of me.

Like Truitt.

Before I could stop myself, I smiled, looking Owen right in the eyes. "I'd love that."

"So the little guy is going to pull through, huh?" Owen asked at dinner the next night.

I poked at my gyro. "Yeah, he should. I was up with him all night, though. I was afraid if I fell asleep he'd be dead when I woke up, but he pulled through."

Owen bit his own gyro, thoughtful. "I'm sure you're

exhausted after staying up all night and going to school all day. I won't keep you out late."

I offered a small smile as the conversation lulled. Again. Owen was being so nice to me, but my heart just wasn't into it. There was absolutely nothing wrong with the handsome guy sitting across from me in the corner booth. Seriously, I couldn't find any fault in him, but there was nothing there. No spark. Just friendship.

I looked up from my plate to find Owen studying me. "What is it, Sadie? Is there someone else?"

My shoulders slumped. "It's…complicated. I'm not cheating on anyone, if that's what you're wondering."

"So it's me, then." He said it so sweetly, I wanted to cry.

"No, it's not you at all. It's just this guy back in Georgia. I don't know if we even are anything or if we'll ever be anything, but I can't stop thinking about him. Can't stop wondering if he'll ever tell me how he feels instead of leaving me hanging. I'm awful, I know."

Owen studied his Pepsi. "You're not awful. I actually know how you feel. This was a big step for me, asking you out."

"Oh, Owen…"

He held up a hand. "I mean, I recently decided to give up on a relationship I've wanted for a long time. I was willing to wait, willing to be patient, but I think she was scared, honestly."

"Scared?"

He nodded sadly. "I guess I knew her back before she really got her life back on track and she's still ashamed of that. Like she thinks that's all I see when I look at her. But I don't. I just wish I could make her get that, but I can't. I have to move forward. I'm sorry. That's probably more than I should say."

Understanding grew inside of me. He asked me about her. She avoided him. It made sense. "Fyn," I whispered.

"Yeah."

We sat there in silence for a minute, both of us wanting something we couldn't have. Both of us knowing what it's like to have a whole bunch of baggage keeping you from something so good. Both of us giving up. The sadness of it all was heavy, like a thick blanket I couldn't shake off. Old Sadie would've gone out with him again, just to spite Fyn. But New Sadie was just too weary.

We finished dinner while avoiding any deeper topics, then Owen drove me home.

"Thank you for letting me take you out tonight, Sadie," he said. I smiled and he leaned forward and kissed me lightly on the cheek.

"Don't give up, friend," he said as he hugged me.

"Back at you." I smiled as he drove away. A sadness and longing I couldn't completely put my finger on filled my chest.

――――― o○o ―――――

When I got home from work Friday night around ten, I made Dad a cup of coffee and took it to him in his recliner. Then I looked around in curiosity. Moose usually welcomed me home like I'd been gone for a month.

"I put him outside this afternoon and he never asked to be let back in," Dad explained when I asked him about the dog.

Oh, no. I ran to the back door, flinging it open. The grass hadn't been cut in months, and Moose could easily be dead out there somewhere and I wouldn't be able to see him. I flipped on my phone's flashlight and began searching desperately, watching my step along the way. Terrified of what I might find. Moose was still so weak.

I finally found him behind the storage building, chewing on some kind of carcass. I gagged as I kicked at the dog with my foot in an attempt to get him to move.

"Get inside!" I yelled. The dog didn't move. Holding

my breath, I reached for the dog, making him drop the dead squirrel. I pulled him to myself and stomped back through the wet, crispy grass that reached nearly to my knees.

Moose licked my face, and I gagged again. I muttered some mean things to him and took him straight to the bathtub when I reached the house.

I filled the tub with warm, soapy water—and dog shampoo, this time—and plopped the dog down into it. The water instantly turned brown as mud. Who knew what else came off the dog and swirled into the water.

"Sadie!" Dad yelled, startling me.

"Yeah?"

"Come here! Hurry!" He sounded panicked. I left Moose and took off running.

"What's wrong?" I asked, reaching his recliner.

"I-I spilled my coffee." He motioned to his shirt and winced.

I knew it was hot, because I had just made it for him— before the Moose fiasco. *Moose.*

As if on cue, the dog barreled into the living room, leaving soapy, muddy footprints behind him.

I stood still for a moment, unsure of whether to help my dad with the burning hot coffee or contain the dog before he ruined the floors for the five-thousandth time.

"Sadie! It's hot!" Dad decided for me. I ran into the kitchen and grabbed a dishrag. Tossing it at Dad, I ran into his room and grabbed a t-shirt, then ran back and helped him change, trying to ignore the bruises and cuts still in the process of healing.

Next, I chased Moose with a towel for several minutes, finally catching him when he burned out of his limited energy supply. I took him back to the tub. After finishing with Moose and drying him, I went back into the living room to scrub the puppy prints off the floor.

"Do you want me to order a pizza?" Dad asked, groggy from the latest round of medication.

"Oh, shoot." Dinner. Right. Somehow I'd completely forgotten to fix him something before I left for work. Now it was almost eleven o'clock, and neither of us had eaten. I decided to finish cleaning up the pawprints before figuring out the food situation.

By the time the floor was mud-free, Dad had drifted off to sleep, TV remote in hand. It wasn't worth it to wake him up for dinner, so I went into the kitchen to find something for myself.

When I got to the kitchen, I noticed the sink overflowing with dishes. They stunk, but I had an essay due Monday I hadn't even started on, and I knew Saturday would be filled with work and dealing with Alyssa.

Stress made my chest feel tight, like a fist squeezing inside of me. Hot tears dripped down my cheeks, and I leaned against the counter, telling myself to breathe. Anxiety gripped my throat, and I had the overwhelming urge to scream, but didn't want to wake up Dad. I was so very tired and every part of me hurt, including my brain. Thanksgiving was next week, and the short break from school couldn't come soon enough. I had so much to catch up on.

"I can't do this, God. I need help!" I whimpered, feeling like my plea didn't make it any higher than the ceiling. I was trying so hard to hold it all together and make God proud of me. Trying so desperately to build a relationship with my dad and "be all there," or whatever Liz told me to do. But everything kept going wrong.

I pulled a frozen bag of vegetable soup from the freezer—the last premade meal I'd purchased from the grocery store two weeks ago—and ran it under hot water until I could remove the block of vegetables from the bag. I dropped it into a large pot, then turned the stove on high. While it simmered, I rummaged around until I found an apple on the counter. I sliced it, then found some special grain bread and slid it into the broiler. I realized I hadn't been to the bathroom in hours, so I left the food to pee.

On the way back to the kitchen, I checked my email and found a note from Greg, letting me know there was a problem with my paycheck going into my account, so I hadn't been paid. I quickly typed out a reply, promising to call my bank as soon as possible. That was grocery money.

As I stepped back into the kitchen, I smelled something burning. I ran over to the oven and threw open the door. My bread was charred black. I reached for an oven mitt and the smoke alarm started going off.

"No!" I said, fanning the air with my hands.

"Sadie?" Dad called from the living room as Moose barked hysterically.

"It's fine! Everything's fine! Just burned some toast!"

I dropped the bread into the sink and ran cold water over it.

"Sadie! The smoke alarm is still going off!"

"Really? I hadn't noticed!" I called back. I dragged a chair across the room, drowning out Dad's response. I climbed on the chair and smothered the smoke alarm with a towel until it finally stopped screeching.

Something sizzled behind me, and I turned just in time to see the soup bubble over the top of the pot and onto the eye of the stove.

"No, no, no..." I switched off the burner and pulled off the soup. I stirred it vigorously with a wooden spoon. Burned black chunks appeared from the bottom of the pot.

I added that to my collection in the sink and plopped onto the floor, my head in my hands.

"Is everything okay in there?" Dad called.

"Yes." I forced my voice an octave higher. "Everything is under control now. I'm just making dinner." I filled the pot with hot water, unable to stop the frustrated, exhausted tears.

"I give up, God," I said. "I can't do this. I tried, I did. But this is too hard. I'm sorry."

I walked over to the fridge, my eyes burning and tears dripping onto the dirty floor.

It was right where I knew it'd be. Right where I'd found it a few weeks ago. I pulled the bottle from the drawer and popped it open with a bottle opener from the drawer by the sink.

"I'm sorry, but I can't take it." My hands shook because I knew I was about to let everyone down—myself and God included—but too at the end of my rope to care. I stood and raised the bottle to my mouth.

Moose startled me with more barking, and I dropped the bottle into the sink on top of the bread, soup, and dishes.

A knock sounded at the door, and I quickly poured out the bottle and threw it away.

I glanced at the clock on the stove. It was the middle of the night. Who in the world was at my house?

I had a vision of someone from the hospital standing on my porch, hand out, demanding payment. Or big, buff Roger telling me he was quitting.

Wiping my tear-stained cheeks with the back of my hand, I flipped on the porch light. Behind me, Moose barked like a straight-up maniac, and I gently shoved him back with my foot as I cautiously opened the door just a crack so I could peek out.

Those jeans with the frayed ends. That Pecan Creek Rec

Department t-shirt. That dusty ball cap and the dark brown hair curling out beneath it. That dimpled chin.
Truitt Peyton.

Chapter Twenty

I slammed the door and unlatched the chain, my fingers shaking violently. I flung open the door and threw myself into those strong arms, wrapping my arms around his neck and burying my face in his coat. I burst into tears. And not just any tears, but full-on hiccupping, snot-running, body-wracking sobs. The gross, uncontrollable type of crying.

Truitt held me, his arms tight around my back. My body gave up on supporting itself and Truitt leaned against the house and slid until we were sitting on the porch. He held me for a long time until I stopped shaking.

"I'm sorry. I'm *so* sorry," I sniffed, wiping my nose on my sleeve. I pushed myself off his lap and onto the porch beside him. "I'm really sorry. I am. I just—"

"It's okay, Sadie."

For the first time, the fact that Truitt Peyton was actually at my house in Seattle, on the other side of the country than Pecan Creek, really settled in.

I pushed away from him and blinked my swollen eyes so I could see all of his face.

"Wait. You're *here*. In Seattle. How can you possibly be *here?*"

I shook my head in disbelief, my hand gripping his arm, afraid I'd look up and he'd just be a hallucination. I hadn't slept much recently, after all.

He laughed, the sound so familiar it brought summer rushing back, even though it was a cold November night. "I'm really here."

"But...you've got school. What are you doing here?"

"My Thanksgiving break is a little more generous than yours. I get a whole week." He shrugged. "Besides, I've been in school all my life. I've earned some time off."

I released his arm, even though I loved the security of him pressed against me. "You're not the skipping type, Yard Man."

"No, but I'm more loyal than any dog hopes to be. To a fault. And I knew I needed to make this trip. You need me. Face it."

"You're so full of yourself, you know?" I said, but my watery grin betrayed me. I shivered. "It's freezing out here. Let's get inside."

"Yes, ma'am," Truitt drawled. "Right behind ya."

I led Truitt into the house, my hand refusing to loosen its grip on his.

"Dad," I said as we stepped into the living room. Dad watched us from the recliner, confusion shading his face.

I leaned against Truitt's side. "This is Truitt Peyton. He's good friends with the Elliots, and we hung out a lot this summer." At the time, it had been way more togetherness than I'd wanted. Oh, how things had changed. "Truitt surprised me with a visit."

Moose intercepted Truitt on his way to Dad's recliner, barking and jumping up on his legs.

"Down, Moose!" I grabbed the wiggling dog. "Sorry."

"Hey, lil' buddy. What's up?" Truitt scrubbed the dog's ears, and Moose returned the love by slobbering all over his hand.

"This is Moose. He's the dog who found his way into my backyard..."

"...And into your heart?"

"Let's not get crazy. I've got posters up around town, but no one's wanted to claim him. Although I don't know why they would. He's a mutant." I couldn't help it; I smiled at the dog before setting him down, and Truitt saw it.

"You're smitten. Why's his name Moose?"

I couldn't go into the Fyn thing five minutes after Truitt arrived. "Hey, so Truitt, this is my dad..."

Truitt crossed the room to the recliner, where Dad watched us in silent fascination. "Nice to meet you, Mr. Franklin." Truitt stuck out his hand.

Dad put his hand in Truitt's and shook. "Nice to meet you, Truitt. Call me Mike."

Truitt grinned, and Dad smiled back. My jaw went slack.

"What brings you all the way out here, man?" Dad asked.

Truitt stuck his hands in his pockets and rocked on his heels. "Honestly, sir, Sadie's a good friend and I missed her. Thought it'd be fun to come see her while I'm on Thanksgiving Break." He winked at me, and my heart jumped. "And I thought she could use some help with...everything."

I held my breath, afraid of Dad's reaction to that. Would he accuse me of complaining about him to Truitt? Would he want to know what all I'd told him? Way to go, Truitt.

"I came as a surprise," Truitt continued, sensing the awkward pause. "Sadie never told me she needed help or anything. I thought mainly she could show me the city."

Slowly, Dad nodded. "You're one of the good guys, Truitt," Dad said. "Sadie could probably use some entertainment besides her dad and football. You see this game against the Falcons last year?" he asked, pointing to the rerun playing on the muted TV.

"Yes, sir. But I'm more of a college football guy, myself. SEC."

I sat on the arm of the couch holding Moose, mesmerized as Dad and Truitt talked sports for ten minutes. When my stomach growled, I realized I still hadn't eaten.

I left them to their guy talk and went into the kitchen, where I rummaged around in the fridge until I found some leftover chicken from the night before. My head was spinning, and my eyes were still stinging from all of the tears. But Truitt was actually here!

The three of us sat in the living room for our midnight feast. Moose spent some quality time in the backyard.

"The chicken's good, Sadie," Truitt said, sitting with some space between us on the couch, but close enough for our knees to bump against each other's. "I like the Italian seasoning you used."

"Thanks. I'm still trying to perfect my baked chicken. It always comes out a little dry." I stabbed a piece of meat and popped it into my mouth.

"Have you tried to brine it?" Truitt asked, using his fork to cut a piece of the meat.

I shook my head. "What's that?"

"You kinda just soak it in salty water for a while. Keeps it juicy and helps the flavor."

I laughed. "I forget you're a pro chef when you're not pulling weeds."

I explained Truitt's lawn care job to Dad, and Truitt said he'd be happy to mow the grass the next day. He even promised to get rid of the carcass Moose had found. I almost cried again in relief. No more losing Moose in the foliage or finding him pigging out on rodent cadavers.

After dinner and decaf coffee—Truitt had just arrived in Coffee City, USA, after all—Truitt yawned and stood. "I know it's not that late yet, but I'm feeling three o'clock in the morning. This time change is no joke. I should go."

I stood, too. Dad watched us. "Go? Where are you going?"

"I don't know yet. I don't think they'll let me check into a hotel. I pretty much just booked a flight as fast as I could and didn't think about the other details."

Okay, that confession was kind of attractive.

I took Truitt's phone from his hand and tossed it on the couch. "Don't be crazy. You're more than welcome here." I didn't chance a glance back at Dad.

"You sure? 'Cause I can…"

"Of course I'm sure. You can sleep in my bed."

Truitt's face shot red. "Sadie, we can't—"

My own cheeks blushed when I realized my mistake. "Oh, no! I meant you can have my room. By yourself. I've been sleeping on the couch to be near Dad, so I don't need my bed."

Truitt hesitated.

"You can sleep in my room." We both turned to look at Dad. "I'm camping out in here these days."

Truit smiled. "I appreciate that, Mike, but if it's all right with you, I'd like to stay out here on the couch. Give Sadie a chance to be in her own space for a few nights."

I sat down. Did Truitt realize what he was saying? Dad needed pain meds during the night, he needed an extra blanket if he got cold, and he needed help adjusting his pillows. Most importantly, he needed help getting to the bathroom. Dad and Truitt didn't even know each other.

"Truitt, that's sweet of you, but I've got it. I already know what to do and Moose is used to sleeping by the couch with me and—"

"Then you'll be able to teach me, no problem."

A stubborn gleam lit his eyes, and I knew I'd be in my room tonight. He always had to be the hero.

After giving Truitt instructions for the night and—at his insistence—filling him in on chores he could do while I was at work the next day, I slipped into my room and clicked the door behind me. The mere sight of my bed brought more tears to my eyes, and I quickly undressed and slipped into a big t-shirt. I pulled back the covers, slid between the cool sheets, and clicked off the lamp on my nightstand. Then I looked up at the ceiling and whispered, "Thank you, God," over and over until I fell asleep.

When my alarm went off the next morning, I instantly smelled coffee. I grabbed my Cannonball's t-shirts off the floor and did a smell test to see which one could pass as the cleanest. Then I dashed into the bathroom for a quick shower and got ready for the day.

By the time I walked into the kitchen, Truitt had scrambled eggs waiting on the table, along with a cup of orange juice and a to-go tumbler of coffee.

"Morning, Sadie," he said from the stove, where he scooped more eggs onto a plate. "Your mutt's outside. That's your plate. Do you have time to eat it?"

I nodded dumbly and slid into my seat. "Why are you up already? You only got a few hours of sleep!"

"Time zone. Truitt time says it's three hours later."

"Ah." I shoveled the eggs down, loving every fluffy bite. After washing it down with orange juice, I grabbed the coffee tumbler and took a sip. "Okay, I'll run home at lunch, then be back again tonight. Please don't feel like you actually have to do anything. Go take a nap or something."

"Got it." Truitt waved a spatula at me. "Go make money."

The sight of him in my kitchen threatened to choke me up again.

"Fine. I'll do a white-glove check when I get back."

I heard him laughing as I whisked myself through the living room, said goodbye to Dad, and went out the door.

Truitt was waiting for me with a salad, apple slices, and peanut butter when I ran home for lunch. "Well, aren't you a regular housewife?" I flopped into a chair at the table.

"Don't get used to it," he said without taking his eyes off his history textbook. "They're my leftovers."

I slugged his arm, and he caught my hand. "Let's talk."

"Okay..." Apples forgotten, I sat across from him.

"So I talked to your dad today. I had something I wanted to run by him."

"Did you ask for his blessing?" I quipped.

He rolled his eyes. "I asked about switching some stuff up. Roger stops by for PT while you're at school, right? I'm here for a solid week and you have school for all but two of those days, so I asked to switch the schedule. I'll help your dad during the day, then Roger will come in the evening. So you'll be able to focus on homework, and then I thought maybe you could show me your city. Your dad and I already lined it up."

I blinked at him. "Whoa. You've been busy."

Truitt leaned back in his chair. "Between making those calls and cleaning up after Moose—who you conveniently failed to mention is *not* totally housetrained, by the way—it's been a full day."

My jaw stiffened. Who did he think he was barging in and interrupting my carefully balanced system? Especially after not even checking in regularly over the past couple months. Never mind the balancing act was falling apart. But I was thankful, right? He'd saved me. At that moment, I realized God had answered a huge prayer. While I was telling Him I couldn't do it anymore and had been seconds away from drowning my pain, Truitt was already on his way.

"Thank you," I whispered sincerely, swallowing my pride. "You saved me."

"I didn't do anything but show up. God does it all." He stood and walked over to the counter for more apples. I followed behind him.

"I just need you to promise me everything will be okay," I whispered, my voice wobbly. "And not a disaster forever."

He studied my face for a moment. Finally, he said, "I can't tell you everything is going to be okay. And I can't tell you everything is going to be terrible, either. But I can tell you it's not up to you to hold it all together."

I hopped up onto the counter to break the thickness of the conversation, leaning back against the cabinet. "God gave me a second chance and I wanted to make Him proud. Prove I was worth it. But now I'm not sure…" I trailed off, studying my knees.

"Hey." Truitt clamped a hand on my knee and gently rocked it back and forth. "Look at me." I looked down at Truitt and wiped my nose with the back of my wrist before it dripped on him. "You can't make God love you any more than He already does, and there's nothing you can do to make Him love you less. He already decided how He felt about you when He sent Jesus to the cross to pay for your sins."

In the past if Truitt had said that, I would've bristled at the preachiness of it all. But now I had no choice but to nod, my eyes focused on his hand which still covered my knee. "You're right."

"Of course I am," he joked, squeezing my knee.

I slid off the counter. "I've gotta eat and get back to work."

"Let me take you. What time do you get off?"

"Ten o'clock."

"I'll pick you up and have dinner ready."

"Thanks, dear." I meant it as a joke, but when I glanced over at him, he was looking at me in a deep way. I couldn't decipher it beyond the knowledge that I was looking at him in the exact same way.

He reached up and swept a piece of hair out of my eyes. I caught my breath before I even realized it. "I don't want you to have to pick me up."

"I'll be there at ten."

Swallowing hard, I nodded and backed away, not trusting my vulnerable emotions enough to stay around him another minute.

Chapter Twenty-One

○○○

I smiled as Truitt walked over to me, dodging a pair of kids as they chased each other out the door.

The place closed in ten minutes, but excited screams and shrieks still filled the building. Truitt reached me as I snipped a wristband off of a sweaty middle school boy.

He leaned over the counter to be heard over the noise. "What did you say this place was called?"

"Birth control."

He laughed, and I raised my pair of scissors in the air. "Team abstinence," I deadpanned. "I've still got a few minutes before I'm off."

He nodded. "Just wanted to see the place. I'll wait in the car, then we can eat dinner."

I snipped another wristband, then glanced at the clock.

"Don't worry," he said as he backed away. "I've got takeout waiting in the car."

He may have been out of place on this side of the country, but his Southernness was even more endearing against the Pacific Northwest backdrop. And that dimple didn't hurt anything, either.

Alyssa came up to me, holding a pair of scissors. I instinctively backed against the counter. She had a gleam of hatred in her eye. "Greg said to go scrub toilets. I'll handle this part."

"That's your job, and you know it. I did them yesterday." I plastered a fake grin on my face as I snipped the wristband off the last kid and waved goodbye.

"Go scrub the toilets, Sadie," she said again, under her breath this time. I glanced around the room to locate Truitt, but he was already gone. It was just me and Alyssa.

"No, Alyssa. I'm finished with my stuff. I've gotta go."

She slammed the scissors down on the counter, and I jumped. "What if I have plans, too? What if I had a date? You don't even care. Just like you didn't care that night when the cops showed up."

"What in the world, Alyssa? You know I didn't call them!"

"You let them in the house. You didn't give us a chance to get away, just opened the door and gave them the grand tour."

"I did not! It's not my fault you were drunk! I didn't pour beer down your throat! I wasn't the one who started yelling obscenities when the cop started questioning you. That was all *you*."

She reached out and grabbed my arm. Hard. "You are trash. My parents found out about that night, thanks to you, and are making me live at home my first year of college."

Her fingers dug into my flesh, and I squirmed. "We each make our own choices."

She released me, and I grabbed my burning arm. "And now I'm making this choice: You will be fired, Sadie. Be sure of that. And you—"

"Whoa! Ladies! What are we doing?" Greg emerged from his office, the unicorn head tucked under his arm.

"Nothing," I mumbled, right as Alyssa said, "Fire her."

"No, Greg, listen—" I held up my hands.

"No, Sadie. You listen. I heard both of you yelling out here. I'm just glad the customers are gone. But I can't deal with all this drama. I've warned you once, Sadie, and I gave you another chance already. You're a nice girl, but it looks like the two of you can't get along to save your life."

"But I was hired first! You love me!" I pleaded. This couldn't be happening.

Greg sighed. "You've got a point, but I still think you need a minute to breathe."

If he only knew…

"Alyssa, let's talk. Sadie, go home. I'll see you the week after Thanksgiving."

"But—"

He pointed toward the door.

"Yes, sir."

Shaking, I exited the building while Alyssa followed Greg to a picnic table in the corner.

The next morning, Truitt and I walked into Raining Grace Community Church just as the band started playing a worship song. If I ever needed church, it was this morning. Last night, Truitt had listened to me rant about Alyssa over our beef and broccoli.

"I feel overdressed," Truitt whispered in my ear, his button-down shirt tucked in and his hands stuck in his pockets.

We slid into the back row of chairs. "At least you're not wearing a bow tie like when I first met you," I told him, thinking back on the night I literally ran into him at church. He'd been wearing a bow tie and an amused grin.

"Hey, I only did that once. And I had come straight to church after a funeral. It was one of those Sunday-best kinds of events."

I blinked at him. "Really? Truitt, I had no idea. I—"

He shook his head. "It's all good. It was for a friend's

uncle. I barely knew him. But that's why I had a bow tie. It's not really my style."

I had to agree with him there, although now I felt bad I'd judged him pretty harshly and called him Bow Tie Boy in my head before I even got to know him. Wow, I could be the worst.

He caught my darkened expression and nudged me with his elbow. "Sadie, really, it's fine. But I *am* glad I didn't pull out the bow tie today."

I smiled. "Brace yourself: the pastor is wearing jeans."

Truitt shook his head, mesmerized. "All I've ever known is Pecan Creek Baptist. Hymns and pews and stained-glass windows."

I watched him out of the corner of my eye in the dark room, unsure of what he'd think of Raining Grace.

But mid-way through the second song, Truitt leaned over, his hand pulling my hair back from my ear. "I love Pecan Creek Baptist, but this place is awesome, too." His voice tickled my ear. I smiled at him, and he put his arm around my shoulder.

I wanted to act nonchalant about it, like it was just a friendly thing for him to do, to reassure me that he was comfortable, but my heart rate jumped a little all the same. The weeks of us being apart had led me to think maybe we were meant to just be friends, and maybe that was best, but my pulse seemed to have missed the memo.

On the way home after the service, Truitt asked, "So which one was Fingernail?"

"Fynnigan."

"Right."

I leaned back in the passenger seat. "She was toward the front with some of the other students. I wasn't exactly up for introductions."

Truitt put on the blinker as he pulled into the driveway. "Yeah, me neither. She hurt you, after all, so she's already on my list."

"Your list, huh?" I rolled my eyes, but secretly, my heart tilted a little more toward his.

———— oOo ————

When the doorbell rang Monday after school, I left my textbook on the couch and went to the door, adjusting my ponytail. Truitt sat on the floor, leaning against the couch and using the coffee table as a desk. Roger had gone home for the day.

"Oh, hey!" I said when I opened the door for Owen. "Come in!"

"Sadie, how are you?" He stepped into the living room and wrapped me in a hug. It caught me off guard, but I hugged him back. I tried to analyze the hug, but came up with nothing. No stomach flutters, no psycho hormones, nothing. Just warm, comfortable friendship.

"I've been worried about you," he said, letting me go. "I didn't get a chance to talk to you before you left church yesterday, and you weren't at Café Graffiti Wednesday."

I ran a hand over my forehead. "Yeah, I'm fine. Just been swamped with everything." I shrugged. "But I'm making it."

Owen handed me the paper bag he was holding. "This is for Moose. I thought he might appreciate some protection against fleas. That would be worse than Sassy Berry." He winked.

I took the bag and looked inside. "Oh, thanks. I um…" I didn't know how to tell him I couldn't afford it and I was praying the Lord would spare Moose of all the diseases during these financially unstable times. "How much…?"

He waved his hand. "Nothing. It's a gift."

I smiled and impulsively returned his hug, grateful for this little mercy. "Thank you, Owen," I said into his shoulder.

Behind me, textbook pages rustled, and I remembered Truitt.

"Hey, Owen, come on in." I led him further into the living room and perched on the arm of the couch. "This is my…this is Truitt. He's a…friend…from Pecan Creek, and he's here for a week pretty much saving my life."

Truitt lightly punched my shoulder. "I'm just in Seattle for the fresh fish. Nice to meet you, man." Truitt and Owen shook hands. Owen glanced over at me, and I knew he knew Truitt was the guy I'd told him about.

"Wanna join the study party?" I asked Owen. Yeah, I didn't want to make things weird, but other than Truitt at home and Liz and Jen at church, I hadn't had time to hang out with any of my friends. "I'll make popcorn…" I bribed.

"Thanks, but I've gotta run. It's my mom's birthday dinner tonight."

I walked him to the door.

"Are you coming to Thanksgiving dinner?" I asked.

Owen nodded. "My family has our big meal at lunch, so I'll be free to come. What do you still need someone to bring?"

"Steaks."

Owen blinked. "Really? You know I don't—"

"I'm joking." I gently shoved him. "You can bring a side dish. Maybe mashed potatoes?"

"Got it. I'm looking forward to Thursday." He hugged me again, and I remembered that he was a pretty huggy person.

After I closed the door behind him, I turned to find Truitt studying me.

"What?"

"Nothin'."

"Spill it, Yard Man."

"You and Owen?"

Was Truitt...*jealous*? I shook my head as I walked over and plopped down on the floor next to him. "No. He's the kind of guy who just makes a great friend. He's so sweet, but not for me."

"He's not, huh? How do you know?"

I shrugged. "Just a feeling, I guess." Or *lack thereof*. Then I pulled the cover off the elephant in the room, keeping my eyes trained on my homework. "What about you and Becca?"

He turned a page. "She's one of my closest friends. She has been for forever. She's amazing in so many ways. But she's a friend." He paused, and I felt his eyes on me.

"Are you...sure?" I asked. "I mean, every time I talked to one of you this semester, you mentioned the other person, or how you were spending time with the other person, or—"

"Sadie."

I stopped blabbering, but kept my eyes on my book. If he was about to admit his affection for Becca, I at least didn't want to watch it happen. "Yeah?"

"She's always going to be one of my best friends, but that's it. And I promise she'd say the same about me. As awesome as she is, I know she's not the girl for me."

I finally looked over at him, and my breath caught. The air was charged with something other than friendship. I could hear him breathing. I thought about how he got my story in ways no one else could. About our kiss. About him holding my hand. About how he'd proven he'd do anything for me, even cross an entire country. "Truitt, I—"

"That's got to be a record," Dad said as he hobbled back into the room, his hair wet from the shower, breaking our trance. "But now I'm exhausted."

I leaned back against the couch and let out my breath. "You did great, Dad," I said, not sure if I was referring to his shower time or that he'd just saved me from something I wasn't sure I had the energy to handle right now.

Chapter Twenty-Two

○○○

Emotions are like bad sushi. One minute, everything's awesome, then the food poisoning hits and you loathe yourself for getting excited about discount spicy tuna rolls.

It happened Tuesday, two days before Thanksgiving. After school, I picked Truitt up to go grocery shopping for the Thanksgiving dinner I was hosting for the Café Graffiti kids.

I wish I could blame exhaustion or PMS or my medication I'd finally had refilled at the pharmacy or something like that, but Truitt and I were both fully responsible for what happened. And like a perfect storm, it came out of nowhere. If I was lightning, Truitt was pouring rain.

I happened to mention I'd decided against college while we compared prices on brands of cranberry sauce.

"What?" Truitt tossed a jar into the shopping cart, and it clanged against the metal.

"I said I've decided to hold off on college for now. Maybe just a year, I don't know." I shrugged.

"Why in the world would you do that?" Truitt looked almost panicked.

"Well, for one, money. There's none of it, and my grades are far from scholarship-worthy." I glanced down at the list on my phone and grabbed another can of cranberry sauce. "Two, I'm still not entirely sure what I want to do."

"That's why they let you take your core classes first, so you have time to figure it all out. And I'm sure you could go somewhere with in-state tuition." He went from panicky to defensive. The nerves in my neck buzzed, like hackles standing up on the back of my neck.

"Still. I'm waiting it out. I'll get a job, save some money…"

"You know if you don't go right into college, you'll never go back to school."

That stung. "Lots of people do! Lots of single moms go back to school. Even old people go back to school after they're retired!"

"But you're not a lot of people."

My mouth dropped open, and my brow furrowed in anger. "What"—I said through gritted teeth—"does *that* mean?"

Truitt shook his head. "That didn't come out right. I meant I don't want you wasting time doing a job you don't love."

I held up my phone. "My father called. He said he wants his job as judge of Sadie's decisions back." I shoved my phone in my back pocket, realizing how cheesy that sounded, but not even caring. "Since when are you the boss of me? Since when is *anyone* the boss of me?"

"I know I am not your boss," Truitt said slowly, enunciating each syllable. "But I think college is a good idea. You know that."

My hands went to my hips. I couldn't believe this was happening, but I was too wound up to stop. Old Sadie was peeking around the corner, and my efforts at shoving her back were failing miserably. "If you think that, then maybe you don't know me at all," I growled, turning to go find the coffee creamer.

"Sadie!" Truitt grabbed my arm and spun me around. Heat shot through me, but this time it wasn't attraction. It was anger.

"Don't touch me, Truitt!" I said a little too loudly. What was it with Truitt and me having confrontations at the grocery store? First, that time in Pecan Creek after I overheard him talking to Mel about my past. And now, as he tried to map out my future. "Stop telling me how to run my life! I know you like to have everything all nice and neat and under control. I know you like your life and everyone in it to appear neat and tidy."

"What does that mean?"

"Oh, you know exactly what that means! You lied and hid your mom's issues from everyone who cared about you. All those bruises you chalked up as baseball accidents. The scratch across your face you claimed was from your cat—a cat I never even met, by the way." My eyes locked into his, and I lowered my voice. "I remember the beer bottles in your trailer. And the smell of whatever your mom had been smoking. You tried to mask all of that. And now you're trying to make me look all put together, too? I appreciate everything you've been doing for me, truly, but I can make my own decisions about my own life."

He was still holding my arm. I tried to wrestle free, and he let me go, even though I knew he was way stronger.

"Let's just finish up and get out of here," I said under my breath.

He followed behind me. "I was wrong about how I handled things with my mom, Sadie. I know I messed up. You said you'd forgiven me. I'm not trying to fix you at all." Out of the corner of my eye, I saw him reach out like he was going to try to comfort me, but I shrugged him away. "I just want you to have the best life possible," he said quietly. "College isn't really an option for me, Sadie, with my mom and everything. And I have my yard business. But I want more for you."

"Well, I want more space," I said, focusing on breathing

and pushing the cart around the corner before he could stop me.

Wednesday was a half-day of school for me, but I had a precalculus test I was positive I'd failed. I was really on a roll with the exams this semester. I'd meant to stay up late Monday night studying, but I'd fallen asleep at the kitchen table. I couldn't even blame Truitt for distracting me with his nonsense because I would've thought I'd be too worked up over the fallout to sleep. I was just so tired. But if I wanted any hope of college at some more distant point in the future, even community college, I absolutely had to pass all of my classes. More than that, I had to do well in them. My previous years of high school (read: partying) had taken a toll on my GPA.

After class, I picked Dad up for an appointment at the orthopedic office.

"Ready for this?" I asked as the elevator stopped on the correct floor of the building. I stretched out my hand to hold the door open while Dad exited, a crutch under his good arm.

He glanced over at me as we made our way into the waiting room. "It'll be nice to have two hands again."

While we waited, I texted the Raining Grace kids to remind them about the Thanksgiving dinner the next day. It was going to be so fun throwing a party where no one—including myself—ended up in a fight or passed out from alcohol or knocked a hole in the wall.

I just wondered if Truitt and I would be on speaking terms again by the time everyone arrived. On one end of the spectrum was the shivery, racing heart thing that happened whenever Truitt was in a three-foot radius of me. On the other end was World War III: Sadie vs. Truitt.

Dad nudged me, pulling me out of my heavy thoughts. We followed the nurse back to the exam room.

After another short wait, during which Dad and I took guesses about how his arm would look once the cast came off, the orthopedic doctor entered the room. He instructed Dad to sit on the exam table and reached for a—

"Is that an electric *saw*?" I gulped.

The doctor nodded. "It will cut right through the cast."

While the doctor slowly cut away the cast with the circular tool, I sat in the corner with an arm wrapped around my stomach. The tinny buzz of the saw made me grit my teeth and break out in a cold sweat. I focused my attention on my lap.

"Hey, Sadie," Dad said once the doctor finished sawing. "It looks weirder than we thought."

Still clutching my stomach, I walked over to where Dad sat, his arm extended to me. I'd never seen—or smelled—anything quite like the cast sitting on the table next to Dad, or the shriveled skin that had been hiding beneath it.

"That's...interesting." I breathed through my mouth.

Dad slid around so that his legs hung off the table. He held out both arms and studied the contrast. "Let's go home and show Truitt."

Truitt. My neck prickled at the thought of facing him. I wasn't really into another volatile encounter.

But when we got home, Truitt was busy reorganizing the storage shed in the backyard, accompanied by Moose who had to sniff and bark at every strange object. Every now and then, I'd look out my window from my spot at the kitchen table and watch him work. Even though it was cold and misty outside, he had still worked up a sweat as he rearranged the lawnmower gas cans, weed-eater, and other stuff I didn't know we owned.

I couldn't figure out what to do. I mean, he *had* come all this way to help me, and I couldn't exactly kick him out of the house. Plus, I surprisingly didn't even want to. But Truitt always tried to be the hero—the fixer. And I always aimed for autonomy.

During dinner, we both tried to act like nothing was up for Dad's sake. We even managed to joke about how we should've brought home Dad's cast to display on the mantle. But there was still a chill in the room. I still couldn't bring myself to make eye contact with Truitt. After we finished eating, I muttered, "Thanks for dinner. I'll clean up," then disappeared into the kitchen. I went to bed early since I was so bummed about the test and Truitt and everything else not right in my life.

Around one o'clock, I woke up thirsty. I shoved my wild bedhead out of my face and headed toward the kitchen for a glass of water.

I rounded the corner into the kitchen. Truitt sat at the table, the stove light the only thing pushing back the shadows in the room. His Bible was open and his head was down. His mouth moved silently.

Truitt, praying?

I turned to leave, not yet ready for this conversation I knew was inevitable, but the floor creaked. Truitt looked up and gave me a sad half-grin. "Hey, Sleeping Beauty."

"Hi." I glanced down at the old, baggy Seahawks t-shirt I'd stolen from Dad's laundry pile years ago and crossed my arms over my chest. "I just...wanted some water."

"Sit."

I obeyed, too sleepy to object to his bossiness. He stood from the table, went over to the cabinet, and removed a cup. Meanwhile, I scooped my unruly hair into a messy bun on top of my head. I definitely didn't look my best, but Truitt had seen me at my absolute worst and somehow hadn't spooked. He'd seen the real me, and that made me feel safe.

Truitt placed a glass of water in front of me and sat back

down, running his thumb over a page in his Bible. "Couldn't sleep." He looked up at me, and I noticed his hair was ruffled from tossing and turning. "So I thought I'd hang out with my Father for a little bit."

The ice around my heart melted. Truitt's dad walked out on his family just a few years ago, when Truitt was thirteen. But God was the Father that would never leave him.

I sipped my water and leaned across the table. "Truitt, I'm…"

He silently shook his head.

So I changed topics. "What're you reading?"

Truitt held the Bible reverently in his hands. "But now, this is what the Lord says—he who created you, Jacob, he who formed you, Israel: 'Do not fear, for I have redeemed you; I have summoned you by name; you are mine. When you pass through the waters, I will be with you; and when you pass through the rivers, they will not sweep over you. When you walk through the fire, you will not be burned; the flames will not set you ablaze.'"

"Wow," I exhaled. "Who is God talking to?"

"Those are the first two verses of Isaiah 43. God is speaking through Isaiah the prophet, promising to rescue his people from captivity. And also, He's looking forward to Jesus rescuing us. So it's a promise to us, too."

"That's an awesome promise." I leaned back in my seat, crossing my arms over my chest again. "I love that."

Truitt smiled. "I thought you would. I was planning to share it with you in the morning." He glanced at the clock on the microwave. "But first, I'm sorry for everything. I know you don't need my guidance, and I know you're the independent type. I just…I told you I'm loyal to a fault."

I nodded, whispering, "Okay," in a wobbly voice. I swallowed, planning to return the apology, but my mouth wouldn't work. Or it probably would've, but then I would've broken down completely.

Then he smiled, and that chin dimple popped and I felt it. That fluttery feeling in my heart and that fuzzy feeling down in my gut. My breathing went shallow when he reached out and put a warm hand over mine.

"It's okay." Truitt squeezed my hand. "You're extremely stressed. I get that. I guess I just want you to have a relationship with your dad since I can't have a relationship with mine. You still have a shot at it, even though that might be hard to see right now. You're gonna get through this rough patch, Sadie," he whispered. "Because God won't let the water drown you or the fire burn you. He's with you."

I swallowed hard. "I just keep asking God to show me the purpose in all of this."

Truitt looked down for a minute, thumbing through the Bible, back toward the beginning of the book, before bringing his eyes to mine and saying, "So you know the Ten Commandments, right?"

I nodded, but also furrowed my brow. What did that have to do with anything? I mean, I hadn't killed anyone, and I hadn't coveted my neighbor's oxen. Carl and Judith didn't even have oxen!

"So Moses is on top of a mountain, and God's giving him the Ten Commandments." Truitt leaned forward as he dove into the story. "This was all a big deal because there was all this thunder and lightning on the mountain and all the other people were scared. It was all so dark and crazy. But God had more to tell Moses. The people were freaked out, and Exodus 20:21 says that 'the people remained at a distance, while Moses approached the thick darkness where God was.'"

I pulled my knees to my chest and rested my chin on them. "I'm not sure I'm tracking."

Truitt closed the book and folded his arms over it. "The point is, while everyone else was freaking out because they couldn't see what was going on, the uncertainty didn't bother Moses. He stepped into the darkness because he knew that's where God was. Nothing else mattered as long as God was with him."

"Help me understand," I whispered in a watery voice.

"Don't ask for a clear path. Ask for the faith to take *one more step* into the unknown. Because God is there."

I nodded and looked right at his face. It took all my willpower to not walk around the table and let him hold me, keep me safe. "Truitt, I..." A tear slipped out beneath my lashes. "I couldn't do this without you. I really don't even know how to say thank you. You've been...you've been everything to me."

"I can't even try to play God for you, but I can try to show Him to you." Truitt tilted his head, and I realized we were alone in my kitchen in the middle of the night and my dad was sleeping in the living room. That feeling they teach you about in fifth grade health class took my attention.

"I should, uh, get to bed." I said that, but my legs wouldn't stand. It was like a magnetism kept me to my seat, looking into Truitt's face.

Truitt closed his Bible and stood first. He walked over to my side of the table and ruffled my hair. "G'night, Franklin."

Then he disappeared into the darkness of the living room.

Chapter Twenty-Three

○○○

I got up early Thursday morning to go for a run. The clouds hung heavy and low, threatening to dump rain on me any minute, but I craved the brisk air that filled my lungs. It was Thanksgiving Day, and I was thankful. In a few hours, I would gather around the table with Dad, Truitt, and a group of new friends God had given me. I planned to think through my to-do list while I ran. But I also needed to process what was going on between Truitt and me, and how much I trusted myself with all of it.

In the past, I wouldn't have thought twice about ending last night with a kiss. Or inviting him into my room. Even though the air was cold, my cheeks burned with the shame of how I'd acted in the past.

But now, I knew I was worth more. Not in a prideful way, but in a deep knowing kind of way. I had purpose and value, and I was made to honor that. And to honor that in Truitt, too. That didn't mean the attraction went away, even if that would be more convenient. But it did mean I could use it as a way to show how I loved God and cared about His purpose for our lives by watching what I did and being wise. Even if that was proving to be way more difficult than I'd expected.

I took a cool-down lap around the neighborhood. While I walked, I gathered handfuls of leaves, admiring each one's unique shape and vibrant color combinations.

Back at my house, I spread out my collection of leaves on paper towels on the kitchen counter to dry. I wasn't much of an interior decorator, but I'd watched a show that suggested spreading these on your Thanksgiving table for a festive feel or something. After a quick shower, I met Truitt in the kitchen to prepare the feast.

Jordan and Claire were joining us at five-thirty that evening, and had volunteered to bring the turkey and pies. Liz was bringing cupcakes. About ten teens had excitedly told me they were coming, which was so cool because I hadn't had the opportunity to get to know most of them well yet. Pastor Theo and his wife even said they would come with their young kids if they had the opportunity. Everyone was asked to bring a side dish, and we had a massive group text for everyone to chime in with what they were bringing.

I was in charge of green bean casserole and, of course, the cranberry sauce. I also had plans to make apple cider in the Crock-Pot for that warm and cozy touch. The lady on TV was all about that autumnal aroma.

The mild ache in my side from my run reminded me that my health would require I watch how much of these rich foods I ate tonight, but even that couldn't dampen my mood. While Truitt fixed a quick lunch in the kitchen and I cleaned up Dad's corner of the living room, Dad and I watched the parade together, commenting on the different floats and assigning our own rating.

I honestly couldn't remember when Dad and I had last bonded like this, laughing together and not arguing. Dad's good mood from the day before remained. He was thrilled to have the cast off his arm, and we looked forward to his leg brace coming off soon, too.

"Two-point deduction for the terrible lip-sync," Dad commented as one of the floats passed by.

"But look how cute the kids are!" I said, pretending to contest his rating.

"They knew you'd say that, Sadie. The cute kids are there to cover up the subpar performance."

I laughed at that as I went in the kitchen to help Truitt.

"What else can I help with?" Truitt asked from where he stood at the counter, opening the jars of cranberry sauce.

I leaned against the counter next to him and tapped my chin. "I think we're good. We have our part of the food ready, the plates and cups are set out, Jen is bringing drinks…"

"Ice." Truitt snapped his fingers. "We forgot about ice."

I rubbed the back of my neck and groaned. "Maybe Jordan and Claire can stop by the store."

Truitt handed me a can of cranberry sauce. "I'm on it. You finish up here, and I'll be back in a minute."

I smiled at him. "Thank you. You're saving the day yet again."

He tweaked my nose. "Don't get mushy, Franklin. You're gonna make me late to the party."

He jogged out of the kitchen, and I finished with the cranberry sauce.

I was just switching the Crock-Pot to the Keep Warm mode when I heard Dad crutch his way into the kitchen behind me.

"That smells fantastic," he said, leaning over the Crock-Pot. The tart cinnamony smell of the cider mingled with the fresh, slightly musky scent of his soap.

"You smell pretty good, too, Dad. Not at all like a couch potato," I joked. Then I turned to look at him, and my mouth dropped open slightly.

He'd shaved the stubble off his face, and his hair was combed and damp, the color matching his eyes. He wore a pair of jeans and a blue plaid shirt with the sleeves rolled up to his elbows. He no longer looked like a guy who'd failed to launch and landed back in his parents' basement playing video games all day. He didn't even look like a weary young widower with a chip on his shoulder. Other than the healing scar across his cheek, he looked like an average guy in his thirties.

I felt a warm pride in my chest that my friends would get to see him as my dad. The foreign feeling brought tears to my eyes as I tried to process it.

"You okay?" he asked, adjusting his crutch under his arm. I saw the reservation in his eyes—emotions freaked him out even more than they bothered me.

I swallowed and nodded. "Yeah, totally. Sorry. You look great, Dad. I mean that."

He smiled, bashful, not used to such praise. That pricked my heart, too. "Yeah?"

"Absolutely." I swiped at my eyes. "Not everyone gets a young, handsome guy for their dad." I was born when my parents were eighteen, so he was relatively young to have a seventeen-year-old daughter, and looking at him now, he could've passed for my brother.

The doorbell rang, and Moose raced past us on his way to the door, already barking like a maniac. "That's probably Jordan and Claire," I explained. "I'll let them in and cage the beast."

Dad reached out and gently ruffled my hair as I left the kitchen.

───── oOo ─────

After an amazing dinner, the group cleared the plates and cups from around the living room and settled in for a wacky game of charades before we had cider and dessert.

Dad ended up engrossed in a sports conversation with Jordan and Truitt and stayed with the group the whole time. Then when Pastor Theo stopped by, he joined in the conversation and the men sat at the kitchen table talking and joking. The group also welcomed Truitt in as if he'd belonged all along. I didn't know if hearts could actually smile, but I was pretty sure mine was all-out grinning.

I'd assumed everyone would leave soon after dessert, but no one seemed ready to go home. I mingled with some of the teens I'd seen at church but had never talked to much before. It was awesome.

The dim spot in all the brightness was Fyn's absence. I knew she'd have the time of her life if she were here, but she had never responded to my open, texted invitation. I couldn't let that stop me, though. I was so thankful to God for all He had done for me, even if this situation still ached. For the first time, I actually thought about the word Thanksgiving. It was all about giving thanks, I knew that, but for the first time, I was truly giving thanks to Someone.

When Dad sat in his chair, a glazed expression on his face, I knew it was time to end the party. I could tell he was trying to still join in, but he was exhausted. He hadn't had this much mobility or social interaction since before the wreck, and it was taking a toll on him. My caregiver instincts took over, and I wrapped things up by ten o'clock. Jordan and Claire offered to help Truitt and me clean up the kitchen so Dad could get to bed that much sooner. Because of his ribs, it was still more comfortable for him to sleep in the recliner, so he stared absently at the TV while we cleaned as quickly as possible so he could go to sleep.

———— ○○○ ————

I stifled a yawn and glanced at the ad in my hand. "Yeah, we're looking for this right here. The early bird deal?"

The sales associate took the paper from me and glanced

at it, before handing it back. "If there aren't any on that aisle over there—" he gestured a couple rows behind us, "then I can check in the back. We've had a run on them this morning."

Truitt and I followed him through the store, dodging early-morning shoppers.

"Why in the world was there a line outside a home improvement store at six in the morning?" Truitt muttered near my ear.

I yawned in response.

Thankfully, the grill that was on the super sale was still in stock. Truitt helped me wheel the box on a cart up to the register, where we waited in line for a solid twenty minutes before I could check out. I thought the small, charcoal grill would be a nice Christmas gift for Dad, now that I was learning how to cook and we'd never had a grill before. Plus, I'd spent a summer in the South and learned every guy needed a grill.

We had one more stop to make before we called it a morning and went back to bed.

Call me a glutton for punishment, but I had to go to that Black Friday pit of no return: the craft store. I wasn't about to knit a blanket for someone's Christmas, but their Christmas decorations were on a crazy-good sale, and I wanted to get a few decorations and some ornaments to use as gifts. Truitt was already dragging behind me, completely unable to understand why I would want to get up before dawn and fight crowds to shop of all things.

There were so many moms in the craft store—some even pushing bleary-eyed preschoolers or sleeping babies in their shopping carts. It was mayhem, the stuff of nightmares. Like Cannonball's for MOPS. Truitt looked like a spooked horse as soon as we entered the store and decided it would be best if he sat out this round. I sent him back to the car, then ventured deeper into the madness.

I squeezed between a woman who was pushing a cart overflowing with greenery and a giant, singing Santa. The Santa was motion-activated, so as I passed by he began knocking his hips back-and-forth, singing "Jingle Bells."

Another woman stood in front of a wall of wrapping paper rolls, loudly shouting into her phone: "Red or Green? Gingerbread cottages or Santa and Rudolph? Glitter? No, no sombreros…"

I didn't hang around long enough to hear the end of that conversation. I finally reached the ornament aisle, only to realize I needed a cart. I couldn't spend much money, but I wanted the decorations to be a surprise for Dad. Christmas had always looked kind of like our Thanksgivings. We'd watch a parade on TV, exchange a gift, order takeout. Really sad stuff.

As classic Christmas carols piped over the speakers, I battled my way back to the front of the store to retrieve a cart. I grabbed a five-foot tall tree, some lights that would blink if I wanted them to, and a star for the top. I found an ornament that looked like a rotisserie and laughed out loud, earning some stares from other under-caffeinated shoppers. I tossed it in the cart. It would remind Dad of my early attempts at cooked chicken. He'd think it was funny.

I'd just found a cute "Baby's First Christmas" ornament to save for Evie, when I heard it:

"You just can't take good advice and stay away from me, can you?"

I swung around and there stood Alyssa. Ruby stepped up next to her.

I dropped the Christmas ornament into my cart but didn't trust myself to respond. I felt the anxiety claw its way up my throat and prayed for help.

"I forgot you're too holier-than-thou to talk to me now,"

Alyssa said, stepping closer. "Too good to interact with us low-lifes when the boss isn't making you."

I cringed. "I don't think I'm too good for you," I said, softly, unsure if the girls could hear me over the din of the shoppers.

"You're obviously not into honesty, then," Ruby piped up.

I wrinkled my brow. "What do you mean? I really don't think less of you or judge you or anything."

"Sorry we couldn't make it to your little party last night."

I froze. How did they know about the Thanksgiving dinner? They definitely didn't go to Café Graffiti.

"Who told you about the party?" I asked, immediately wanting to clamp my hand over my untrustworthy mouth.

Alyssa crossed her arms. "What? You mean you didn't want us to come? Ouch. You *do* think you're too good for us. Too high and mighty! Too straight and narrow to hang out with *sinners*." She spat the word like it was profane.

I tried to turn away, *so* over this conversation, but she grabbed my shoulder and pulled me back to her. "We're not done talking."

"Yeah, I think we are." This time I grabbed my cart and wove through the crowd to the back corner of the store. The framing gallery, where less people were. I needed to breathe for a moment.

I jumped as the girls stepped up to me.

"No, we're not done talking," Alyssa said.

I hadn't been too scared of them until now, when I realized we were less visible. *God, help me get out of here without breaking someone's nose.* "We're finally going to talk about how you ruined—"

"You're a bully!" I said loudly.

Alyssa looked like I'd slapped her, her face red and angry.

She stepped forward, and I drew in a breath as she drew back her hand.

Alyssa's eyes narrowed. "You—"

"Sadie! There you are. Aubrey and Nolan are waiting on us!" My eyes went wide as Fyn reached out and grabbed my arm, dragging me and my cart away from Alyssa and Ruby. "Sorry to cut this short!" she called to the girls over her shoulder. "Aubrey needs her coffee or there will be injuries."

Before I knew what was happening, she'd led me all the way to the check-out line. They actually had all of their lanes open for once, but the wait was still insane. I considered abandoning the cart and this entire, bizarre situation. I actually started to walk away, but Fyn still hadn't let go of my arm.

"Not yet," she hissed. "They're probably waiting for you."

Finally regaining words, I asked, "Who is Nolan?"

Out of all the questions I had, I didn't know why that one seemed to be the most important one for my brain to find words to ask, but there it was.

Fyn smiled and said, "Fig's real name," reminding me that absolutely nothing about the Larcy family made sense. "They're technically in the car waiting for me, and if my mom doesn't get her coffee soon, it won't be pretty."

I didn't know what to do with this information. So I tried another question: "How…?"

We shifted forward in line. Fyn finally dropped my arm, and I rubbed the spot where she'd gripped me too hard. She stared straight ahead as she spoke.

"I was getting framing ideas for a painting of Gran I've been working on for my dad's Christmas gift, when I saw you cornered. Not gonna lie, a part of me wanted to leave you there. But the part of me that reminds me I'm a Christian told me to step in. What did you do to those girls to make them so ticked at you?"

We stepped forward a few more feet. "They're the ones I've been avoiding all semester, remember?"

"Oh, boy." She released a breath. "Did they show up at your party? Maybe I shouldn't have invited them." She laughed nervously.

"Wait, what?"

"Good morning! Find everything you were looking for?" The cashier bubbled, her eyes too bright and her ponytail too bouncy for this time of morning.

"I'm not sure," I mumbled as I unloaded my cart on the belt. Turning back to Fyn, I said, "What do you mean you invited them? How could you?"

She crossed her arms over her chest. "First, I didn't know that tall one was *the* girl who's friends with Ruby. Second, I've been kinda depressed recently, and I wanted to meet some new people. But then I realized Ruby was a snot, so I decided to invite them to a youth group event instead."

"The one I was hosting?"

"I was just thinking they needed to be exposed to the Lord. And I knew I wouldn't be there."

We stared at each other, the cashier beeping things beside us. I mean, what did I say to that?

I opted not to say anything until I was outside with my cart, with no sign of the girls. I turned awkwardly to Fyn. It was so uncomfortable—like we'd gotten so close, so fast, and now we were strangers. "Hey, Fyn, thanks for saving me."

She offered a small smile. "Thanks for letting me. Look, I've been a jerk, I know that. Yeah, I'm hurting, but I forgive you. And I'm sorry for my part of it. You know I'm an all-or-nothing person. I can't pretend to be okay when I'm not."

I nodded, slowly. "Thank you." I didn't know how to proceed.

"I'm not all that used to real friends." Leave it to Fyn to fill the silence.

I lifted a shoulder and let it drop again. "I'm not so great, either. So…where do we go from here?"

She sighed. "I am sorry, and I do forgive you, but Glenna is still my sister, and she's really upset after your dad dumped her."

"He what?" How did I not know that?

"Yeah. A couple weeks ago. She says you made them break up. She's been in a mood."

"Yikes. That wasn't my fault. If that's what happened, it's because Dad made his own decision."

"Even so, she says you were completely against it, and that influenced your dad. So I just need some time before I hang out with you again."

"I get you." It just felt like it's what I should say, even if I didn't mean it. Fyn looked like she was about to step up to me and hug me, but after a pause, she said, "See ya around, Sadie."

I could only nod. While Truitt slept in the driver's seat and I loaded the Christmas stuff into the trunk of the car, I couldn't help but wonder if Fyn and I would ever get back to a healthy place.

But maybe that's what happens when two broken people try to have a whole friendship. It's bound to be messy.

Chapter Twenty-Four

○○○

"Where are we going, exactly?" Truitt asked later that afternoon. He clicked his seatbelt then popped the top on a Diet Coke.

I smiled because I knew it was bothering him that he couldn't be all macho-protector and drive for me. "Oh, don't get your briefs in a bunch, Yard Man. Enjoy the ride."

"First," he said, sipping from the can again, "I don't wear briefs. Second—"

"Okay!" I interrupted. "That's far beyond too much information." I pulled out of the driveway and took a deep breath, silently praying for the strength to survive what I was about to do. I couldn't explain it, but somehow I knew this was my next little step into the darkness.

Even though I hadn't been there in nearly a decade, I knew the directions by heart from all of the times I'd started the journey, but then chickened out. But now I had someone by my side and I had God.

We drove for about thirty-five minutes. We talked a bit, but I think Truitt sensed the weight in my heart, and he gradually stopped joking around.

Finally, we turned onto a gravel road. Tall fir trees lined the way, like fluffy soldiers standing guard outside a palace... protecting something sacred. I checked the notes I'd jotted on my palm only once so I'd know which way to turn. It had been sunny all day, and I was thankful for that. Rain would make things way too dramatic.

After checking my hand once more, I stopped the car, grabbed the package at my feet, and slowly opened the door.

Truitt exhaled slowly. "Are you sure?"

I nodded and reverently shut the car door behind me. I walked about fifteen feet until I arrived where I was going. Where maybe the past eight years had been leading me.

I felt a warm, steady hand on my shoulder, and I took a deep, stuttering breath.

"Truitt," I said softly, yet confidently, "I'd like you to meet my mom."

I spread my hands in the direction of the headstone.

Melody June Carter
Beloved Daughter, Wife, and Mother
Great is Thy Faithfulness, Lord, Unto Me

Beneath the line from her favorite hymn were her date of birth and her date of death. The date she entered the world in Augusta, Georgia, and the day she left the world on the way to my soccer practice in Seattle, Washington. Neither event, I now knew, had been a surprise to God.

I watched our breath in the nippy air. I was shaking but not from the weather. I led Truitt over to a little stone bench, which had been placed there in case I ever wanted to come visit. I could only recall sitting on it once before. We sat in silence, side-by-side, until I lost track of time, both of us looking at the place where Mom's body had been, unmoving, for now over half of my life. Finally, I looked down at the bouquet of pink carnations in my hands, studying them.

Then I stood slowly and made my way to the headstone, where I knelt down and placed the flowers in the concrete vase.

I sat on my knees, the cold from the ground seeping through my jeans, and adjusted the flowers.

"You know why I hate pink? Why I don't wear it? Why I nearly had an anxiety attack the first night I slept in Trissy's bubblegum-pink bedroom?" I asked into the stillness. If Truitt wondered why I chose to break the silence with such strange questions, he didn't let on.

Instead, he asked, "Why's that?" He leaned forward, but stayed on the bench, giving me space.

"It's because the day of the funeral, everything was pink. All of the flowers and wreaths and cards and even the fancy dress I was wearing." I also knew Mom had been buried in pink, because Melina had come to the house to pick out an outfit for her. "All my memories of that day are pink. Freaking *pink*, Truitt. I didn't even get to see my mom—just the spray of pink flowers on top of the casket." My shoulders slumped as I explained all I hadn't told anyone else before—not even Melina. I wasn't entirely sure why I was unloading it all on Truitt now. "Do you know the last time I saw her? She was being carried into the back of an ambulance. I didn't know it at the time, but she was already gone. My next memory is of all this pink. Stupid *pink!*" My throat was thick, and I coughed in an attempt to clear it. "Her favorite color became my least favorite because it reminded me of all I'd lost." I felt Truitt come close beside me, his shoulder brushing mine as he sat in the grass.

"Did you know she was so gentle and kind and loving, Truitt?" I said, staring straight ahead. "Did you know she truly loved God and wanted me to love Him too? It took me nearly nine years to get here. But she prayed for me. She prayed for Dad. She was so…" I couldn't take it anymore. I crumpled into myself, wrapping my arms around my middle, and wailed. "I miss her, Truitt!" I cried. "I've needed her so much, but God took her!" Truitt pulled my shaking body toward him until his chest was against my back, and his arms were securely wrapped around mine. "And I know God has a plan, I do, but I miss her. I brought her pink flowers because they're her favorite and that's more important than how I feel. All I want is my mom!"

I don't know how long we stayed there in the grass by the headstone under the tree, but I didn't care. I was finally able to grieve. Sure, I'd cried and processed over the summer. But I'd never shared so much with anyone, fearing I couldn't handle it. But this? This felt like permission to breathe more deeply than I'd breathed in so long. This felt like healing.

When I'd cried until the tears wouldn't come anymore and I was exhausted, Truitt helped me stand. Then he pulled me into a hug, holding me until the shaking stopped. When I finally pulled back, he put his hands on my shoulders.

"Your mom left an incredible legacy," he said.

I scrubbed my nose with the back of my hand. "What's that?"

"You."

I looked at him through swollen eyes. "Me?"

"You're her legacy, Sadie Grey Franklin. You're living, breathing proof that God is faithful and that He does have a purpose. I know you're into purpose."

Lyrics to Mom's hymn slowly played in my mind until I could see them clearly, almost hear her singing them: *Pardon for sin and a peace that endureth. Thine own dear presence to cheer and to guide. Strength for today and bright hope for tomorrow. Blessings all mine with ten thousand beside.*

Ever since I lost my mom, I'd bristled at the idea of God's faithfulness. After all, He was seemingly absent my whole life, especially in the tragedy. And while it could be tempting to believe He didn't care now, I couldn't deny He loved me and had a purpose for me. He'd forgiven all the wrong choices I'd made. And He'd given me strength for today and bright hope for tomorrow. No matter what happened, I'd be okay. Because the same God who welcomed my mom home nearly nine years ago was with me now.

I looked at Truitt and smiled slowly, wobbly, whispering, "You're the answer to a prayer I never dared to pray."

He wrapped his arm around me as we took one more look at the grave. "Right back at you."

———— oOo ————

"Highlight of my trip, easily," Truitt said, patting his stomach.

"Seriously? A piece of fish is the best moment of this past week?" My arm brushed against his as we strolled through downtown Seattle after a late lunch. My boots clicked against the pavement as we headed toward the waterfront, and I smiled to myself when he took my hand and squeezed it.

"A close second would be that time you accused me of being a dictator," he said. I bumped against his side with my elbow, and he winked.

To say the week had been an emotional rollercoaster would be an incredible understatement. From the tears to the sweet moments to the growing feelings I was too weary to fight—and wasn't even sure I wanted to—to the prayers to the arguments and that moment in the cemetery the day before, it had been a full week. In some ways, it felt like Truitt had only been here a couple days and the time had flown by; in other ways it felt like he'd been here forever.

So that's why, for Truitt's last day in Seattle, he'd convinced me to show him the city since Cannonball's was closed for the holiday weekend while Greg lived it up with his extended family in Yakima.

It was kind of fun playing tourist with him, especially

since it'd been a while since I'd paid attention to the sights. We started the day early, grabbing big cups of coffee and sharing an umbrella as the sky drizzled and we walked around the city. We stood in the shadow of the Space Needle and admired the wacky exterior of the EMP Museum. Truitt promised to bring a passport next time and I promised we'd catch a ferry and explore Victoria, British Columbia.

We explored the Olympic Sculpture garden, and I showed Truitt the original Starbucks' location. We added our own chewing gum to the Gum Wall—which was just as gross as it sounds. He was thrilled to no end at the men throwing fish at Pike Place Market, and we explored all the shops under the market. He grabbed my hand, pulling me over to a Bigfoot sculpture and begging me to take his picture with it. Which reminded me of Fyn's tourist game and made me sad. But I forced myself not to think about her. Not today. Not when Truitt was here and we were exploring my city together.

After that, we bought tickets to go up the Columbia tower. I'd never done that before, but supposedly, you could go higher than the Space Needle for a lower price, and since the sky had cleared, the view was amazing. We entered the elevator and began the trip up to the seventy-third floor, while I chattered on about different places we could eat dinner. I hadn't noticed he'd grown quiet beside me until we reached our stop.

I stepped out and turned to find him still in the elevator. "Are you coming?" I asked. I thought I saw him gulp. "Are you okay?" I reached out a hand to keep the elevator door open so it wouldn't take him back down to the ground floor. He nodded and slowly stepped out, staying against the wall.

I cocked my head and looked at him. "What's wrong?"

He stuffed his hands in his pockets and leaned against the wall. "I'm actually not the biggest fan of heights," he said so quietly I had to lean in to hear.

I chuckled. "You? Afraid of heights? Please."

He arched his brows. "I'm completely serious."

I lowered my voice to match his as another group of people exited the elevator. "Why didn't you say something before?"

He shrugged. "I wanted to see the sights, do the tourist thing. And you were so excited to show me everything, so…" He trailed off and I saw him bend his knees slightly.

I looked around. I definitely wanted to check out the 360-degree view, especially since the sky was clear enough. And we'd paid for it. "We'll go back down." I pushed the elevator button.

"No, I'll be all right," he insisted. He took a deep breath and exhaled. Reaching for my hand, he said, "Let's see Seattle."

I let him hold onto my hand. His hold was more like a scared child grabbing his mom's hand than anything remotely romantic. His palms were clammy, and it was all I could do not to let go and dry mine off. We slowly made our way over to a window. "Oh, hey, cool!" I said, pointing to a sign on the wall indicating how high up we were. "This says we're—"

"Please don't." Truitt said. I couldn't stop my laugh. He truly couldn't handle how high up we were. I thought Truitt was fearless when it came to things like that. Or anything else, really. He gripped my hand tighter and I heard him take another breath as we looked out over the city.

"Holy cow," he exhaled.

"Ditto." We stood there in silence for a minute or five, him drawing strength from me for once, my hand held firm in his grasp. I looked down at the map in front of the window. "We should be able to see the Space Needle from here."

"There," he whispered, pointing out the tower. We toured our way around the room, finding other landmarks. We found two of the Hammering Man sculptures scattered throughout the city, pointed out boats in the water, and gazed at Mt. Rainer in the distance. After a while, Truitt sat down on a bench toward the middle of the room while I continued my self-guided tour. I could've stayed up there all day, but Truitt started to look a little green, so we made our way back to the elevator.

"How in the world did you survive the plane ride over?" I asked when we were safely back on the ground.

"I spent most of it in that closet they call a bathroom." He laughed. "Flying was an experience."

I turned to look at him. "That was your first flight?"

He smiled, and his chin dimple popped. "Yeah."

"Wow." It hit me again how much he'd done to be here for me. Flying for the first time, knowing heights made him squeamish. Spending all that money on tickets, navigating airports…

Later, as we made our way back to the market to eat before dark, I asked, "When did you decide to come, Truitt?"

My hand in his, Truitt gently swung my arm as we walked. "It wasn't even a decision. I just did it. When I finished talking to you that night, after you told me all you were dealing with, I booked my flight. Then I convinced Kurt to drive me to Atlanta and give me a crash-course on all things airports."

"But heights freak you out…"

"The thought of you hurting three thousand miles away freaked me out more."

He held a door open for me, and we entered the restaurant. We ate on the second floor of an old building overlooking Pike Place Market. I was tired from the day, but as wide-awake as I'd felt in months, all at the same time. I contentedly ate my fish as Truitt caught me up on his plans to expand his lawn care business in the summer and potentially launch his own company.

Now, as we walked down to the Puget Sound, the sun

sinking toward the water, the reality that I was about to be forced to jump out of this dreamland and into the real world again began to sink into my heart.

"A lot of people like sunrises the best," Truitt said, his arms folded on the railing as we looked over the water. The Sound seemed extra alive tonight, like the rain had given everything a renewed energy. "But I'm a fan of sunsets."

"Why? Because sunrises require waking up at insane hours?"

Truitt chuckled. "That too. But to me, a sunset is like God saying, 'See? Told you you'd make it through the day. I'm faithful.'"

"I like that," I admitted softly. I'd seen so many sunsets recently, but never thought of them as a sign of God's faithfulness. More of just a reminder that darkness was on its way.

A few yards away, a musician played soft jazz on a saxophone. An older couple stepped away from the railing and began dancing. I smiled but felt sad. I wondered what it would be like to be old and known and still enjoy somebody's company like that, but I couldn't see beyond the struggle I currently faced to imagine that kind of contentment.

"Wanna dance?" Truitt's voice brought me back, and I realized he was holding out his hand.

I shook my head. "Absolutely not. Sadie Franklin doesn't slow dance." I'd done my fair share of party dancing, but wasn't much for a soft melody.

Truitt wouldn't take no for an answer. He grabbed my hand and tugged me to him, just firmly enough that I couldn't pull away, despite my protests of having two left feet and an affinity for stepping on my partner's shoes and bumping into nearby objects.

Truitt just laughed as we figured out a rhythm. It was a

simple dance where we just sort of shuffled our feet, one of my hands in his, the other resting on his shoulder, while his other hand rested lightly on my waist.

"What's up?" he said, and I realized I was staring at him.

I focused on my feet for a minute. "This is going better than my middle school dances."

He laughed again as the saxophonist began playing a soulful rendition of "What a Wonderful World."

My world was so not wonderful. In fact, it was currently very broken, and I knew the hard times weren't over yet. Truitt hummed along, purposefully off-key, making me laugh despite my deep thoughts. I didn't want to forget about things, because they'd still be there when the dance ended, and remembering would make me feel discouraged all over again. But I couldn't turn my eyes away from the guy who held me gently, yet made me feel so very secure. And so we danced.

I couldn't deny the way my breath synced with his. Or the way my pulse pumped too quickly for our slow dance. Or the way he saw me when he looked at me—not all of my junk and all of my heartache, but *me*. And not even just me. It was like he saw more than me. Not who I was or what I'd done, but what I could become.

A tear slipped onto my cheek before I realized I was crying. Without interrupting our dance, he brushed the tear away with his thumb.

"Thank you," I whispered, my voice thick with the rest of the tears waiting for their chance to escape.

He kind of smiled with one side of his mouth. "Couldn't let it stay there. Might mess up your makeup."

I shook my head and removed my hand from his shoulder to brush the bangs from my eyes. Behind us, the saxophone sang on. "No, not just for that. For. . .everything. Absolutely everything. For coming to Seattle, for helping me through this nightmare with my dad, for…" I drew in a shaky breath, "for *seeing* me, Truitt. You see me, and yet you're still here."

He shrugged, "I'm still here *because* I see you. I've decided you're terminal to me."

I raised an eyebrow, pulling back slightly so I could see his whole face. "What does that even mean?"

"It means I'll never get over you."

The music stopped, and the musician prepared to play another song. Truitt took my hand and led me over to a patch of grass.

We sat there, side-by-side, and stared at the rich Pacific Northwest sunset screaming vibrant colors of pink and orange and yellow. "So, if I'm terminal…" I wove my fingers into the soft, chilly grass. "What does that mean for us?"

I'd never had a problem with boldness around guys, not even around Truitt. It was so weird because we were so close in other areas, but for some reason, I felt shy talking about this. About *us*.

Truitt leaned back on his elbows, his eyes never leaving the sky. "I wish I'd never made that promise to your uncle," he muttered.

"What?"

He tilted his head to look at me. "I promised Kurt I wouldn't start something I couldn't finish."

"What does that mean?"

He sighed. "Look. I'm about to travel three thousand miles back to Georgia while you stay up here. Never mind the fact you're the first girl I've ever really cared about—"

"Wait." I put my hand up. "What do you mean by that? Haven't you dated?"

"Let's put it this way," he said. The color in his cheeks deepened, and it had nothing to do with the shadows lengthening around us. "That kiss in the hospital? That's the first one I've ever given."

My ears warmed at his vulnerable confession. I thought back to the night my baby cousin was born and I saw Truitt for the first time since we'd both worked through some big stuff, since I gave my life to Jesus and Truitt chose to get help for his mom and her addictions. The kiss was quick, but I could still feel it months later. Even still, I couldn't believe that was the first time Truitt had kissed a girl.

"That wasn't a real kiss, Truitt." I couldn't help teasing him. The moment was too thick and needed some laughter. "That was like stamping a postcard or something."

"Oh, really?" He cocked an eyebrow. "Then how's a real kiss different?"

I looked over to where the musician was packing up his instrument for the evening. "A real kiss is like. . .a song."

He laughed. "Where did that come from?"

I tossed my hands in the air. "I don't know how to explain it. It just felt like something profound to say."

"I've never been good at reading music," Truitt eased himself up off his elbows and turned to face me. "So maybe you could play it for me."

And then he leaned close and I closed my eyes so I could see it all at once and his lips met mine and the whole moment felt like I was free falling. Like the ground opened up beneath me and caught my stomach and stole my breath. And then when he brought his hands to my face and I felt his smile against my own, I realized I *was* falling. I was falling for the small-town Georgia boy with the annoying Southernisms and frustrating stubbornness and heart bigger than the Puget Sound.

And I didn't want anyone to catch me.

Chapter Twenty-Five

oOo

Truitt's flight left early the next morning, so we stayed out until the sun had completely disappeared, then drove home. We'd planned to go to bed sooner, since the cab was scheduled to pick up Truitt at four-thirty in the morning. But we ended up sitting at the kitchen table, drinking coffee and talking about anything and everything. About him and me and what we could look like. About faith and purpose and how I needed to stop trying to prove myself to God and just live like His beloved daughter. I was so tired, but I didn't want to sleep. Because although I knew I'd be visiting Georgia in just a few weeks, that seemed too far away.

Finally, though, Truitt said he was going to bed, so I went into my room. I thought I'd be too caffeinated to sleep, but I was out as soon as my head hit the pillow.

Truitt must have slipped me decaf.

oOo

"Sadie!"

I moaned and burrowed deeper into my blankets.

"Sadie, wake up!"

Now I felt a hand gently shaking my shoulder. I slowly sat up, squinting at the light from the hallway coming into my room. A shadowy figure stood over me.

"My cab's going to be here in a few minutes," said the figure. I was finally conscious enough to realize it was Truitt.

"What?" I frantically reached for my phone. "My alarm. It was supposed to—oh." I dropped my head back against my pillow, realizing I'd set the alarm for *PM*, rather than *AM*.

I sat back up and pulled my hair into a ponytail. "I was gonna make you coffee—"

"I'll get some at the airport. I'll wait out there," he said before slipping out of my room and closing the door. I flipped on the lamp sitting on my bedside table and shuffled into a pair of sweats and a hoodie. I scurried into the bathroom to brush my teeth, then found Truitt in the kitchen.

"Okay, I told your Dad goodbye last night," he said as if rattling off a mental list, handing me a cup of orange juice. I accepted it, but knew I was too frazzled to drink it right then. Plus, fresh breath and everything. I looked down into the juice, and my eyes clouded.

"Hey," he said softly, so as not to wake my dad in the next room. "I'll see you at Christmas. You're gonna be okay."

I nodded, afraid if I looked up at that chin dimple and those brown eyes and that hair curling out from beneath that ball cap, my heart wouldn't be able to take it. Instead, when he opened his arms, I accepted the invitation, stepping into the warmth and security and stability that was Truitt Peyton.

"Don't forget about me," I whispered.

"Sadie, I can honestly say you are always the last thing on my mind."

I pulled away and stared at him, my brow furrowed. "Ouch."

He winced. "Sorry. You are always the last thing on my mind, and always the first thing on my mind, too," he finished, laughing. He pulled me back into his arms. I'd never been one for mushiness, but somehow along the way, this boy's cheesy way of talking grew on me. "Besides," he mumbled into the hair by my ear. "We've got some serious praying to do, and we'll need to talk some more about...all of this." He gently pushed me back so he could look at my face. "Because right now, all I know is I don't even want to think about what's next if it doesn't include you, Sadie Grey Franklin."

I could parrot the same back to him. Truitt had so clearly been placed in my life for a purpose. For friendship, for stability, and now?

I glanced at the clock on the stove. *4:25.* Five minutes.

I leaned up and kissed his cheek. Old Sadie wouldn't have known so much restraint, but the moment felt sacred and pure somehow, and I wanted to honor that. "Thank you," I said, smiling. Outside, a horn honked once, brief.

I walked Truitt to the door, where his luggage waited.

"Well," I shrugged, trying to keep the moment light. "Later, Yard Man."

Unexpectedly, Truitt pulled me to him, kissing me like the first time back in Georgia. Gentle, but with more promise. It wasn't long, and it wasn't very deep, but it would have to be enough for me to hold onto until we could figure us out.

Truitt hugged me tightly, then swung his backpack over his shoulder. "See you soon, Franklin."

And then he slipped out the door, taking a piece of my heart further away with each step toward the waiting cab.

We set the Christmas tree up Sunday night. Dad had moved to the sofa, where he sat with a mug of hot chocolate in his hands, Moose curled up beside him, watching me. Truitt's visit had been so good for Dad. He'd needed some guy time to talk football and yard equipment and whatever else they were discussing that time I walked in on them having a conversation over a bag of beef jerky. I turned on some Christmas music and began fluffing the fake tree I'd bought. It was a little patchy in places, but I hoped the ornaments would hide its lack of quality.

While Bing crooned about a white Christmas, I reverently opened the box of ornaments. Most were handmade by me when I was a little kid. So many tiny Sadie handprints. Dad asked me to help him stand, and Moose hopped off the couch and began sniffing the ornaments in the box.

"Oh no, you don't," I told him. I hadn't yet figured out how to keep him away from the tree, but I did know all of the best ornaments would be placed out of his reach.

Memories flooded my mind as I hung the ornaments. I saw these decorations every year, of course, but their impact never stopped hitting me. We'd hung these—as a family—when I was a little girl. Or if Dad wasn't home, Mom and I decorated the tree. Either way, Mom was always there. A constant.

A few minutes later, Dad came back into the living room, holding a small box. He opened it and pulled out a glass ball ornament with my parents' wedding date hand-painted on the outside.

"Wow," I breathed. "I haven't seen this one in forever."

Dad reached up and placed it near the top of the tree. "Decided we might as well use it to decorate."

"What's that inside?" I asked, wondering for the first time why the ball was stuffed with paper.

Dad finished hanging the ornament, carefully bending the hook around the branch so it wouldn't slide off.

"Those," he said slowly, "are our vows. You're mentioned in there."

I studied the ornament through cloudy vision as "What Child is This" faded into the background. I was mentioned in those vows? It made sense, I guess, because they already knew I existed. I was the reason they got married, after all. The reason they did the "right" thing to try to make up for the "wrong" thing that was the night that led to me.

"I guess if I hadn't happened, we wouldn't have this ornament." I brought my hand to my mouth. I totally didn't mean to verbalize my train of thought.

"That's true," Dad said, and his confession stung a little. My parents' relationship had always been rocky, and I'd had to realize over time that I couldn't blame their unhappiness on my existence.

"But," Dad continued, carefully shoving Moose away from the tree with his good foot. "You were the motivation I needed to make a commitment."

I set down the plastic gingerbread man I was holding. I'd never heard him talk like that before. "Seriously?"

"There was no way I'd leave Melody alone to raise a baby. You were just as much mine as hers, and she was the mother of my kid. A man takes responsibility for his family, even if he's still a kid himself. Just because you're a dad and a husband doesn't mean you automatically grow up, but it does mean it's your job to take care of your family."

I was honestly speechless—a rarity. I'd never heard any of this before. I'd always thought my parents got married to cover up what they did. But the marriage was actually Dad owning up to the responsibility he'd been given? And he said Mom's name. I hadn't heard him call her by her name in so long.

"Dad..." I began, but my words caught in my throat.

"I've never been anywhere near perfect, Sadie," Dad said when I didn't continue. "But we didn't get married out of obligation because your mom was pregnant. Yeah, that was a big factor. But we got married because we chose to. We chose to build a life together and give our child a house with a mom and a dad."

Tears trailed slowly down my face. I'd never heard my dad say so much at once without yelling in anger. But to think that my parents decided to own the life they'd been given when they found out Mom was pregnant was a game-changer, a world-rocker for me. They had decided to fight the odds and opposition and give me a shot at a decent life. Mom had been his other half, even if the other half sometimes looked like a puzzle piece that didn't quite fit.

"See that one?" Dad pointed to one of the first ornaments I'd hung. It was a little porcelain dove with a banner that read *peace*.

"That one's pretty."

"You know your mom was carrying twins, right?"

I nodded, slowly. I'd just learned that this summer, while I was in Georgia. The doctor told me one of the effects of my medical condition was that I might one day have trouble conceiving a child, but if I could get pregnant, my chance of having multiples was higher. Then I learned my mom also had PCOS...and she had carried twins until one of the babies died early on. So not only did she get pregnant when she didn't think it was possible, she'd also carried two babies. Me, and a brother or sister I'd never met. It was all so crazy and amazing at the same time. My whole life, I'd felt like a mistake, when my life was actually a miracle. This summer Kurt and Melina helped me see that God had a very specific purpose for my unlikely life. That's when my world changed.

But now, back in my living room with my dad and Celine Dion singing on the TV, I nodded. "Yeah," I said softly, "I know."

Dad reached out and touched the dove with two of his fingers. "I got this one for your brother or sister on your first Christmas to help us remember."

I had to sit down. I pulled Moose into my lap and kissed

the top of his head. I'd seen that ornament every year of my life but never knew it belonged to the memory of my brother or sister. I never knew my parents carried that added grief. I knew Mom had lost the baby before they could even know the gender, but still. It was their other baby.

"Dad," I said, looking up at him. So tall from where I sat on the floor. "Thank you for telling me that."

Dad glanced at something across the room, his eyes misty. I'd never seen him so visibly process emotion before. It was unsettling and comforting at the same time.

But just as soon as the moment had started, the heaviness left as Moose jumped out of my arms and ran to bark at a car driving by outside the window.

I stood back up and wiped my eyes, then went back to putting ornaments on the tree.

The music changed again, this time to "Jingle Bell Rock."

"So you're leaving in a couple of weeks," Dad said. Man, he was talkative tonight. It was a statement, not a question. I hoped that meant he was okay with it and the bonding moment we'd just shared wouldn't be killed with an argument. Instinctively, I braced myself.

"Yeah. I'm getting my ticket this week." I smiled at the thought. I'd done it—I'd saved enough money to pay half. Kurt and Melina would pay the other half as a Christmas gift.

"And you're coming back, right?" Dad asked. I knew he was joking, or at least I thought so, but it still wasn't an easy question to answer. Truitt's visit had made me more homesick than before, and leaving while Dad and I were getting along would make the holiday even sweeter.

"I'll be back New Year's Day."

Dad nodded, adding a little sledding Santa to the tree. "I think it's good you're going."

That was the last thing I expected him to say. I looked up from prying a plastic candy cane from Moose's jaws. "Really?"

He nodded again, more slowly, more thoughtfully. "Your heart hasn't been here since you were there. I saw how you brightened when Truitt showed up. You're thinking about that place all the time. You've been counting down the days to when you can go back ever since you got here."

Had he seen the countdown app on my phone? I focused on adjusting the tooth-marked candy cane on the tree.

"And I think they want you there, too. Truitt flew all the way across the country just to see you." He chuckled. "I like that guy."

The praise of Truitt should've thrilled me, but I was stuck on what he'd said earlier. "You can still tell that's always my focus?"

"Oh, yeah. You want to make Kurt and Mel proud. You want to try for a chance with Truitt. You even work at a kid's place, of all the jobs, because you miss being around your cousins. You need to be where your heart is."

The way he said it made me think of what Liz told me earlier in the fall: "Wherever you are, be all there." She told me to look up the rest of the quote, and I hadn't done it. Now I couldn't remember where the quote was from. I'd have to text her about it.

I suddenly wanted to know where Dad's heart was. After tonight, I wanted to think it had been with Mom all along, but what about Glenna? Would she be back one day? I certainly didn't want to bring that up again. That wasn't a conversation either of us was ready for.

We finished decorating the tree, then Dad went to the kitchen for some popcorn and I set up my childhood nativity on the mantle. Out of all the uncertainties in my life, one thing was sure: This Christmas would be different than any I'd ever experienced.

Because this year, I knew that Baby in the manger.

———oOo———

Somehow, life settled back into a rhythm. Dad was searching for jobs during all of his downtime, and he'd found a few options to check out as soon as he was healed enough to work. In the meantime, since he was more mobile now, Roger no longer came to our house. Instead, I took Dad to his physical therapy sessions, where I sat in the waiting room working on homework...and researching airline tickets to use in just a couple of weeks.

I missed Truitt more than ever, and the feeling of Christmas everywhere made me long for my family in Georgia. I needed to order the tickets by the end of the week so they didn't sell out during the holiday travel season. Now that I'd saved enough money, I could only pray there were still some good flight options left. School would end a handful of days before Christmas, and I planned to fly out the next morning, giving me about a week and a half in Georgia before I had to be back to finish up senior year. It wasn't much, but it would have to do until summer. Just thinking about summer made me bounce up and down. I'd been spending way too much time around Moose.

After I bought my tickets, end-of-semester projects and studying for exams kept me from focusing on anything other than passing my classes.

I still saw Fyn at school, and we were civil, but it wasn't the same. We survived our presentation without any casualties, which I chalked up to a miracle. Though we got along during the presentation, awkwardness still lingered, like an invisible wall neither of us knew how to climb. We could see each other, but we couldn't actually communicate. I was so torn between fighting for one of the only true friends I'd ever had and trusting God to do what was best. It wasn't fun. But one fun thing was watching Fyn and Owen begin to interact at Café Graffiti. That gave me hope that maybe God wasn't finished with our friendship yet.

I wrapped my cousins' Christmas gifts and packed them into a box I could mail so that it would meet me in Pecan Creek. I arranged for Moose to stay with Owen so Dad wouldn't have to keep up with him, and I arranged for Dad to spend Christmas Day with Jordan and Claire. Dad had said he'd think about it. That was enough for me.

It was weird—Dad was gaining his independence again, and I was even sleeping in my own bed. But I still felt the need to handle everything for him. I was so glad he was getting better, though. I knew if he'd spent one more week recliner-bound, we both would've lost it.

Chapter Twenty-Six

○○○

I'd just rolled out of bed to go to the bathroom when I heard movement in the kitchen. I followed the noise over to the sink, where I stumbled over Dad on the floor.

"Dad! What's going on?"

I flipped on the light and knelt down. He was soaked in a cold sweat and shaking with chills.

He pulled himself into a sitting position. "I—I don't know." He paused to hack some more. "This strong pain in my leg made me dizzy, and…"

"Oh, Dad." My stomach rolled. I knelt down to steady myself and get a closer look at his leg. I couldn't see much with the splint, but I could tell his leg looked red and angry around where one of the screws went in. "I'm taking you to the ER."

"No, I'm fine. Get me back to—" He attempted to stand, but dropped back to the floor. That couldn't feel good to his healing ribs.

Pushing aside the thought of the exam I had the next day, I helped him to his room. "Let's get you changed and to the doctor."

He didn't argue this time, just bit his lip to keep from moaning in pain.

I helped him put on a clean t-shirt and a coat, then drove him to the ER.

When we finally arrived at the hospital, we sat in a corner

of the waiting room. He gripped the arms of his chair with his hands as a cold sweat broke out on his forehead again. I felt helpless.

A nurse stepped into the room and called Dad's name. I stood and helped Dad to his feet.

"I'll go back there with you so we'll both know what's going on." It's not like I hadn't been invading Dad's privacy every day of his life over the past couple months anyway.

But Dad shook his head. "No, I'll be okay."

I wasn't convinced, but I sat down to wait.

So while I waited, I stared at the sad little fake Christmas tree set up in the corner. The colored lights flickered sporadically, and the angel perched on top leaned dangerously far to the right. The ornaments looked like snowflakes someone had cut from coffee filters.

When the doctor finally emerged without Dad, he said they were going to admit him to the hospital for surgery.

"What's going on?" I asked the doctor.

"Your dad has an infection in his leg," he said, looking over a chart.

No. Oh, no. "Are you for real?"

The doctor nodded. "Yes. We're going to go in and clean out the infection, then get him started on IV medication to take care of it."

I followed him to the desk. "How did this happen?"

The doctor shook his head. "It's at one of his incision sites. Sometimes bacteria can get in."

"Is he going to be okay?" We needed another setback like Moose needed more energy.

"As long as he takes the antibiotics we give him, he should be fine. He'll just need to be on the medicine for a few weeks."

"And how long will he be in the hospital?"

The doctor offered a soft smile. "Hopefully just a couple of days. They'll get him home soon."

I hung my head, exhausted by this latest update. And by the fact it was somewhere in the middle of the night. "Okay, thanks."

He patted my shoulder, then gave me instructions on where to find Dad.

I was glad he didn't seem to want me to stay because I feared I would have a meltdown. After checking in on him, I went home to catch a couple hours of sleep before my exam.

True to the doctor's word, the hospital released Dad two days later. After picking him up in the afternoon, we went through the drive-thru at the pharmacy to pick up his prescription. On the way home, silent tears rolled down my cheeks while Christmas tunes crackled through the radio. I was *so* very tired of being a caregiver. So very tired of pausing everything in my own life to help someone else survive theirs. So tired of PT and doctor appointments and painkillers and antibiotics. Already tired of Dad's grumpy mood that was sure to return with this new setback. So tired of setbacks, period.

It was supposed to be the most wonderful time of the year. The season to be jolly. Joy to the world, and all that. Next weekend couldn't come soon enough.

Sure enough, Dad's dark mood returned stronger than ever. I imagined he was probably even more over his issues than I was. Even though the infection wasn't as bad as it could've been, I couldn't blame him for his frustration. He was so close to being healed, and now he was immobile again while the medicine fought for him. Home help stopped by once a day to check in and administer the drugs via IV, and I was back to caring for him whenever I wasn't at school.

His mood also meant no more sweet father-daughter moments around the tree, reminiscing. Instead, he watched TV all day.

I was able to sneak away to the tacky sweater Christmas party at Café Graffiti two Fridays before Christmas. I'd taken the whole afternoon off work so I could clean the house, study for exams, and stop by the party.

"Sadie! What's up? How's your dad?" Liz popped up next to me as I decorated a Christmas cookie shaped like a little sweater. She was wearing her Christmas tree costume from Halloween.

I took a bite of the cookie, knowing I'd regret eating it later. "He's improving. And I haven't felt like passing out whenever I see the PICC line stuck in his hand for the IV."

She high-fived me. "Way to go, Sadie!"

"What did Sadie do?" Owen stepped up next to us and looked me over, a curious expression on his face.

"Sadie hasn't fainted."

He grinned and handed me a cup of apple cider. Raising his own in a toast, he said, "To Sadie!"

Liz laughed. "Here, here!"

Owen turned to talk to another guy, and I pulled Liz aside. "What was that quote you told me a while back? I never looked it up."

She sipped her cider. "Which one?"

"The missionary."

"Oh, Jim Elliot?"

I nodded and sipped my own cider before wincing. Way too hot. "Yeah. That one."

She looked off into the distance over my shoulder as she recited it: "Wherever you are, be all there."

I nodded, encouraging her to go on. "But you said there was more to it."

"Oh, yeah. There is."

"Liz! Come on!" Jen grabbed Liz by the arm and dragged her toward stage.

"I'll text it to you!" she called over her shoulder.

I found a seat near some of the people who'd been to my house at Thanksgiving. After we sang a few carols, Jordan spoke for a minute before the games started. I made an honest attempt to just enjoy the games and the friends around me, but I was so anxious to get away from the Fyn drama and the Dad drama and the school drama and just be with my family. My mind was constantly in a state of countdown.

I even carried on the countdown with my cousins. Each day, I texted a picture of myself holding up the number of fingers that matched the days before I'd see them again. Then they'd send a picture back.

School ended on a Thursday, and Christmas was on Monday. My flight went out on Friday morning. My precalculus exam went miraculously well, and it took all of my restraint not to burst into song and skip out to my car afterward. Instead of taking a victory lap around the city, I took Moose to Owen's, surprised at how emotional the goodbye turned out to be. He'd been my little buddy through everything, and I knew I'd miss him like crazy, even though it was only for a couple of weeks. Besides, I for sure couldn't afford a plane ticket for a dog. I had checked.

When I got back, Dad was walking around the house. A great sign. He was even sleeping in his own bed again, which meant our living room no longer looked like a frat house. It also meant he would be okay without me for a little while.

"How are you feeling?" I asked, slipping out of my coat.

"Better. What time is your flight Friday?"

"Six-thirty in the morning." Hey, I didn't believe in wasting time. I was already losing sleep over my excitement.

He didn't say anything, just pulled a leftover container of tuna salad out of the fridge and grabbed a fork before returning to his chair.

I followed him into the living room.

"And you're sure you'll be okay?" *Please, God, don't let him change his mind!*

"I'm fine, Sadie. I'm moving around again and I'm clear to drive. I can take care of myself."

That last statement was a little tense. "Right."

"What does that mean?" He stuck his fork in the tuna, but didn't eat any yet.

"Nothing. It just means you're right—you *can* take care of yourself. Oh, and before I forget—Raining Grace is having a candlelight Christmas Eve service. It's at seven, and—"

"Sadie." Tuna forgotten, he just looked at me.

"I just thought—"

"You know better than to suggest I go to church."

I should've left it at that, I know, but I felt this strange need to defend God—even though I knew He could handle it Himself. "But don't you think you should go? God kept you alive with a miracle. God helped you heal."

"God let me lose my job. God let me go through a horrible accident. God let me get an infection. God made me a widower before I even turned thirty. God let the only girl I've dated since your mother get away. Should I go on?"

I shot back, "Why are you so negative?"

He didn't say anything more, and I wanted to throw my hands over my mouth. But I stood there, staring him down.

"Give me some space, Sadie," he finally said.

"Gladly. By this time tomorrow, I'll be on the other side of the country, completely out of your space."

"You know what I mean."

"I know exactly what you mean. I'm going for a run."

I changed clothes, then slipped out of the house, taking off down the street. "Why is he so impossibly difficult?" I prayed out loud. "Why doesn't he realize how much I've sacrificed for him and done for him? How hard is it to even say 'thank you'? I mean, really!"

I was angry, and my breath came ragged. I hadn't stretched or warmed up, just taken off, full-speed ahead.

After I ran and showered, I sat in the middle of my floor, my biggest suitcase beside me with a pile of jeans spilling out, wishing Moose were with me for moral support. Packing was the worst.

I texted Truitt: *12 hours.*

He replied a moment later: *So glad you get to spend Christmas where your heart is home.*

Okay, that was extremely sappy, even for Truitt.

Are you watching Hallmark Christmas movies...?

I need to know if Laura can forgive Steve for dumping her in high school!

I laughed. He was *so* messing with me. As I crawled into bed, my phone dinged again. Truitt was probably about to spoil the ending of the movie for me.

Instead, it was a text from Liz. *Finally remembered to text you that quote. Sorry! It's:*

"Wherever you are, be all there! Live to the hilt every situation you believe to be the will of God."

I didn't know what "to the hilt" meant, so I asked. A moment later, she replied:

It means all the way. Wholly. Fully. Completely. Totally.

I thought that over for a few minutes as I burrowed deep beneath my blankets, making a little cave. Live fully in every situation I believe to be the will of God?

I was so new at the whole faith thing. I only knew the basics about being a Christian, much less any inside info about

God's will. His will was whatever He wanted for my life, right? Like my purpose?

I reached over and clicked on my bedside lamp. Grabbing my Bible off my nightstand, I flipped open the cover to the handwritten note Melina had penned before they gave the Bible to me as a gift. I'd read it so many times before, but this moment of confusion seemed to call for the clarity it offered. I skimmed until I came to the middle of the note:

> *Remember this moment. Remember when God felt closer than your next breath and His love felt more constant than your heartbeat. When life spins out of control and you don't know what's next, remember this moment when you realized God's love for you is the most real thing in all the world. Always remember. And when you can't handle it on your own, give up. Dare to trust Him and watch Him do the impossible.*

I traced the pretty letters with my fingertips, reading them in Melina's voice. Trust. I'd said I trusted God, but looking back, I was really trusting in myself to hold it all together and make myself worth God's time.

Slowly, something shifted inside me. I'd had it backward all along. Truitt told me that, but I hadn't really listened. I still felt so sure of my own capabilities. It was like I needed to prove to God I was worth saving. He'd moved heaven and earth for me, so I needed to show Him it wasn't a waste. But then, wasn't the purpose of it all the fact that Jesus lived the perfect life I could never live? In my place? Kurt and Mel assured me I could never earn God's love, but I could never lose it either. I just needed to trust.

Could I really trust in more than me? In a God I never heard speak? I had no choice. This faith thing was all or nothing.

"All I want is You," I whispered to the God who hadn't

given up on me. Not when I lived my own, self-destructive way, and not when I tried to work hard to prove I was worth loving. "I don't want anything else anymore. I only want You."

And it started with being all there. Now, on my last night in Seattle for a little while ... and tomorrow, when my thirsty heart got to soak up all of the love of my family. I clicked off the light and burrowed back beneath the covers, Truitt's and Jim Elliot's words blending together in my mind.

Where your heart is home...be all there.

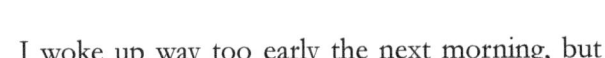

I woke up way too early the next morning, but I didn't mind at all. I wheeled my suitcase down the hallway and into the kitchen for a quick cup of coffee, even though I was already jittery without the caffeine. My heart was going home.

I'd actually convinced Dad to drive me to the airport. I think he was just so anxious to leave the house after not driving in so long, he probably would've driven me straight to Georgia.

Or maybe not.

While I waited for him to emerge from his man cave, I anxiously sipped my coffee in the living room. I flipped on the tree lights and smiled. It had been so long since I'd felt this kind of anticipation.

In the summer, I'd reluctantly left Seattle. Who would want to travel across the country for a summer with people they barely knew? But that's what I had done. I had no choice—Dad was sending me away. I'd needed the chance to start over, whether I wanted it or not.

And by the time summer was over, I hadn't wanted to leave. I tried to talk Melina into homeschooling me with the rest of her kids or enrolling me at Pecan Creek High. I even promised to help out with the kids for free. But she told me I couldn't run away forever. I had to go back and try to fix things with Dad and everything else I'd messed up.

I glanced at my phone. We needed to leave in five minutes.

I walked down the hall and knocked on his door. No answer. Maybe he was in his bathroom getting ready. He was still moving slowly, after all.

After a couple more minutes, I knocked again with no answer.

I dropped to the ground and looked under his door. The light wasn't on.

Standing back up, I slowly turned the doorknob and stepped inside. The light from the hallway spilled into the room as I walked over to the bed, where Dad slept.

I grabbed his phone off the nightstand and checked his alarms. They weren't set.

I gently shook his shoulder. "Dad. Dad, get up!"

He groaned and slowly opened his eyes. Running a hand over his face, he asked, "What time is it?"

"Time to leave for the airport!"

"My alarm…"

"Yeah, about that. It wasn't set." I tried to hide the panic creeping into my words.

"Oh." He struggled to sit up, wincing at the soreness of his ribs. "Give me five minutes and I'll be ready."

I clicked on his light as I left the room and heard him groan again.

About ten minutes later, he finally emerged to find me doing some burpees by the light of the Christmas tree. Exercise was how I dealt with anxiousness.

"Let's go!" I jumped up and grabbed my coat.

"We might need to arrange a ride for you," Dad said, leaning against the wall.

"Why? You're up."

"I'm having a hard time moving around."

Excuses. I sighed. "Why is that?"

He tried to take a step, but his leg bowed under the weight and he cursed under his breath.

"Dad, what's going on?" I went over to him and helped him to the couch. He pulled up the leg of his sweats, where his leg was swollen and a dark, nasty bruise covered it.

I sucked in a breath. "What happened?"

"I fell getting out of the shower last night. I took some pain killers. That's why I overslept. I thought it was just a bruise, but I can't..." He hissed as I gently touched just below his kneecap. It was the leg he'd broken. The one he usually had a brace on.

"This might be broken again," I said, fearing the worst. "We need to get you to the doctor as soon as they open." Without thinking, I stood and went to go get an ice pack out of the freezer.

"Go catch your flight."

I gasped and glanced at the clock on the wall. *Oh, no.* If I didn't leave right now, I'd miss my flight. But I couldn't just leave my father in pain and with a messed-up leg, could I? And who knows how many painkillers he took the night before. I usually measured them out for him. And was he even supposed to take those with his antibiotics?

I hesitated for only a moment. I couldn't see the path ahead, but I could take one more step into the unknown, trusting God was there.

I held out my hand to help him shift on the couch and elevate his leg. "I'll catch the next plane."

And that's how God spoke.

--- oOo ---

The bone wasn't broken, but it was badly bruised. The

doctor secured Dad's leg in a brace, then sent Dad home with something for the pain. A part of me wished the doc would slip me something, too.

When daylight arrived, I sent out a text to half the population of Pecan Creek, letting them know about my delay. I was seriously bummed to have one less day in Georgia, but I knew I couldn't leave Dad like that.

I helped him to the recliner when we got back and handed him a cup of coffee before turning to leave.

"Sadie."

I stopped and turned to face him. "Yeah?"

"I can't get on board with your ideas about a God who cares—" he motioned to his leg, "—but I can honestly say there's something different in you. A few months ago you would've left me on the couch with a broken leg to catch your flight. I don't know what's different, but…thank you. You deserve a great Christmas in Pecan Creek."

I watched him for a minute, his cast propped up on the foot rest, the pain etching lines into his face. I nodded and slipped into my room, clicking the door closed behind me. I hauled my laptop onto my bed to change my plane ticket, tears blurring the screen in front of me.

Chapter Twenty-Seven

○○○

Christmas Eve morning, I rolled over and checked the time on my phone. *8:45.* It might as well have been a quarter to six, I was so tired. I stayed up really late the night before, talking to Melina, basically crying my way through an update of everything I'd avoided admitting to her.

"I don't know what I thought," I confessed, running my hands over a soft blanket on the couch. "I guess I thought being a Christian would make things a little easier."

She laughed softly at that. "Oh, Sadie Grey. It's not a matter of life getting easier, but rather, it's knowing God is holding onto you through it all. And trusting He has a purpose. God is your anchor. He'll hold you steady."

"Yeah, but…"

"You don't find the anchor bobbing along on the surface, where everything is bright and sunny. You find the anchor when you hit rock bottom. Down in the cold darkness where there's nothing else to hold onto and nothing else to see."

I sighed. "I've definitely been at the bottom of the ocean these past couple months."

"You have. But can I tell you I'm so proud of you? I cry just thinking about it."

It was my turn to laugh. "You? Melina Elliot, crying? I'm so talented to get so many tears out of you."

"Right. But I'm proud because you've listened. You've

paid attention to God's nudging and did what He asked of You. He sees that, I promise." She sighed. "Now get to bed. Tomorrow's Christmas Eve."

And so I went to bed, with a bruised, yet hopeful heart. Was that what joy felt like in the middle of pain? It wasn't the same as circumstantial happiness, but it was still there, deeper somehow, giving me the courage I needed to make one of the toughest decisions I'd ever made.

Because now that I felt how much real love could hurt, I wondered if I'd ever truly loved before.

I lay in bed until nine o'clock, then made my way into the kitchen.

"Merry Christmas Eve," I stifled a yawn as I walked over to the coffee pot where a fresh pot waited for me. It smelled like heaven and home.

Dad looked up from his cereal. "Morning, Sadie."

I fixed my coffee, then sat at the table, quietly drinking my coffee and looking out at the cold, foggy morning.

"You can still get there if we work the system right," Dad said, his voice surprising me in the silence.

It was so tempting, but I shook my head. "I'm choosing to spend Christmas with my dad."

He smiled. "If I can stay awake, I can try my hand at hot chocolate once you get back from your church service tonight."

"Many have tried, but few can mix the powder into the milk like Sadie Franklin."

Dad laughed reached for the cereal box. "Whatever."

After breakfast, I went back to my room to get dressed and break the news to Truitt.

The phone stopped ringing and I dove in before he could say hello. "I'm so sorry. I'm not going to be there for Christmas."

The silence that followed was long enough to make me pull the phone away from my ear to make sure Truitt was still on the line.

Finally, he said, "I know."

"What? How?"

"First of all..." His tone was light, and I heard the grin in his voice, "Your aunt is like your publicist when it comes to updates on your life. She texted me this morning."

I dropped onto my bed and covered my eyes with my hand. "Are you mad?"

"No way. Before Mel even told me, I knew you'd stay."

I sat up straight. "How?"

"It was a gut feeling." His voice dropped in pitch. "Your heart wants to be home."

"Yeah, but—"

"God is your home. Doesn't matter where you are—Seattle or Pecan Creek or anywhere else on the planet. You belong to Him, and you'll only feel at peace when you're where He wants you to be. Right now, He wants you and your dad to keep growing your relationship. Y'all have come so far already."

I sniffed back tears. "But what about you? Us?"

"I can't even let myself think about how much I'll miss you. So instead, I'll think about how much I admire your commitment to loving your dad. You've inspired me to continue working on my relationship with my mom once she's home."

I leaned back against the pillows and looked up at the ceiling, a smile filling my face while tears trailed down my cheeks. "Some guy once told me it's not about asking for a clear path, but about asking God to give you the faith to take one more step into the unknown."

Truitt laughed. "He sounds like a keeper."

Even though Truitt couldn't see me, I shook my head in amazement. Somewhere along the way, I'd forgotten about my list of goals and just focused on living fully right where God had me, trusting Him to handle the crazy pieces of my life and lead me forward one step at a time.

After ending the call with Truitt, I finally got dressed and joined my dad in the living room.

The rest of the day passed like any other. We camped out on the couch watching Christmas movies, the lights on the tree reflecting across the dimly lit room, flickering off the window panes and picture frames. A Christmas candle burned next to the TV, making the house smell like a real Christmas tree. I burrowed under a red and green quilt on the couch, while Dad held down the recliner. Outside, rain fell quietly. Seattle snow.

Wherever you are, be all there…

That afternoon, I helped prepare and serve a Christmas Eve dinner at Raining Grace to those who otherwise wouldn't have a meal. The other teens all had plans with their families, so it was just me and a few adults. I worked the food line with Claire, plopping baked chicken, mashed potatoes, and green beans onto plates, then cleaning up while Pastor Theo read the Christmas story to our guests. After dinner, I went home to quickly change for the candlelight service. I slipped into a dark green dress, a pair of leggings, and some boots. I quietly grabbed my coat and a scarf from the hook by the door, careful not to wake up Dad. Then I climbed in the car for the eight o'clock candlelight service.

When I entered, the room had once again been transformed. All of the tables were cleared out, and the rows of chairs were back. On the stage, the wooden cross still stood, this time with a crude wooden manger in front of it, straw and a scratchy blanket spilling over the edge. The way the spotlight hit sent a shadow from the cross over the manger. I shivered.

The room was dark, and a guy played Christmas carols on an acoustic guitar. Someone handed me a candle, and I found a seat toward the back, surprised at how the room had filled up so quickly.

Everything started right after I found my seat and removed my coat. I clutched my little white candle, fiddling with the paper ring that was supposed to catch the dripping wax.

"Welcome to Raining Grace Community Church," Pastor Theo said from where he stood by the manger. "We're honored you've chosen to join us as we celebrate the night God became a man. He didn't come as a mighty, conquering king like people were expecting. No, He came as a newborn baby. The Creator was fully dependent on His creation. The One who spoke the universe into existence whimpered when He was hungry. He who never sleeps napped in the arms of a teenage girl. The One who commands legions of angels couldn't lift his own head. This is Jesus. And this,"—he pointed to the cross, "—is the reason He came. Our sin separates us from God, so God made a way for us to have a relationship with Him. What an act of love. That He would send His Son—as a little, helpless, perfect baby—to die the cruelest, most humiliating death so that the ones who turned against Him can know they're loved. This is Christmas. God saw, God came, God stayed. And He's still here. He's Emmanuel, God with us. Let's sing to Him."

The guy with the guitar played the chords of a Christmas song as people began lighting candles at the ends of the rows of chairs.

O holy night! The stars are brightly shining...

The girl in front of me turned to light my candle, and I realized it was Fyn, standing next to Owen. "Merry Christmas, Sadie," she whispered, the light dancing across her warm smile. She tipped her candle until mine caught the tiny, flickering flame. We needed to have another conversation soon. A real, honesty conversation to work through our pain. But for now, it was enough to have this brief moment of hope. I smiled back at her.

...It is the night of our dear Savior's birth...

Meanwhile, the crowd continued to sing as little lights began popping up throughout the room.

...Long lay the world in sin and error pining...

I caught my breath because, for the first time, I saw myself in that song. I had been caught in sin and error, desperately trying to climb my way out of the mess, resisting the realest Love I could ever know.

...Till He appeared and the soul felt its worth...

Me again. I'd felt purposeless and hopeless, and God interrupted everything and showed me I had value because He wanted me.

...A thrill of hope—the weary world rejoices...

Wasn't that what I was learning? That hope and joy existed even in the darkest days? I fixed my gaze on my candle, my eyes watery as I watched the flame dance close to my heart, its little light ensuring the darkness around me wouldn't swallow me. A reminder that God truly was with me in the unknown.

...For yonder breaks a new and glorious morn...

Morning was coming. I'd been through the darkest night, but I survived. It wasn't over for Sadie Grey Franklin.

...Fall on your knees! O hear the angel voices!

I closed my eyes, tears dripping off my chin. Unable to fall on my actual knees, but falling on my knees in my heart. *Thank You*, I whispered to the sky. *You rescued me. Saved me. Never gave up on me. Not when I was doing everything but loving You, and not now as I'm learning to hold onto the only thing that matters. I don't need a perfect life. I just need You.*

...O night divine, O night when Christ was born!

My relationship with Fyn was still fractured. So was my

relationship with my dad. My goals hadn't been checked off quite as neatly as I'd wanted them to be. I wouldn't be able to see my family until next year—nearly a whole year since I'd last been with them. My heart ached just thinking about it. But the One who arrived in a stable and stayed on the cross for me was with me now, reminding me that just one thing matters.

O night divine! O night, o night divine!

The song transitioned into another verse, and I quietly whispered the words.

Truly He taught us to love one another. His law is love and His gospel is peace...

I couldn't take my eyes off the manger and the cross. Beside me, something rustled, and I felt someone brush against me. I glanced up and caught my breath. Mike Franklin stood beside me, one hand holding his crutch, the other hand clutching a little white candle.

He looked at me, the light from my own candle flickering on his face. Maybe it was the lighting, but his eyes looked damp. Had he been crying?

Instinctively, I shifted closer to my father. Not to feel safe and not to feel protected, but because we were in this crazy life together. He was my dad. I was his daughter. Our relationship was far from perfect and had so far to go. But he was here, with me, in this moment. And somehow, that was enough. As much as it depended on me, I would live fully where God's will had placed me. I would live it to the hilt.

Dad leaned down and whispered next to my ear, "Please don't give up on me yet, Sadie Grey."

Sweet hymns of joy in grateful chorus raise we, with all our hearts we praise His Holy name!

My heart was joyful. It felt whole. Despite all of this, just one thing mattered. And by God's grace, He loved me.

Christ is the Lord! Then ever, ever praise we, His power and glory ever more proclaim!

I tilted my candle toward my dad's. The flame jumped to his candle, the light swallowing up a little more of the darkness.

Acknowledgments

○○○

Aside from telling the story, writing the acknowledgments is my favorite part of the book process. A few words at the back of this book hardly convey my gratitude, but there's no way I'd miss out on the chance to thank everyone who's cheered me on along way.

To you, the reader: Thank you for loving *All of This*—Sadie's first story—enough to ask for more. And to those of you who are picking up one of my books for the first time, welcome to the party. I'm so happy you're here! In a world where you have countless entertainment options, you chose this book and invested your time in Sadie's journey. You're the best. Seriously.

To Mom: For tirelessly reading rough drafts, answering questions, and telling me to keep going when I'd rather just take a nap. You gave me a love of stories, and I'm forever grateful.

To Dad: For teaching me to use jumper cables, and for helping me understand the world of insurance. But more than that, thank you for your support and presence in my life.

To my four siblings, who are my very best friends:

Erin, though I'm the most squeamish person on the planet, I somehow find myself writing about medical stuff. Thank you for always answering my weird questions and supplying your nursing knowledge whenever I need it (any remaining plausibility issues are totally my imagination's fault).

Abby, thank you for giving me the initial plot detail that shaped Sadie years ago. And for listening to the text-to-speech version of the rough draft for six hours straight, yet still being interested in what I write. Trouper.

Josh, thank you for the tacos and listening ear that time when I was overwhelmed by this project. And for all of the prayers and encouragement along the way. Best brother-in-law ever.

Ellen, you're my littlest sister, biggest cheerleader, best buddy, and real-life Trissy. I can't wait for you to read Sadie's stories one day. But for now, I'm cool with you staying a kid for a little while longer.

To Granddaddy and Grandmama: Thank you for faithfully walking through the story God has written for you. And for your support, prayers, and unwavering enthusiasm.

To Emily: For the amazing, spontaneous trip to Seattle a few years ago that influenced this story. You've stood by my side through everything for over half of our lives. Thank you for your loyalty, my sweet friend.

To my Southeastern Seminary community, including my boss, coworkers, professors, roommates, and friends: Thank you for believing in God's call on my life and giving me incredible opportunities to write for His glory.

To my small group family: For listening, and for praying me through this thing.

To my writing community: Ruth Anne Crews, thank you for being my wonderful writing buddy who's always up for a brainstorming session. And for reading multiple versions of this story. Look at us—We survived this book! Your turn, friend.

Tessa Emily Hall, thank you for your encouragement and support along the way. I'm so glad to know you.

Stephanie Morrill, thank you for your mentorship through

Go Teen Writers, your eagerness to answer questions and support my writing, and for connecting me with my book team.

Rachelle Rea Cobb, thank you for your editing expertise, your kindness, and your excitement for Sadie's journey.

Roseanna White, thank you for designing the perfect cover for this book. You caught the heart of Sadie's story, and I'm so grateful.

And to all my friends and family: My word, I can't thank y'all enough. I wish I could list you all by name, but just know you mean the world to me. I couldn't chase this dream without you.

Most of all, thank you to Jesus: For saving me, giving me a purpose, and allowing me to share the best news ever through my stories. You are my reason. My life, words, and every opportunity are Yours and only Yours. Thank You, God, for all of this.

Also by Anna Schaeffer

*A girl running from her past. A quirky Southern town.
And a summer that could change everything.*

Before senior year in Seattle, Sadie experienced a
life-changing summer in Pecan Creek, Georgia.
Read the beginning of Sadie's journey in *All of This*,
available online from your favorite book retailer!

CPSIA information can be obtained
at www.ICGtesting.com
Printed in the USA
FFHW021847261119
56120831-62234FF